THE JOURNEYING MOON

Other Sailing Classics

Ernle Bradford

THE JOURNEYING
MOON

GRAFTON BOOKS

A Division of the Collins Publishing Group

LONDON GLASGOW
TORONTO SYDNEY AUCKLAND

Grafton Books
A Division of the Collins Publishing Group
8 Grafton Street, London W1X 3LA

First published in Great Britain 1958
This edition published by Grafton Books 1987

British Library Cataloguing in Publication Data

Bradford, Ernle
  The journeying moon.
  1. Mediterranean Region—Description
  and travel
  I. Title
  910'.091822   D973

ISBN 0–246–13227–2

Printed in Great Britain by
Robert Hartnoll (1985) Ltd, Bodmin

To
MARIE BLANCHE

IN HIS loneliness and fixedness he yearneth towards the journeying moon, and the stars that still sojourn, yet still move onward; and everywhere the blue sky belongs to them, and is their appointed rest and their native country and their own natural homes, which they enter unannounced, as lords that are certainly expected, and yet there is a silent joy at their arrival.

SAMUEL TAYLOR COLERIDGE

Notes to
The Rime of the Ancient Mariner

IN THE few seconds before you drop off to sleep you are conscious of the many sounds that make up the silence of the sea. There is a clatter from the galley, where they are washing-up after supper, and a small squeak and sigh somewhere just overhead—one of the jib sheet blocks could do with some oil. A gentle stirring noise, like a bird's wing lifting, is followed by an almost inaudible flop as a coat on a hook lifts and subsides with the yacht's movement. There are odd rustles and mouselike squeaks; a steady background of minute unrelated sounds.

Nothing else? Yes, all the time, an inch or so away from your ear, there is the purring lisp of water. Sometimes it runs past softly and dreamily like summer streams; at others it mounts to a high-pitched hiss, as though a giant soda-syphon were being sprayed against the wooden hull. You know then that the yacht has heeled to a hard puff of wind, or that she is sliding fast down the long green back of an Atlantic roller. These sounds are part of your silence. Any interruption, or change in them, will bring you scrambling from your bunk, even though a few seconds before you may have been as deep down, and as far away, as the Seven Sleepers.

Tonight she is going easily and well. The galley noises recede. The innumerable small voices fade. Only the endless hush-hushing of the water past the ship's side remains. Sleep.

'Hey there! Wakey wakey!' Drops of water are falling on to my face.

'Come on, you lucky sailor! It's ten to four on a wet and windy morning!'

Slowly I swim up out of the dark fathoms of sleep. I have been a long way down tonight. Arne switches on the light above my head and leans back against the opposite bunk. He takes out a pack of cigarettes, lights one, and then offers the pack to me.

'What's it like out?'

'You can see. . . .' He shakes the water off his cap. His face looks raw and cold.

'You'll need plenty of clothes. The wind's pretty steady, about three to four. North-west. We've got all plain sail on her. Logging a nice five and a half. There's quite a bit of cloud coming over.'

On my way through to the galley I pass Bob, my watchmate, stumbling about in stockinged feet. He is swearing to himself.

'Some basket's pinched my sea-boots. I put them under the table just before I turned in.'

'I did. I shifted them into the oilskin locker. They'd slid out into the passageway. I was afraid of someone breaking their neck over them.'

Arne laughs. 'You'd have to climb over them first—then fall off.'

Bob takes fourteen in shoes. The size of his feet provides a constant target for the wit of our small world.

The galley is warm and reassuring. The light gleams on the stainless steel stove, on the coffee-pot steaming gently, and on a large plate piled with sandwiches.

'That's a good idea.' I help myself.

'Mine,' says Arne. 'Thought we might as well get rid of that German cheese. It's still all right, but I wanted to be quite sure that it was the cheese and not Bob's socks that's been making the after-locker unendurable.'

A splatter of rain drives against the galley window as I stand there with my hands cupped round a mug of coffee. Arne grins.

'It's a bit wet on deck. But you can't help it. She's going along well, but every now and then you get a big one and she digs her nose into it. The drizzle's letting up though.'

I follow him through the galley to the chart table. The clock says three minutes to four, and the barometer is standing at 1016 millibars. I look in the log-book and see that it has been steady for the past four hours. While I am reading through the middle watch entries, the hatch behind me opens and Ronnie's face appears.

'Log reading "Thirty-one and a half".'

I enter it in the book. One thousand two hundred and thirty-one and a half miles. From Falmouth towards New York.

10

Aboard the yawl *Kay*. The First of May, 1956. Our twelfth day at sea. Bob pushes past me and opens the hatch, letting in a thin spray of salt water.

'I'll take her first, if you like,' he says over his shoulder.

'I'll be up in a minute.'

I finish my coffee and am just lighting another cigarette, when Ronnie comes into the galley. His eyelids are red and puckered, his face is misted with a straggling, half-grown beard, and his hands are crinkled like an old washerwoman's. He holds them out over the stove.

'Why the hell don't you wear gloves, Ronnie?'

'I can't get the feel of the wheel if I do. She's steering pretty easily, though. We're waltzing along. If it wasn't for the cold it'd be perfect.'

Ronnie comes from South Africa. He is more sensitive to the cold than the rest of us, who are either English or Swedish. As he stands there in the brightly lit galley he looks like an advertisement for Michelin tyres, his oilskin suit bulging as though it were inflated with compressed air, and a wet towel sealing the suit around his neck. Under his sou'wester he is wearing a woollen cap pulled down over his ears.

I put out my cigarette. 'I'd better go up top. 'Night, Ronnie. 'Night, Arne.'

But Arne, having stopped only to pull off his sea-boots and oilskins, is already fast asleep in his bunk. Frank and Stig, the other members of the crew, are also asleep. Frank lies sprawled on his back, one large hand hanging just over the edge of the bunkboard. It drifts gently to and fro as the yacht sways and rises over the sea. Stig, who sleeps in one of the quarter berths, has pulled the curtains across so that the light from the chart table cannot disturb him. I hear his deep breathing as I make my way up to the hatch. He lies, I know, snugly hidden away in a frowst of warm, damp clothes; sea-boot stockings; woollen blankets; and whatever dreams haunt the deep sleep of Swedish fishermen.

When you come outside from the glow of the chart-table light at first you can see nothing. But you feel the cold. It bites into the skin of your face, and you take a few deep, shocked breaths as though you had plunged into icy water. You pull on your gloves quickly and sit down in the nearest corner of the cockpit, waiting for your eyes to adjust to the dark.

'The moon's just gone down behind that bank of clouds. We're going along well.'

I can see Bob's face, lit from beneath by the soft glow of the compass. He is sitting just to one side of the wheel, a little tensed, and watching the card carefully. Bob is not quite sure of himself as a helmsman. He will probably never make a good one, for he does not seem to have the necessary 'hands': that sure, relaxed touch of the man who feels like part of the boat, and who can tell—even without looking at the card—whether she is on course, and if the sails are drawing well.

I look at the Kenyon speedometer. It is flickering between six and seven knots. The wind is fairly broad on the beam, and the yacht is driving along at an easy angle of heel. Just occasionally an errant wave jumps over the bows and flies aft in a flicker of spray.

'Got the torch?'

He hands it to me and I climb out of the cockpit and walk forward on the weather side, holding on to the guard-rail with one hand. By the mainmast I pause and shine the torch aloft. The varnished mast, the spreaders, and the white wing of the mainsail spring out of the darkness. Seventy foot above me the top of the mast describes its gentle arc against the sky. A few seconds later the moon breaks out from behind the clouds and transforms the night scene. Its light induces a certain confidence, subduing the lonely dark, and the indifferent sea.

We are in a fifty-two-foot yacht, over a thousand miles out from Land's End, headed west for America in the early spring of the year. Our destination is New York, and our only aim to deliver the yacht safe and sound, ready for the Bermuda race in two months' time. We are not doing it in a barrel, nor backwards in a bathtub, with an eye to lucrative publicity and heroic tales in the popular Press. Why then? The question is worth asking, but I suppose the answer would be different for each one of us. Stig alone is doing it for bread-and-butter. He is the only professional seaman in our crew of six.

I go forward into the pulpit, turn my back to the advancing waves, and gaze up along the luff of the jib. The sail curves away in a smooth arc, as beautiful and nearly as efficient as a gull's wing. Maybe, though, the jib is sheeted in a little too hard.

'Bob!'

I hear his answering shout.

'Can you check away the jib a little? Only a little.'

A few seconds later the sheet-blocks tap on the deck. They strain upwards and creak. There is a faint, rasping sigh as the wet jib sheets ease themselves through the blocks' swollen wooden mouths, and the sail seems to give a slight shrug. A flutter runs from its foot, up over the belly, and dies away at the head. The sail resumes its shape, only now it is a fraction fuller, and the yacht seems to move more easily. There is more of a 'cushioned' feel about her as she rises over the north-westerly swell, or shoulders her way down the backs of the waves.

'That's enough!'

I make my way slowly aft, checking the lashings on the dinghy, and coiling up a wandering rope's end as I pass. Bob is struggling with a cigarette, and I sit down beside him.

'Here, I'll take her for a bit. Why not go below and fix us some tea? Or see if there's any of that coffee left. I'll have a tot of rum in mine.'

'The hard-drinking mate! Okay.'

He gets to his feet and opens the doghouse doors. The light streams up, catching his wet, unshaved cheeks, but only for a second, and then the doors are closed and I am alone. Except for the glimmer of light from the galley windows there is nothing to show that I am not the only man alive in the world. Something to do with the peace, the solitude, and the feeling of self-reliance—is that why one does it? Partly.

The spokes of the wheel drift through my hands and the compass light glows soft and steady, a friendly glow. The moon has gone again and there is another dark bank of cirrus cloud moving over us from the north. Mindlessly—it requires no conscious control any more—my body shifts and sways, easing itself to the scend and movement of the sea.

We are steering 250°, just a little south of west. Yesterday our noon position was 45° 15′N., 25° 34′W.—some four hundred miles north of the Azores, almost in the centre of the Western Ocean. And it is spring, the ripe breeding season for North Atlantic gales, the cold, dour season when the thermometer stands at thirteen degrees Centigrade, and the flung spray bites on your skin like a vicious mouth with small, salt teeth. But there is little love in it.

'Here's yours. There's as much rum in it as coffee.' Bob settles back in his corner, lights two cigarettes in the screen of his jacket and hands one to me.

'The barometer's falling. It's back to 1015.' A millibar in the last hour. Still, it may not mean anything. The wind seems steady and there is no sign of any increase in the swell. Bob begins to sing softly to himself. He has a wide range of old songs, Victorian drawing-room pieces, and bawdy ballads.

> 'Once I was a serving girl,
> Down in Drury Lane,
> My master was kind to me
> My Mistress was the same. . . .'

Curious how many of us either hum or sing on watch, men who when ashore would rarely sing, even in the bathtub. Perhaps peasants and fishermen, and most simple people, sing because the quietness and simplicity of their lives need a thread of sound running through them.

You know how the dawn comes over the Atlantic at that time of year? There is a faint lightening of the sea's surface and the air seems different. It is rather as if during the night watches one has lost one's sense of taste and smell. They are only restored by the new day. For the first time you can savour the air on your tongue, salty and yet with a wonderful quality about it as though all those thousands of miles of ocean have rinsed it clean. Then you begin to notice the smell of the boat, the teak of the decks, wet cordage and sailcloth, the tang of damp metal fittings, and the curious chemical smell of oilskins. Your hands become visible.

The sea begins to glow softly like old, unpolished pewter, and the cloud base—as it races overhead—becomes, for the first time in hours, varied in texture. You see now that not all of it is dark and ominous, as you had imagined, but that here and there it is dappled with white puffs, and combed with threads of grey, like trailers of smoke. Only in a few places does it sag in dark, pregnant folds, or bulk itself like threatening shoulders against the horizon. The light spreads and the sea seems to glow from within. You know now that the sun will be up in less than half an hour. You light a cigarette, and it seems as if the others you have smoked during the night have had no taste. With a fresh cigarette and a cup of coffee, you face the new day with a sparkle in your blood.

The sea is no longer a dark, moving mass, but resolves itself into individual waves; some humped; some crested; some sliding in long green, sibilant rushes; others marching with a curious and imposing silence.

'Look!' Bob points on our starboard bow. 'Look, there they are!'

One after another, leaping, diving and playing, the dolphins glide past and around us. Sometimes one of them jumps so close alongside that we can hear him snort as he takes another breath. Strange beauty! They seem so remote from us, and yet they, too, are mammals; and their play seems often to have a conscious, almost human quality about it.

' "When the sea-hog jumps, stand by your pumps",' Bob quotes. 'What about that?'

'Oh, only sometimes, I guess, Bob. I've seen them for days on end in the Mediterranean—and never a breath of wind.'

'I'm not so sure about it out here, though. And those damn chickens are back again.'

I had not noticed them before, but now, as I follow the direction of his gaze, I see two or three Arctic terns, 'Mother Carey's Chickens', scuttering their webbed feet along the water as they search for plankton.

The sun comes up over our quarter, pale yellow like old straw, and the horizon has a hard, sharp look about it. But the barometer, as we go off watch at eight o'clock, is steady. Stig has the wheel. Frank takes over the watch from me. His bald head shines in the early light and, although he has only just woken, he is cheerful as ever.

'I'll call you at nine with a lovely breakfast. One of my specials. Egg, bacon, and tinned tomatoes.'

By ten o'clock, when we have all breakfasted, washed up in hot salt water, and tidied the boat, the wind has backed round to the west. Frank comes below with a worried look.

'I've had to fall off to two hundred and twenty degrees, Arne. I don't like the way it's backing. The horizon's nice and clear though.'

'Too clear. What's the glass doing?'

'Steady.'

It begins to fall at noon. Not much at first, just a half millibar drop. But the fall is continuous, another half millibar in the next hour, and all the time the wind is backing into the south-west. At two o'clock, just as those of us who are off watch are getting snugged down for an afternoon's sleep, there comes the call I have been expecting—'All hands!' Even down below it has been noticeable during the past hour how much more the yacht is increasing her heel. She has started to stumble and to hesitate in her long rushes down the flanks of the waves. Earlier on we have fallen off to a north-westerly course, and the motion of the boat is awkward for we are now plunging into the swell left over by the wind of the past two days.

Arne has the helm.

'Reefing stations, Ernle. But first of all, we'll shift to the number three jib.'

Ronnie and Bob stay aft in the cockpit to cope with the sheets, while Stig, Frank, and I make our way forward. The spray is coming over in cold-driven sheets. Our language keeps us warm as we wait with frozen hands (gloves are useless for this work) to take down the large, fair-weather jib. Stig stands by the halyard, while Frank and I hang on, ready in the bows.

Here she comes! The sheets start, the halyard is eased, and the sail—with a long-drawn sigh—begins to crumple. Frank and I leap on it, shouting and swearing as if it were an enemy. As fast as we can, we tear it down the windswept forestay, beating it to the deck with our fists and fingers. Then the sodden sail is parcelled and secured along the deck, while its successor, a smaller jib cut high along the foot so that it clears the spray and the sea, is hanked on to the forestay.

'All ready!' I shout as we grasp the halyard. The sail soars aloft, takes the wind, and begins to shake like a mad thing. But then—as the cockpit crew haul in on the sheets—it suddenly comes to heel. Bridled, the sail takes up its working curve against the grey sky, and begins to haul us along like a team of horses. Only now that the job is over, do I realize that my old Spanish beret has disappeared during that fight with the sail. Frank holds up a dripping thumb.

'Caught it on one of those —— hanks!'

The blood falls to the deck, making small oily spots—until a green wave bursts over and washes it clean again.

We take a reef in the mainsail while the yacht is still on the wind. It is more difficult this way, but we try to do things much as if we were racing. Taking a reef while the yacht is on the wind means that the sail remains full almost every second of the operation. The boat does not lose way, but keeps going hard all the time.

'You take the winch handle, Frank. Stig will look after the main halyard. I'll back up on the pennant.'

Arne signals that he is ready. Slowly the sail is started. Frank gasps with the exertion as he cranks in on the winch. All my weight is on the rope that I hang on to with hands from which all feeling seems to have disappeared.

'She's coming all right!'

Then I hear Stig cursing. Something wrong? No. He waves reassuringly when I glance in his direction.

The folds of wet canvas sag down along the foot of the boom. The wind gathers in the loose belly of the sail which gives a quick angry flap. All down! A mad scramble follows as all hands, save the helmsman, leap for the reef points and make them fast along the boom. We have taken a deep reef—right down to the second row of reef points—and the mainsail is now as small as we can get it. If it blows any harder, the sail itself will have to come down and the storm trysail go up instead.

Despite the intense cold you find that you are sweating under your layers of clothing. Your hands give small spasmodic jumps as they relax from the tension of physical effort. To sprawl for a few seconds in the cockpit and take a few deep breaths is luxury— like easing your body into layers of cotton wool—and then the first cold sweep of spray sends you below again.

'We're still a bit slow on this reefing, Arne. The trouble is the pennant doesn't render properly through that cringle.'

'I know. We'll work some tallow into it, and see if that helps.'

Arne stands behind the wheel, his body swaying from side to side, drops of water falling off the peak of his cap, and a sodden cigarette between his lips.

'She's easier on the helm now. And we're still making seven knots.'

But the barometer goes on falling and the wind continues to

harden. It has steadied at west by south. There are all the signs of a real blow impending. I glance in the log as I go below for a cup of tea. The noon entry reads: 'The North Atlantic is strictly for the birds!' And Arne has added, during the afternoon: 'I never did think much of the First of May. I see no reason to reverse my opinion.'

Frank sticks a piece of plaster round his thumb and hands me a scalding mug of tea.

'No point in turning in now?' he asks.

'No.'

'We'll be up there getting the main off her within the hour?'

'I expect so.'

At that moment *Kay* lies over to a heavy sea which breaks onboard with a great roar. Frank slips sideways and falls to the deck. Tea-pot and cups fly across the galley, and I end up halfway over the ice-box, clutching an empty mug. There is tea on the deckhead, tea on the floor, and tea running down inside my sweater.

'All hands!'

A quarter of an hour later we are wallowing gently along under our stormsails: a small nylon jib and trysail. The furled mainsail humps itself along the coachroof, and the wind flicks at an untidy lashing, making a strange buzzing sound like a bee trapped under a jam jar. The sky is ten-tenths cloud, mainly nimbus, the rain-bearer, although a great arch of anvil-headed thunderclouds bars the western horizon.

'Good luck, chum—and a very merry watch to you!' Arne hands me the wheel.

'The sea's just beginning to get up,' he adds, 'wouldn't be surprised if we don't have to take the lot down before nightfall.'

Yes, we have done that before, only once though on this voyage. When the wind and the sea get too strong and too high for the yacht to carry even her stormsails, we lower all sail and run back before the gale under bare poles. It is exciting and a little nerve-wracking, keeping her stern presented to the following seas—aware that if you get off course you will invite a large wave to break clean over the boat.

'I think it's more than likely,' I say as he goes below. I take the wheel and, in between conning the boat, watch the dolphins. They have been with us all day—school after school of them.

They are leaping clean out of the water now, wonderful gleaming arcs of flesh and sinew.

We have altered course so that the sea is on our quarter and, out of the corner of my eye, I see four large dolphins riding a fifteen-foot wave like surf-bathers. Their bird-like snouts project through the sliding wall of water as they balance themselves in the sea's rolling advance. Then one of them hurls himself clean out of the moving wall of water, to dive without splash or sound into the dark trough beneath him. The others follow —jump, flight, dive—jump, flight, dive—one after another, and then the *Kay*'s stern lifts to the roller and a wet tongue of water slides over the canvas splash screens and slaps my face.

At sunset an apricot light flickers along the dark cloud base and the sea is the colour of gun-metal, save that here and there the sliding hills of water are becoming flecked with white as the wind blows the crests headlong. The barometer is down to 1010 millibars. The thermometer is twelve degrees centigrade, and the wind is steady at Force 8—gale force.

Arne pokes his head through the hatch and looks inquiringly at me.

'We're travelling too fast,' I say. 'Our wake's beginning to disturb the waves. They've got a tendency to break already. How high would you estimate them? Fifteen?'

He peers around and purses his lips. 'Fifteen or even twenty. Forty—if I were a journalist!'

They are imposing enough, though, when seen from a height of four or five feet above the water. They seem to tower over us. We climb and climb up their long backs, hesitate in the whistling rush at the top, and then plummet down their steep faces as though we were on a roller-coaster.

'Yes,' he agrees with my unspoken suggestion. 'With night coming on, maybe we'd be better to run before it.'

'Safer. You can't see which ones are dangerous in the dark.'

We both know that running back before the gale means throwing away hard-won miles. It means retracing our steps and adding more days to the voyage.

'Ah, well, what do the books say? "Patience is a virtue learned at sea." All hands!'

We have just got the storm jib and the trysail down, and are lashing the latter securely in place—ready to run up again the minute the weather eases—when Frank gives a shout.

'Look at that!'

Away on the western horizon, lit from beneath by the dying sun, a huge cumulo-nimbus cloud towers into the sky. A fantastic structure, like a baroque cathedral, the cloud soars in thousand-foot pinnacles and then sags at its base as though it cannot support its weight. Below it, descending from some two hundred foot above the sea, three dark pillars hang down into the ocean.

'Waterspouts!'

Like giant elephants' trunks, they writhe and twist beneath the cloud base as if they were searching for water. One of them suddenly gives a shiver and collapses in a smoky heap, but the other two still stand erect. Then a dark finger seems to poke out of the cloud; it straightens a knuckle, and elongates itself. Another water spout is being born.

'I hope to God we don't come across any of those during the night!'

Fascinated, we stand and watch them. The whole horizon, lit by the last flares of the dying sun, has a majestic and unearthly look about it.

'*Gotterdammerung!*' says Bob.

Stig swears in Swedish. Ronnie combs his bedraggled beard with broken fingernails.

'Time for a drink?'

'I could do with one!'

Shorn of all her canvas, the yacht runs sweetly and smoothly before the wind and sea. We have paid out long lengths of rope astern to comb the advancing rollers, and to check our speed. Even with no sail up, we are making five knots from the pressure of the wind on the hull, the mast and the rigging. It is fast enough for comfort, but not too fast for safety—although we are sadly aware that every mile we are running off is a mile to be regained as soon as the weather clears.

Dance music from America murmurs in the saloon. The bottles are out in their fiddles on the table.

'I'll have a rum.'

'Say when.'

'How'd you like to be in New York with a doe-eyed blonde on your arm?'

The gimballed paraffin stove sways gently to the swing of the ship, and spreads its warmth around the friendly panelling. For supper there are frankfurters, potatoes and sauerkraut, tinned lobster soup and peaches. You could hardly complain of that for a menu in a small boat running before a spring gale in mid-Atlantic.

'It's been quite a day.' Bob eases off his boots.

'Yes, quite a day.'

And tonight, I think, is going to be none too pleasant. To-morrow, too, will be cold, wet, and windy. But bad weather does not last for ever. Quite soon we will have it fine again.

We shall lounge on the deck and feel the sun on our bare skins, and trail lines over the stern for fish. We shall set the light-weather sails, and the spinnaker will loom like a great bubble over the bows. We shall hear the gentle crunch of the forefoot as she shoulders her way through a summer sea, and the wake at night will be a shining path of phosphorescence. Quite soon it will be like sailing through silk.

2

I T WAS an early spring morning in Alexandria when it all
started. Well, to say that it started then is an over-statement.
It would be truer to say that it was at that moment something
inside me crystallized. It may take years for passions and en-
thusiasms to form, but year by year they build up, drop by drop
like stalactites. And then, 'How extraordinary!' we remark as
the trusted lawyer absconds with the funds, or the businessman
sails for Tahiti, or the quiet citizen leaves home and family to
turn Trappist. No, it did not start then with me, it came to a
head rather. The last drop fell into place, that was all.

It was an odd thing to have been doing, perhaps, in wartime
Alexandria, but that morning I had been reading Tchekhov—I
had found a sun-dried edition of his works mouldering in a
French bookshop, and had bought them for a few piastres. I
had twenty-four hours' leave before rejoining my ship, a Hunt
class destroyer, and it was my twenty-first birthday.

In the morning I had shopped and strolled about that pleasant
cosmopolitan city with the comfortable feeling of having nothing
to do while all the rest of the world was busy, and in the evening
there was to be a party. There were always parties in those days;
hectic rowdy parties, flowering and expanding like rockets in the
air—and driven upwards by a similar pressing urgency. There
is only one springtime, and when it is one's own, and when it is
threatened daily and hourly, then the force that drives in young
veins becomes unnaturally accelerated. A birthday party—and
my twenty-first at that—was certain to be memorable.

I had this pleasant feeling of anticipation inside me, all day
with nothing to do, and the satisfaction of being twenty-one
and alive.

I unwrapped the books in the cocktail bar of the Cecil Hotel.
A number of army officers were drinking whisky at the bar. They

were trying to pinch the gully-gully man's chickens, and a friendly 'dug-out' commander from the Ras-El-Tin base came in and raised a hand in greeting.

' 'Morning, Sub. Hasn't your ship finished boiler-cleaning yet?'

'Finishes today, sir. I've been lucky and collected twenty-four hours' leave.'

The sun spiralled in through a long window. A Sudanese waiter brought me a John Collins and I opened the books. I took them in to lunch with me and read bits and pieces of them while I ate. I was a little drunk by this time—just comfortably expanding in a warm glow—the only way to be drunk and the right way to be at that time and at that age. Odd sentences and scraps of dialogue were transferred from the page and printed on my brain. They had more evocative power than they would have had for a sober man: they had acquired that mysterious transference which is the magic spell that all writers seek, and few find.

It was while I was dreaming happily over my first cup of coffee and my second brandy that I suddenly stumbled on the key words. They came to me as such a profound revelation that I can quote them now without looking at them. In fact, I would not know where to look, for it is years since I lost that edition of Tchekhov and I cannot recall whether they were in a play, a short story or a letter. But I can remember them.

'Life does not come again; if you have not lived during the days that were given to you, once only, then write it down as lost. . . .'

I went down to the beach and swam and lay in the sun during the afternoon. The words haunted me. They seemed to me then —as they seem to me still—to have the simplicity of truth.

Yes, I thought, as I lay lizard-like on the beach, I have no certainty but this one life, a brittle gift and menaced every second. For the past two years I've not been living as I wanted to —how few of us ever do—but living according to the designs of my country. One day, though, if I survive the war, I'll have my own life to live.

At twenty-one the gift of a life seems the promise of endless freedom.

At six o'clock I went to the bar at Mary's House and waited around for my friends to join me. It was a good bar at Mary's; the drink was reasonable, the measures just; the food eatable—and

23

upstairs there were a few rather tired girls for those whose simple appetites were not revolted by a communal dish.

I was no virgin myself, but I preferred a little personal discretion in my pleasures. I was lucky, for some months previously I had made the acquaintance of a French widow—who shared her favours equally between myself and a Greek submarine officer. Fortunately, he was away on patrol at the time.

It was not long before Andy came in. He was our gunnery officer, a schoolmaster in civilian life, a man gifted with a dry and civilized wit. He was my best friend in those days. Soon afterwards several more from our wardroom joined us, the friends from other Hunt class destroyers in our flotilla. The evening began to warm up genially and slowly—an unforced pressure mounting inside young heads and bodies. The braying sounds of Ronny Dewar's hunting-horn were heard over the babble at the bar. The clarion call of the Hunts! We were away into a rose-pink evening through the tired streets of Alexandria, which were steaming here and there where shopkeepers had tossed out pails of water; tired streets smelling of bread and ordure, of cooking camel steaks and tropical flowers—the improbable pot-pourri of Egypt.

'Where first?' I asked as our gharry rattled into Mahomet Ali Square. A drunk Aussie jumped on the running-board, shouted 'Whoo-oop!' and fell off again.

'To the Long Bar,' said Andy. 'All the others are going there. It's our excellent intention to get you very stewed before the evening's out. We'll dine at Maxim's and then beat up some of the cabarets.'

It was an evening like many others. And yet to me, in retrospect, it seems the peak and the very symbol of all those wartime parties. One cannot recapture that atmosphere; an atmosphere that was pressurized by the underlying tension of our times.

There was a moment I remember at random out of the charged, high-flowing evening, when we were in some sailors' cabaret in 'Beer Street' (I never learned its Egyptian name but it was always 'Beer Street' to us then), when cheap champagne was spurting stickily over our faces and Ronny had climbed into the band and taken over on the trumpet. A fight between two English stokers was raging in the doorway entrance. A plump French *poule* was sitting on my lap. 'Mac', the bearded navigator of one of our flotilla, had appeared wailing on his bagpipes; and Andy had just bought from an itinerant, pox-ridden street-vendor his entire basket of gardenias. Champagne was spurting, gardenias flying through the air, and at any moment the M.P.s would arrive and separate the fighting stokers—and I was very happy. I think I never was so happy before or since. In those few, brief crazy moments I seemed to understand what it was all about.

I shouted my new-found wisdom across the table. Andy blinked uncomprehendingly. I dug out from my pocket the envelope on which I had written down Tchekhov's words. He looked at it with a wry smile and said nothing.

Later on, as we were driving through the night to a further cabaret, he handed me the bottle out of which he had just taken a swig and remarked: 'Well, I agree with Mr. Tchekhov. I agree entirely. But it all depends on what you call living. I shall be quite happy to go back to my humdrum teaching. And to my wife and child.'

He was killed six months later on a Malta convoy.

'I don't think I want that,' I said. 'Of course, I don't know. I haven't got a wife and child. I think I just want to be free.'

Andy laughed. 'You'll be lucky. If it wasn't your twenty-first birthday I'd quote some truer words than Tchekhov's to you.'

'What?'

'A Greek philosopher. I can't remember his name—"We live not as we would wish to, but as we must".'

The shine of other lights, the chatter of another bar, the sentimental murmur of more dance music lured us in out of the night.

There was an air-raid early next morning. I heard the distant banging of the guns through the thick veils of alcohol and sleep and physical fatigue. My companion was up and out of bed. 'Being very French,' I thought drowsily. 'Excitable French.'

She kept up a running commentary from the window. There were a few planes over bombing the ships in the harbour. Nothing much. Once there was a loud crump! as a 'stick' fell somewhere in the town. She darted away from the window, abusing the dirty 'Boches' and the murderous war. I slept again until the alarm went off at five. I had to be back on board before eight o'clock colours.

'*Au revoir*, my darling.' She rolled over lazily. 'I will see you soon?'

'Yes. Not so long this time. In about a week, I hope.' (And I hope that damn Greek's still at sea.)

'Only a veek? Oh-oh—*mais c'est merveilleux!* Only a veek!'

A little worried. Oh, well, I wasn't. It didn't really matter to me. I shaved with a shaky hand. Her dead husband's razor—a cut-throat. I wondered if *his* hand ever slipped after a night on Bolanachi's poisonous gin and brandy? Perhaps that's exactly how he . . .

'*Au revoir*, Minou!'

I had two hours in which to get on board. Plenty of time. How good the dawn air seemed! Damp off the sea, effacing and erasing the hot fatigue of the city, it came in every morning like spring over the tired land.

I was still a little tight, but pleasantly so. My body had the easy grace of health, and I felt that if the blind beggar on the corner had hailed me with the old salutation 'O King, live for ever!' for me it would have been true. There are times when one is young that it seems impossible one should ever die.

Near Ramleh station I sat down in a working-class bar and ordered a *café* and a *fine*. A group of ragged-trousered Egyptian workmen were chattering in the corner. They laughed a lot together and I rather liked them, they robbed you with a smile— which was more than you could say for some of our Mediterranean allies.

The café proprietor shambled over, one hand lodged inside his shirt scratching a hairy paunch.

' 'Ullo, Captain—you up early, eh?'

'Uh-huh. Cigarette?'

He shook his head and flopped into the chair opposite me. The lilac sky behind his head began to harden in colour. Time I was going. I hailed a passing gharry and told him to drive to No. 10 gate. From there I could always get a felucca to sail me out to the ship.

We clop-clopped our way down the *Rue des Sœurs*—'Sisters' Street', the sailors' bar-and-brothel quarter. It was quiet now in the early morning, with only the odd barman sluicing down the pavements or rattling up the shutters. I stopped at a street cart and bought a couple of hard-boiled eggs and a roll.

'Eggs and bread! Eggs and bread!' I could hear his monotonous chant as we rattled towards the harbour.

A bend in the road—and the whole Mediterranean Fleet lay sleeping at anchor in front of me. In that still, early light the pale grey ships had all the grace of a peacetime regatta. There was a drift of smoke here and there from galley funnels, and a motor-boat with despatches was heading out towards the *Warspite*. Beyond, lifting slowly into sight as the night mists blew away, lay the still, impersonal sea.

The last drop fell into place. Ever since a child I had had this passion. It was strange that, even in wartime, I could have it and suffer no disillusionment. It was like waking and looking at the face of a woman who has betrayed you—and knowing that your own affection is unchanged.

Abdul, the felucca man who looked after our ship when she was in harbour, hailed me.

'Hey, Captain! Mister Johnny! You want to go back? All right?'

He wiped the stern sheets carefully with a sponge—his boat was always well kept—and gave me an arm as I got in.

'Good night—good girl, eh, Captain?'

He had an engaging grin that disclosed his back teeth.

We cast off and I took the tiller while he ran up the lateen sail. There was a breeze funnelling through the anchored shipping, a northerly breeze that came all the way from Cyprus and Turkey.

'You take her, Captain? I look after sail, eh?' We tacked through the lines of shipping. I let my hand trail in the warm water and put my feet up on the centre thwart.

'You sailing soon?' Abdul began to peel an orange. His huge cracked feet, whitened by years of salt water, were propped on the gunwale. I said nothing.

'You sailing about noon, I think, Captain.'

There were few secrets in Alexandria harbour.

'Not as we would wish to, but as we must.' But one day, perhaps, we would be able to make our own decisions. 'Life does not come again . . .' Should I ever be able to face an office in London after this war? A puff of wind swirled round the bows of a cruiser, and Abdul with an oath slackened the sheet. The felucca rose on her side and buried her lee gunwale.

One day I would come back and sail this sea for my own pleasure, and in my own time and way.

'All right, Captain. I take her now. We coming up to your ship.'

I looked beyond the destroyer's keen bows and saw, far away and low on the horizon, a tiny line of cumulus clouds spreading. False cumulus clouds. They were ack-ack bursts. Some convoy was getting a torpedo-bomber attack.

The Alexandria sirens began to wail as I jumped on to the gangway. Red warning flags drifted to the yard-arms of the assembled ships, hung loosely for a moment, and then blew out stiff in the morning breeze. We were sailing at noon for Tobruk.

3

SHORTLY after the war I married and tried to settle down to a life in London. Like most of my generation, though, I was infected by restlessness. Early in our lives we had been given a taste for the world of action, and too much adrenalin had gone through our systems for them to adjust easily to the routine of 'nine to six'. Our palates had been spoiled for the softer nuances of contentment. The after-lunch doze with the Sunday paper, the clatter of the lawn-mower, and the distant scrape and fiddle of B.B.C. tea-time music seemed insipid after fevered nights in leave-time ports.

Of those who failed to make the adjustment, some emigrated, some took to drink, and some climbed mountains. Others—and I was among them—attempted the return to post-war living, found it unsatisfying, and then cut out new paths for ourselves. The Welfare State was designed for the generation that followed us.

London was strange and uneasy in those immediate post-war years. It had something of the same smell about it that conquered Naples had at the time when Naples was the leave centre for our Anzio troops: a little dust; much decay; and the smell of corruption. I remember the night-clubs thick with black-marketeers; the well-fleshed smiler who knew where you could get whisky, and whose new Bentley echoed nightly with the giggles of loose-legged girls. People never fight for the world they get. They fight for the world they remember. Perhaps that is why so many returned soldiers make poor citizens.

I had an acquaintance, a Labour M.P. in the post-war Government. He had never dined nor dressed so well in all his life before.

'What are you belly-aching about?' he said one night. 'We're making a new world for England, don't you see that? Social justice, fair shares for all. . . .' I listened to him booming away through the fog of cigarette-smoke. Like most people he had his share of sense but, like ninety-nine per cent, he put himself first. Well, that was an aspect of self-preservation we had all learned during the war. '—— you, Jack. I'm inboard.'

'If you don't like it,' he said. 'Why don't you get out of it? It's a big world, my boy.'

You're right, I thought, I will. Just give me time, just let me save a little money, and I'll get going.

We were living then in a small flat in Chelsea, that old Bohemia which was being rapidly overlaid by the flats and houses of those who, before the war, would have lived in Mayfair or Knightsbridge. My wife had been thirteen when the war started. She knew little of the world but England under bombardment, shortages and rationing. When I talked nostalgically of the sunlight on Table Mountain, the long swell of the South Atlantic, or the decline of day over the Eastern Mediterranean her eyes would light up.

'Was it really like that? I expect you're laying it on a bit. Did you ever come across flying fish?'

'Yes. If it's quite quiet you can hear the thin scuttering sound their wings make as they leave the water.'

In the evening, walking home along the Embankment, I would stand and watch the tugs slipping down on a full tide, the barges swaying drunkenly behind them. The autumn was the worst time. Then, as the sun began to recede every day earlier and earlier from our northern world, I would listen to the tugs on the river at night. . . . Those deep nostalgic voices calling out of the damp and the mist.

> 'I should like to rise and go
> Where the golden apples grow . . .'

I came back one night and it was raining. The Korean War had started and the evening papers were selling fast. The faces on Underground and bus were tired and worried. It's all beginning again, I thought. Now she will never see anything but a world at war—and now I shall never sail my own boat through peaceful seas.

The decision was quickly made. We would get rid of our flat, sell our furniture, cut our links with England, buy a boat—and go. For a long while Janet had been hoping that I would make up my mind instead of havering. A keen sailor herself, she had little use for the conventional domestic life of the town-bred woman. 'Hens in cages!' she would exclaim. I had acquired a taste for the free life during the war, but there are some who are born with a knowledge of it in their veins. For them the conventional life is a kind of torture. They hate it more than the domesticated animal would hate freedom.

Janet was of their rare number. Even during the years in which we had been married she had hardly ever failed to escape once a week to go dinghy-sailing on the Thames. Her favourite reading was the history of sailing ships, and she could tell you without hesitation under which captain, and on what date, the *Thermopylae*, the *Flying Cloud*, or the *Cutty Sark* had made their record passages. The first woman to win the Little Ship Club Trophy for seamanship and navigation, she was possessed by a passion for the sea that I have rarely seen equalled. While my own motives were obscured by the conflicting desires to visit again the sun-drenched countries and to record them, as well as to sail free and in my own sweet time, Janet's devotion was single-minded. She was one of Baudelaire's elect company *'les vrais voyageurs qui partent seulement pour partir'*.

We sat up late that night—our decision made—and discussed the many changes which we should have to make to our lives. We were still talking when the dawn came up grey over the London roofscape—tangled chimneys covering eight million sleeping heads—still talking, and finishing the remains of a bottle of brandy that had been full a few hours before. The sun in the grape stirred my memories, and I remember looking through the open windows over the city. It was already turning pearl-grey and pink as the sun rose, and I was taking a kind of dream flight over the huddle of the town. I could see the Aegean islands raising their opal heads out of a May morning, smell thyme on the wind, and hear the sea.

Four months later we left England for France. We had been waiting for two days inside the bar at Chichester harbour while a spring gale blew itself out down the Channel. The wind was dying now and the barometer was rising. Janet took the tiller while I heaved in the anchor. The voyage had begun.

Our boat, *Mother Goose*, was a ten-ton cutter. A Dutch boeier, with a draught of only two feet, she was forty years old, clinker-built of galvanized iron on iron frames. She was as tubby, as solid, and as dependable as a Dutchman's ideal *hausfrau*. Her decks were teak, her curved aerofoil leeboards (which threw great fan-like shadows on the deck) were of oak, and her saloon and interior were panelled in polished mahogany. With her dark blue hull, her tanned red sails, her curved gaff, and her elaborately carved tiller—which ended in a goose's head—she was a romantic boat. Some had their doubts about her.

'I wouldn't mind her on the Broads,' said an ocean-racing friend. 'But I wouldn't like to be out in her in any real weather.'

'You'll never be taking that, midear, any far way from land,' remarked old Jack, who was coxwain of the Fowey lifeboat. 'Why, look at them there leeboards! No, midear, you want a good keel under you when you get out to sea. Them there boats is all very well for the Dutch.'

I heard many such arguments. When questioned closely as to where I really intended to take her, I hedged or remarked casually, 'Well, we might pick a quiet day and run over to France.' I never disclosed my real intentions. Certainly, even I never realized that within the thirty-foot length of *Mother Goose* we should make our home for two and a half years.

The first time that you make a departure for a foreign coast-line in your own boat is as unforgettable as first love. There is a tension and a suppressed excitement about your actions. Even routine details like taking a pair of crossed bearings to fix your point of departure assume a strange and satisfying importance.

Outside the bar we found that the wind had died but the sea was still running lumpily up the Channel. The grey sky was touched with faint light along the edges of the clouds. I sighted along the hand-bearing compass and called out the bearings to Janet who had the chart splayed out in front of her on the saloon table.

'One nine oh degrees—the Nab tower.'

She repeated it back.

'Two three oh degrees—Culver Head. One degree easterly deviation on the compass.'

Fixed. The simple 'mystery' of the navigator's art now held our small swaying world of food and books and iron and wood and us, located in one pinpoint on the Channel chart. The intersected lines that marked the boat's position marked the start of our new life. In the act of taking two bearings we had crossed our Rubicon and established for all our lives the point of no return.

The kettle feathered a wisp of steam through the open hatch, and soon we were clasping mugs of hot coffee as we sat in the cockpit and listened to the suck and swallow of the sea against the ship's side. The wind died away, and the sails hung empty as a sailor's pockets. I started our small twin-cylinder diesel engine, waited an anxious moment until its first asthmatic cough had settled down to a steady snore, and then lashed the tiller while the two of us lowered the sails.

Even under power *Mother Goose* left a clean sweet wake. Her rounded stern settled down or rose to the sea like a bird's blunt tail. She lifted easily over the swell, and ran down its sides with a smooth, unhurried movement.

We were twenty-four hours out from Chichester Bar when we sighted Le Havre light vessel blinking and groaning in a cold white mist. As the lights of Le Havre faded against the dawn and went out we altered course for the nearest whistle buoy, whose sigh blended with the melancholy morning. The broken buildings and the stark lines of the reconstructed city came up past the headland. Shipping thronged the fairway, and a Chinese cook, carrying a vast tea-pot along the decks of a merchantman, gave us 'Good Day' with a flash of teeth.

Janet and I looked at each other and smiled. The damp night air had crinkled our hands, and it sparkled in our hair.

'Made it!'

The first leg of the voyage was over. Now we could confess to each other what we had never confessed to inquisitive long-shoremen or even to friends: that this was not just a casual trip to France 'only if the weather's fine'. This was the end of one life and the beginning of another. We were bound up the Seine for Paris and beyond—through the canal for Lyons, then down the Rhône to Marseilles. Our course lay eastward to the dolphin-haunted waters; to the islands of thyme and silver rock, and the high noon that leaves no shadows.

The Channel weather followed us up the Seine. The rain drove down in iron-grey spears. The trees leaned to the hissing water, and we lived to the melancholy drip of sails and cordage. At the end of our first day I was looking for somewhere to secure for the night when I sighted ahead of us a long line of barges moored to the bank. It was our first encounter with the *mariniers*. I wondered what reception we should get from these hard-bitten bargees of the French inland water world. I need not have worried.

'*Vous permettez?*' I called up to the first barge as I idled *Mother Goose* against the stream. Janet held up a warp on the foredeck.

'But certainly.' A squat bull-neck turned and shouted something into the barge's fo'c'sle. Two men appeared on deck.

'Let us assist you. Better if you got a little further ahead. Let Jean jump aboard and give you a hand with your fenders. The tide runs fast here! You need to be well secured for the night.'

It was the beginning of a long and pleasant acquaintanceship. Communists to a man, the French *mariniers* were unfailingly kind and courteous to us in our voyage through their canals.

'My aunt,' said the barge skipper, 'runs a *bistro* a quarter of a mile up-river from here. If you care to come with me you can get good wine. Food if you wish it. Tomorrow morning she will have fresh bread ready for us before we leave. If your lady needs bread I will order some for you.'

A good friend! Two days later, when we were anchored in the stream a few yards off the small village of La Bouille, I met him again. We had been ashore for dinner the previous night and lay late in our bunks listening to the swirl of the Seine an inch or less from our ears. The sound of moving water makes for deep sleep, and I was far away next morning when a noise like a bull snorting slowly down the ship's side brought me out with a rush. Still half asleep I leapt into the cockpit, and looked up to find a barge towering over me. The skipper and the crew laughed at my sleep-stained face.

'Pardon for waking you, m'sieu. You aren't in trouble? Ah, good. I saw your small boat anchored here and stopped to ask. Well, we shall meet in Rouen then.'

He went back to the wheelhouse. The barge's bows fell away

from *Mother Goose*. His diesel engine rumbled and then, with a plume of smoke and a wave, he was off into the soft spring morning.

Some weeks later in Marseilles, I was to hear from a distinguished English yachtsman of the 'insolence and rudeness' of the French bargees. He was a man who lived under the conviction that the working classes of the world—and particularly foreigners —should respond readily to a shout of 'Hey! You there!' There are many like him. May their boats yearly be squashed in Seine locks, may longshoreman steal all their ropes, and may gigolos from Nice seduce their wives!

At Rouen we lowered the mast, ate snails in the shadow of the cathedral, and drank too much at Stockholm Jack's bar. It rained steadily the two days that we were there. It was still raining when we left.

'Let's get going. The sea and the south!' Janet took the tiller.

'I've had my breakfast,' she said. 'There's fresh tea in the galley. Bacon and eggs in the oven. Croissant on the table.'

It was good to sit below and listen to the steady mutter of the engine as we drove up the river. It was good to eat breakfast with a book propped in front of me and hear, outside my small world of warmth and comfort, the plash of rain on the coach-roof overhead. I browsed over *Saint Anthony* with added appreciation. A few miles from here, on this wet and windy river, Flaubert might have written his words especially for us:

We go South, beyond the mountains and the great waters, to seek in perfumes the reason of love . . . the stars tremble like eyes, the water-falls sing like lyres, intoxicating are the opening flowers; among those airs your spirit will grow wings. It is time, the wind is rising, the swallows are awakening, the myrtle leaf has fled away!

'Hey there!'

I put the book away and stacked my cup and plate in the sink.

'There's a wind getting up. The clouds are thinning.'

We anchored that night, clear of the main stream in the lee of a small island. I looked at the waterways chart—the Grande Ile d'Orival. From a village, hidden round a bend in the river, we could hear the strange brassy voice of a steam roundabout. The murmur of a fair came to us in drifts on the wind. The lights of the village, and the fires and lights of the fair stained the low-lying clouds with orange.

Janet woke me early next morning.

'Come on outside. It really is a day!'

I looked at the clock over the bookshelf. Six.

'What?'

'I heard the cable rattle as we swung to the tide, and got up to see if the anchor was holding. It is. Come on up.'

The rain had stopped, and a soft mist sprawled over the river and the country. As we sat in the cockpit over breakfast, *Mother Goose* seemed to float suspended in a gossamer world. Spiders' webs, spun between the lowered mast and the coachroof, trembled under a million beads of moisture. The damp earth smelt rich with grass, trees and flowers—the distilled essence of spring. The Seine was cool silver, and fine gossamer strands blew in our faces as we lit our cigarettes and prepared to start the day.

The anchor came up clean from the river bed. I washed down the cable and the foredeck with icy water that made my toes curl. Janet put the engine in gear and we headed out into midstream, leaving a slick of oil behind us on the calm river. We were motoring through an innocent world—a morning such as one remembers from childhood. The rising sun brushed away the mist, but like an untidy maid, left it hanging all day in hedgerows and hollows: forgotten patches pooled under plane trees or round the roots of willows.

'Listen!'

Above the bumble of the engine we could hear the cuckoo shouting from copse to copse. A liquid sound—his voice had not yet broken—each note seemed to burst like a soap bubble, leaving behind it an almost iridescent film on the air.

Two days later we were nearing the outskirts of Paris. It was a heavy thundery evening and the midges were steaming up off the river.

'Let's make fast for the night and run on into Paris tomorrow.'

Janet nodded. 'Yes. We can't get much further anyway. There's a lock half a mile ahead and it'll be closed by the time we're there.'

We brought up alongside a solitary barge, the *Persée*. Her skipper, hitching his bony body against the gunwale, commented on the fact that, like himself, I smoked Gaulloise and settled down for a talk. Like most French working men he was obsessed by money and food. As he talked he spat with precision, over the gunwale and into the river, to punctuate his sentences.

'My employers—sons of bitches—hrrch! pwwhhtt!—they're all the same, all employers—we work only to eat. We've no money left for diversions—pwwhhtt!—or for new clothes, by the time we've paid for our food and wine.'

His wife, hitching her skirts to disclose dead-white legs stained with broken veins, clambered over to inspect our galley and saloon. She patted Janet on the shoulder.

'It's a hard life, my child, living on board a boat. But then you do this for pleasure? Incredible! If I had the money for your little boat I would buy a farm with it and never more travel on the water.'

Meanwhile her small daughter, a sloe-eyed urchin of six, played with her rag doll. It was a simple game, and consisted in letting down the doll's skirts and sitting it carefully over the stern of the barge in a position that called for no speculation.

They were hard people, but friendly. We exchanged glasses of wine for whisky. The skipper drank his with a wry face, then patted his belly.

'What fire! This may account for the Scottish soldiers!' He slapped his wife's backside.

'Watch out for yourself tonight!'

As we left in the morning his wife called out to Janet: 'Don't shop on the right bank in Paris! Go to the left bank behind the Eiffel Tower.'

The skipper shook my hand as we cast off.

'We load with cement today. Tomorrow we come up to Paris. But I'd rather be here.' He waved his hand over the muddy banks and the rising mist. 'It's sad to be in Paris, and not be able to divert oneself. Whereas here—no temptation.'

He laughed and spat into the widening gulf between our boats.

We berthed finally a few yards away from the Pont Alexandre III, within sound of the Champs Elysée orchestra—of the ceaseless drumming of traffic, the squeal, squeak and bray of brakes and car horns. We spent ten days there moored alongside the Yacht Club de France: I had work to do, articles to be typed, and photographs to be printed. Apart from that, we were tempted to linger, for Paris exerted its old familiar charm—like a drug or a lover from whom one must break free or die. We had far to go and we could see our limited foreign currency blowing away down the light wind. Then we would remind ourselves that every franc spent in Paris would be better spent in a fishing village south of Naples.

Waking in the morning was easy those days. Who would not wake with pleasure if, by raising an arm and sliding open a hatch, he could uncover a view of the Seine powdered with May morning haze? Under an idle air the trees were twisting their new leaves, and the Pont Alexandre was catching the early sunlight on the lavish busts and thighs of its gilt figures.

'Hurry—or we shall miss the market!'

Janet swung her string bag and we were off into the soft morning.

The night before we left a group of friends descended on the boat and took us away on one of those fiery electric evenings that seem to occur less and less the older one grows. Even before raising the first glass in Harry's bar we knew that we would see the dawn come up over the river. By four in the morning there were five of us, the hardy remnant of an early dozen, sitting in a café in the Rue Jacob. Our cab driver, whom we had collected at the Crillon early in the evening, was still with us. A man with a magnificently gross face, he had a deep laugh that rumbled like distant thunder in his belly.

'*J'aime brutaliser les femmes!*' he remarked suddenly and then, pursuing some inner vision of God knows what delights, shook with submerged laughter. A minute later, having learnt that one of our friends was a Scot, he accepted a cigar from him and remarked with grave candour.

'The Scots—Ah, the Scots are as grasping as Jews!' He lit Mac's cigar and beamed through the smoke.

Loaded with flowers (our last call had been at the flower market) we stumbled back aboard *Mother Goose*. The Seine was sliding past shiny with morning light and the city had a faded pastel air. It was time to go.

'Good-bye, then! Good-bye!'

The engine rumbled and we drew away from the bank. Another landmark was behind us. Although it was now early

June the river was in spate. The rains had come late and heavy over France, and all the mountain streams were discharging into the swollen river. It was no easy business battling upstream with a small engine which could give us six knots at the most. In the centre the Seine was running close on five knots, but we followed the low-powered barges and watched how they hugged the banks and how they worked the bends and eddies in the river.

Our voyage nearly came to an end in the small village of Champagne-sur-Seine, under a rainy sky and against the muddy banks of the Seine. The weir there was broken by the floods and the full force of the river hurtled across the entrance to the lock gates. It was unsafe for any except the most powerful barges to attempt to rush the lock gates, and so we waited there in company with an ever-increasing number of barges. Secured next to a cheerful group of Belgians we waited and listened to the drumming of the rain on the coachroof and the steady hiss of the angry river against the side. Our only diversion was to watch the attempts of the more powerful, or more confident, barges to mount against the stream and enter the lock without damage. One of them hitting the bank at an angle of forty-five degrees, was spun on its side by the force of the flood water and all but turned over. Another had his stern set down against the concrete wall and broke his rudder. I spoke to her skipper afterwards in the small *bistro* by the lock.

'It's making anything from seven to eight knots in the centre,' he said. 'And the water's still rising. You'll have to wait a day or so yet with your little boat. And now I have to convince my owners that it was not negligence that caused me to break the rudder. If they hadn't ordered me to get to Lyons at all costs I would have waited a day or two. They won't like this! A new rudder and the boat out of service for two weeks will cost them more francs than they pay me in a year.'

We had a glass of Marc together. It was the right drink for that grey weather, disinfecting the throat and exploding like a depth-charge deep down in the belly.

'We can't go yet,' I said to Janet when I got back. 'The river's still rising.'

We were having breakfast in the cockpit next morning, watching the barges coming downstream, when suddenly it happened. A powered barge—I noticed her name, the *Vega*—

had just left the lock gates with a trot of three deep-laden cement barges in tow behind her. She was crossing into midstream when the current from the broken weir struck her stern and swung her off course. She just missed the far bank, straightened up in time and whirled downstream, two of the towed craft following her obediently. The third, spinning out from the line and pointing her bows in our direction, burst from the tow-rope like an arrow from a bent bow and came hurtling across the river. I heard the Belgians inboard of us give a yell and start leaping for the bank, even before I had realized our danger.

There was nothing that Janet or I could do. It was only a matter of seconds from the barge breaking her tow until the moment when she thundered into the bank astern of us. Thank God she was deep-laden! The projecting top of our mast, which was lowered into a cradle over the cockpit, stuck out some eight foot from the stern of *Mother Goose*. The bows of the barge passed clean under the mast. If she had been a few feet higher in the water the barge would have broken the mast to pieces; if she had been pointing a few feet higher up the river she would have come clean through the cockpit where we sat.

Her skipper who had been fighting the heavy tiller, trying with all his might to avoid us, fell to the deck as the barge struck the bank. A wave of dank Seine water bounded high and drenched us where we sat. Our dinghy, which had been lying alongside, was lifted on the bow-wave of the barge, broke its painter and came down with a crash on deck. *Mother Goose* rose to the wave and fell back heavily against the side of the Belgian inboard and carried away two fenders. Drenched and stupefied we sat there for a moment not sure whether we were dead or alive.

The skipper picked himself up—his barge was stuck at right angles into the bank and held there in the soft French mud. If possible, he was more shaken than we were, for he had seen all along what was likely to happen.

'My God!' He leaned over and looked down at us. 'Are you all right? I had my whole strength on the tiller, m'sieu. I thought she was certain to hit you.'

I clambered aboard and we shook hands, then together we secured his barge to the bank until the *Vega* should come back and tow him clear. Reaction had set in by now and we all needed a drink. His wife purred over Janet like a cat over a recovered kitten.

As soon as the river was down we joined the string of barges and pressed on upstream. June had come at last, with a warm sun and fleecy clouds grazing over the moss-green countryside. We had met many *mariniers* already, but now we were entering their private world—the long silver canals that cut across France like softer, more feminine versions of the Roman roads. Unlike England, the canals of France are not dead; they are alive and busy with traffic. In this world of locks and grass-lined waterways the *marinier* reigns supreme, a tired-eyed man, usually with a plump wife and a growing brood of children. His barge is as clean as his hands are dirty; he has little time for his owners, and he knows that the working man in France will never fight in any other war—on anybody's side. For many days now we lived their life on à thread of water, through banks lined by cattle, to the throb of diesel engines and the sight of the long, low barges striding out of the landscape.

'Happy?'

'Who wouldn't be?' Janet looked up from some splicing she was doing. She rolled the splice under foot to finish it off and then got out the sailmaker's thread to put a whipping on the rope. The exhaust rumbled contentedly as the flower- and reed-lined bank flickered by. The stove was going for supper and there was a soft haze over the water. Tonight we would find a lonely bank with a prospect of distant hills. We would secure the boat carefully and have the quiet tapestry country all to ourselves.

The Canal de Bourgogne had one major drawback, and it did not take us long to find it. Weed, muscular and sinewy as a wrestler, infested the quiet water. Once it had wrapped itself in a green taut bundle round our small propeller a groan from the engine and a cloud of black smoke would soon bring us to a halt. There was nothing one could do but dive overboard with a knife and unravel or slice to pieces the clogging bundle—no easy job, for the weed tied itself into hard Chinese knots, the one superimposed on the other. The canal was icy cold and reputedly typhoidal. The shock on entering the water seemed to stop my heart, and I would have to dive and saw away with a knife sometimes for half an hour.

It was a good thing Janet was strong in the arms. One grey

afternoon I got so frozen and had cut my hand on the propeller blade into the bargain that I could not drag myself back on board. She got her hands under my armpits and hauled me over the side and within a minute had me swathed in a bath-towel, seated in front of our paraffin stove, drinking Marc out of a half-pint tumbler. I put it down to the quantities of Marc I drank in those days that I neither got typhoid nor pneumonia.

Now we were beginning the long climb over the range of hills behind which Dijon lies. For mile after mile the gentle, civilized land mounted in front of us. The thin grey ribbon of the canal was increasingly broken by locks—locks which we would always try to enter in company with a barge, for the *mariniers* would work the lock gates. When we were travelling alone, on the other hand, Janet would have to take the tiller while I jumped off onto the bank, some fifty yards ahead of the lock, and ran up to help with the gates. The job of lock-keeper in France is usually given to war widows or war wounded. Either old or incapacitated, they rely on the traveller to do his own donkey work.

Fine people most of them, they are poor but with dignity. Their cottage and their vegetable garden go with the job, but their pay is little more than five pounds a month. We found them glad to barter with us: coffee for fresh eggs, corned beef for apples or lettuces. One old woman, brown and crinkled as a walnut, came running up just as we were leaving her lock.

'Madame! Madame! The coffee you gave me was too much for only six eggs. Here, a small gift. I've nothing else with which to thank you.'

She bent down and gave Janet a dark rose out of her garden. We looked back and waved, and she was still waving when the next bend in the canal hid her from sight.

Just before one reaches the crest of the mountain range the canal dives into a dark tunnel, to emerge on the far side with the trim escalator of water dropping away from you all the way to Dijon. It was strange that tunnel. It took us nearly an hour to motor through the dank vein of water between the sunlight on one side of the hills and the sunlight on the other. The engine was running badly and I had an unreasoning fear of something going wrong; it was unreasoning because the next barge on its way through would have found us and towed us clear.

The sound of the exhaust echoed ominously round the

dripping walls. At every hesitation in its mutter I would feel a constriction in my stomach. Janet stood beside me, shining the Aldis lamp ahead of us.

'I'll be glad when we're out of here.'

'Me, too,' she said. 'I've got the feeling that we might never get out.'

It was good to see the shining eye that marked the far end, and better still when the rich scents of the country and the glow of the evening sun lit the water. There was something akin to the old Mysteries of Eleusis about that dive into the dark, and the resurrection into light and life on the far side. From this point on we knew that all the canals and rivers flowed homeward towards the sea—not the cold sea that we had left behind us, but the warm summer Mediterranean.

'Good evening, monsieur and madame.' It was an old friend, the skipper of the barge *Romeo*, moored against the bank, who greeted us as we emerged. He took our lines and helped make us fast for the night.

'Come aboard and have a drink,' I said. I had found that all the *mariniers* liked a tot of whisky.

'It's all easy now,' he said, pointing ahead of us. 'All downhill.' The canal dropped away from us in silver stages towards Dijon and the Saône.

'Take a skipper at Lyons,' were his parting words. 'Take a pilot for the Rhône, m'sieu. It's not like other rivers. Don't imagine that the Rhône is like the Seine. It's a dangerous river, a real boat-eater!'

Motoring downhill was easier and pleasanter than the long steady trudge to which we had become accustomed. The locks filled with the rushing of descending water all in a few minutes, and the only worry was that the eight foot of mast which projected over our stern might get sprained against the stone walls. We watched over *Mother Goose* with the tenderness of parents. She was not only our home; she was our capital, and our only passport to the world of wind and sea. When I had bought her, boat prices had been low, and I knew that her insurance value could never buy anything half as good. I have sailed with rich men for whom their boat was no more than the means to a sport, just as a bag of golf clubs might be. They could never have understood that to us a boat was more than a plaything; it was the means to a way of life.

43

But what do you do all day, people sometimes ask, living in a boat? There is plenty to do if you live in a boat as we did for years, always on the move. There is the job of sailing and navigating yourself from A to B to start with. After that—if you have any time left—there is the steady work of maintenance; engines, bilge pumps, lavatories and lighting systems to be maintained; as well as keeping the boat inside and out as clean as a frosty morning. When all these things were done, Janet would cook or sew or mend, while I wandered about with the camera, or sat at the small saloon table and typed out the stories and articles that helped feed us and pay for the upkeep of our journeying home. We had a small library on board, that included—stowed in a long rack in the fo'c'sle—the *Encyclopaedia Britannica*. We read much in the quiet evenings. Now, while we descended the stairway of locks towards Dijon, Janet was working on her Italian and I was trying to transform my schoolboy Greek into a working knowledge of the modern tongue. If one is living a full life there is no need for cinema, radio, television, or any of the things that distract urban man from his unhappiness. There is always plenty to do.

We fell on Dijon and the rich plunder of the Burgundian countryside like crazy Goths. For two days we indulged Balzacian appetites—vast puddings heavy with fruit, glazed brawns, wines and liqueurs, thick piles of chocolate, and sweet waves of cakes and pastries. With appetites sharpened by health, fresh air, and exercise, we gave ourselves a brief spell from home-cooking. Two days was more than enough for stomach and purse. We left several pounds fatter and many francs lighter, to push on to St-Jean-de-Losne where we left the canal behind and joined the River Saône.

We were three weeks out from Paris, and in just over 400 kilometres we had passed through 218 locks—nearly a lock a mile, and small wonder that I had biceps like Sugar Ray. The marks of our dawdling struggle through the French countryside were to be seen on *Mother Goose*'s stained but undamaged sides.

'Isn't it just wunnerful,' said an American woman whom we met aboard a large motor yacht in Dijon, 'just wunnerful gliding through the French country? So peaceful. Kin' of timeless.' Her paid skipper gave me a slow wink. He knew, as we did, that there is more to it than that. Canal travelling is peaceful, and it is timeless, but what gives it its savour is the concentration and hard work involved.

'They get so bored,' he said to me afterwards, jerking his head to where the 'afterguard' sat over their evening martinis. 'Sometimes they quarrel. Sometimes they drink. The rest of the time they spend trying to make up their minds whether to swop partners before we reach Marseilles or after!'

We were washing down the decks next day, when Janet remarked: 'I'm glad we're not rich "yachtsmen". How dull things would be if all we had to do was to watch our sailors doing this for us.'

It was the 29th of June when we slid down the Saône, fast-running and muddy after the late rains, and secured in the heart of Lyons. The Roman theatre was glowing under a tawny sunset on our right, and on our left was all the shouting bustle and colour of the great market.

'Now it really is downhill all the way.' We shared a smile. The river stumbled against the boat's side and made a broken babbling round the rudder.

'I must overhaul the mainsail.'

'I'll do it. I'm handier with palm and needle than you.'

'We'll stop at Arles and get the mast up. I must get the engine decoked before we push out to sea.'

'That'll be the day!'

Our pilot, seventy years old, white-haired and tanned, with the alert figure of a young man, stepped aboard.

'My name is Pacquet. Pleased to meet you. You will be ready to leave tomorrow morning? At six o'clock, then. Yes, we enter the lock just after six.'

'Will you have a drink?'

'No thank you. Never anything but a little wine with my meals. That's how my father lived to be ninety-five.'

We walked down to the Rhône and looked at it—the huge, boat-eating river, swirling southward in the sunset.

'She's a big river, all right.'

'Yes. The last stretch of fresh water we'll see for some time.'

Mother Goose did not feel fresh water again beneath her keel until we anchored in a river in Greece. But that was two thousand miles and a year away.

4

M ONSIEUR PACQUET warmed his hands round a cup of coffee and balanced the tiller against his thigh.

'We'll stop for the night at Montelimar,' he said. 'There's a place where we can turn the boat and go alongside comfortably. Then, if we leave early, we shall get through the "Chute" at Donzères by seven o'clock.'

'The "Chute"?' I queried.

'Yes. You know that the Rhône dam is nearly completed? But the canal isn't open yet. Just for the moment they've left a space about thirty metres wide for the barges to pass through. It's not dangerous, you understand—but it's not easy. That's why I asked you when we left this morning to make sure that everything on board was well lashed down. At Donzères the whole of the Rhône is diverted through a small channel. As you can see'— he waved his old hand over the hungry river—'the river is in spate. When we get to the "Chute" there's a slight waterfall. That's because the stream is running over a concrete bed they're laying in the river.' He smiled at Janet. 'Nothing for Madame to worry about. We shall do it easily.'

I did not like the sound of the 'Chute', but I soon had confidence in our pilot. We were racing down on our first bridge, the engine giving us five knots and the current another six, when I noticed Monsieur Pacquet putting the helm carefully over to starboard. We spun down towards the central span of the bridge at an angle of thirty degrees to the stream, and I made a gesture of protest. He smiled.

'Watch now!'

No sooner were *Mother Goose*'s bows level with the beginning of the stonework than she lurched to port, straightened up, and went through dead in the centre.

'There's a side current,' he said. 'That's something no chart or diagram could show you. How would you have undertaken that bridge if you'd been by yourself?'

'I'd have aimed for the centre.'

'Yes, of course you would.' He took a light off my cigarette. 'And so would anyone else who didn't know. And then, what would have happened? Suddenly you'd have found the bows fall off to port and—unless you were careful—you would have been swept into the arch. The Rhône isn't easy, particularly for a boat like yours that hasn't the power to beat the current.'

The sun came out. Grey, broken castles on high peaks guarded the river. Vines mounted in trim escalators up the warm flanks of mountains. I took the tiller while the pilot ate his lunch, and listened to his old water-voice telling me about the Rhône. Fifty-three years he had spent as a boy, deck-hand and pilot on these waters. The descendant of men who had navigated the Rhône for centuries, he had been born in a village on its banks; in a small house which had belonged to his family for generations. The sound of the river and its changing face from spring to winter had been the background of his life.

'Careful now.' He looked up. 'You see this bridge ahead? Go through the centre span. I'll tell you what to do with the tiller. Two years ago a Danish yacht came down here. Her captain was a great sailor. He'd taken his yacht over many seas, so—when he came to the Rhône—he said: "No thank you. No pilot." Put the helm hard to starboard!'

I did so and turned *Mother Goose* nearly broadside to the stream. I could hear the hungry mouthing of the water as it piled up round the arches.

'Yes,' he went on. 'This poor Danish man, he does what anyone would do who did not know better. He heads straight for the centre.'

As he spoke *Mother Goose* shivered, twisted sideways and sailed under the main arch at almost double her previous speed, pointing straight downstream.

'You see?' He lit a cigarette and stood up. 'I'll take her now. Yes, he enters the bridge in the middle, not knowing about that current. His boat was crushed on the arch and he, his wife, and one of the crew were drowned. Only two survived, the cook and the small son of six. The cook swam ashore with the child in his arms—somewhere just near here. He probably

47

fetched up on that sand spit. That's where the river would carry you.'

Evening came down as we neared Le Teil, the village near Montelimar where we were to secure for the night. Since leaving the lock at Lyons in the morning we had covered 158 kilometres —in the canals we had thought thirty a good day's average.

Monsieur Pacquet pointed ahead.

'There—you see that derelict barge? We'll go alongside that for the night.'

A few hundred yards above the barge he began to turn the boat round so that we faced upstream. The engine was running at almost maximum revolutions, yet we were still being borne backwards by the current. Keeping *Mother Goose*'s bows at a slight angle to the stream we edged slowly astern in a crabwise movement towards the bank. Just as the barge's bows came level with our quarter he motioned me to give the engine full boost. I opened the throttle as wide as it would go. Close in by the bank the current was less and we found that we were just stemming it.

'Good. Now ease her a bit.'

We came alongside as gently as thistledown, and in a few minutes were made fast. Janet and I looked at the old man with admiration. He was seventy years old, yet he had stood at the tiller all day long, only resting himself to sit down for half an hour while he had lunch. Now, with a practised ease and a strength of arm that many a young man might have envied, he swung himself up onto the barge.

'I must catch my bus to Montelimar—where my wife awaits me. I will see you tomorrow, Captain. At five o'clock? *Entendu.* Please don't forget to see that everything is well secured before we leave. I wish you good night, madame.'

We watched him stride off towards the road and his bus home.

Later that night, as we were eating dinner, Janet suddenly motioned for silence. She laid down her knife and fork.

'Listen!'

The night was quiet, the boat still, and against this emptiness we could hear the voice of the Rhône. Our iron hull resounded with an icy, continuous hiss. This was not the gentle whisper with which the Seine and the Saône had lulled us to sleep. This sound was peremptory and demanding. Sometimes a floating branch would thump against our bows, and then make its way down the ship's side—tap! tap-tap!—with ominous fingers. Occasionally an eddy or side-current would boil up against the yacht with a chuckling, sucking noise.

We were awake by half past four next morning. I think neither of us had slept well. While Janet made breakfast I went carefully round the boat checking all the lashings, seeing that the mast was firmly bedded in its cradle, and putting another rope's end over the anchor on the foredeck.

'All ready?'

Monsieur Pacquet stepped aboard and looked about him with his quiet, old man's smile. The boat was soaked with dew. Whatever one touched left one's hand cold and wet.

'All ready,' I said.

A few seconds later we had cast off and were slipping downstream through a grey morning mist. You could hear the noise of the river even above the engine.

We had been going about an hour, and the sun was beginning to break through, when I noticed that the current was running much faster. I had gone forward to check the oil level in the engine and was just making my way back to the cockpit when Monsieur Pacquet raised his arm and pointed ahead.

'Donzères!' he said. 'The dam!'

Across more than three-quarters of its length the Rhône was blocked by a dark line of concrete and masonry. Above this great wall cranes and derricks raised their sharp heads like sentries. On the left, where the river still ran unrestrained, a huddle of buildings, cranes and huts straggled back into the fields.

'That's where the canal will run when the dam's completed,' he said. 'It will be easy then. For the first time in all its history the Rhône will be tamed. Next year it will be completed.'

I knew he was retiring next year. I think he was pleased to go before the face of his river was altered.

'Get out the klaxon, Captain. We are supposed to warn them before we make the passage of the "Chute".'

The horn brayed awkwardly in the early morning. 'Childe Roland to the dark tower came.'

But no one appeared on any of the ramparts ahead of us. No

flags broke from the battlements. There was no signal. Monsieur Pacquet looked a little worried.

'Again,' he said, 'sound it again.'

But perhaps the guards were at breakfast, or perhaps they never heard the weak sound of our klaxon above the roaring of the river. It would have made no difference. It was too late now to turn back, even if we had been ordered to. The Rhône had caught us in its teeth and was sweeping us downstream like a stick between a dog's jaws.

'We go through that bridge span?' I shouted. He nodded— a little grimly. The span was quite plain now, a narrow passage little more than thirty yards wide. Beneath it poured the full force of the river, the Rhône in spate making an ugly, grumbling noise as it felt the restraint of the cement dam. The bank was sliding past increasingly quickly, like countryside glimpsed in a dream. A large notice on the foreshore loomed up: 'Canoeists, small boats and those unfamiliar with the river, stop here! Before attempting to proceed, it is advisable to inspect the passage ahead. DANGER!' Over the bridge itself another notice in red letters several feet high announced 'PASSEZ-ICI'.

Now that we were only a few hundred yards away from the dam, we could see what effect it had on the waters of the Rhône. Beneath the span of the bridge a confused white mass of water was flanked by sinister green arms of side-currents. The 'Chute' itself was an overfall caused by the concrete foundations that were being laid on the bed of the Rhône. As tons of concrete were pumped below the surface, so the level of this submerged base rose, and the river grew more and more disturbed.

We were rapidly nearing the bridge, making straight for the centre of the arch, and we could see how hazardous the 'Chute' was. The river dipped smoothly downwards for a few yards like a line of stretched silk and then, every now and again, bubbling up from the surface, an opposing wave would build up to break against the main current of the river. As we drew close I saw one of these waves collapse with a boom and sizzle like surf breaking on a beach.

I glanced at Monsieur Pacquet. He was holding the tiller with both hands, his feet braced against the well of the cockpit, his eyes fixed on the surface ahead. Then I realized, from the speed with which we were making our approach and from the sinister heave of the water in front of us, that we were going to enter the 'Chute' at the very moment that the opposing wave was ready to break. Monsieur Pacquet gave a small unquiet whistle. Janet looked into both our faces and went below, closing the hatch after her.

'Stand by the engine controls!'

I jumped across and opened the throttle, as we had arranged, to three-quarters. The pilot braced himself. I held on with one hand on the throttle, the other round the main boom as we dived downwards, with an ugly lurching movement like a seagull overbalanced in an air current. The next few minutes were timeless—rather like being under a dive-bomb attack, with one's stomach compressed in a ball and one's senses anaesthetized.

As *Mother Goose* dipped her bows into the 'Chute', the propeller was flung, roaring, clear of the water. At the same moment, the wave which had built up in front of us broke like thunder on our bows. For a split second, as the water rolled over the fo'c'sle and swept aft along the upper deck and over the coachroof I thought it was certain to sink us. Warps and spars, boathooks and fenders rose up under the press of water and floated aft—as far as their lashings would allow them—in a confused heap. Now I knew why the pilot had been so concerned about everything being lashed down. One rope trailing over the side to wind itself round the propeller would have left us helpless. As it was, the yacht was out of control. At one moment the propeller and rudder would be clear of the water. At another, they would be dug down into such conflicting currents that they were impotent.

I glanced at Monsieur Pacquet. He gave me a tired smile, then shrugged his shoulders as if to say: 'You see—there's nothing I can do. Except keep hold of the tiller!'

We were through the 'Chute' itself by now, and out in the wild welter on the far side of the bridge. *Mother Goose* was swung broadside on to the force of the stream, shipping great waves over the cockpit. Both of us were soaked to the skin. A sudden twist and an unexpected roll threw open the saloon hatch, just as a wave broke clean over the boat. Half of it went down below, and there was a crash of breaking crockery. Janet popped out like a jack-in-the-box. She had thought that the yacht was turning over, and that either I or the pilot had opened the hatch to let her escape.

There were a few more violent rolls, another wave which knocked the cover off the compass and shot a wicked wet hand down the saloon hatch, and then we were in comparatively calm water. For the first time since we had entered the 'Chute' I could hear the sound of the engine, purring away reassuringly. Monsieur Pacquet smiled and squared off *Mother Goose* on her course downstream.

'I would have turned back as soon as I saw what it was like today,' he said. 'But then we couldn't, could we? Not once the old lady had us by the throat.'

Out of the chaos of the saloon we fetched cigarettes and a bottle of brandy.

'Yes, perhaps today—it's against my rules, but perhaps today I will have a drink, too.' He swallowed. 'Very good brandy! Here's to the success of your voyage. I think you have the worst of it behind you!'

The inside of the boat was chaotic. Cups, glasses and plates had been hurled from their racks and lay scattered over the soaking deck. Books had been thrown from their shelves and lay miserably among spilt marmalade and tea. Things which would have stayed secure throughout bad weather at sea had jumped loose with the boat's sudden and contradictory cavortings. The radio had broken its two retaining screws and leapt bodily into my bunk.

'*Ma foi!*' Monsieur Pacquet peered below. 'Your poor wife—she will never forgive us for this!'

The worst of the Rhône was behind us. Now, with every mile that we drew nearer to Arles the stream decreased as the river spread out into a grandeur of unruffled water. Avignon went by in a glow of ancient walls, its broken Roman bridge defying the current of the centuries. The sun was warm. The fields were rich. The smell of summer was in the air.

At Arles we said good-bye to Monsieur Pacquet. He left us to catch the train north to Lyons; tomorrow morning he was due to pick up an oil barge and make the trip south again. At seventy he still had the firm body and the clear eye of a young man. A fine dignified human being, may he live long beside his river and go to sleep with its deep susurrus in his ears!

It was midday in Arles and Janet and I were alone again; alone in our own boat and our home; with work to do, and a meal to eat, and a whole town to explore. Midday was drowsy with the high, ceaseless dynamo of the cicadas, and the sun was spread like golden butter along the boat's sides and over the deep-gleaming varnish of the coachroof.

'You think we're cheating?' I showed Janet the headlines of the local paper. Korea was in flames. Women and children were dying under napalm bombs in the same sunlight.

'Can you change the world?' she said. 'I expect there were times during the war when you were having hell when there were people living happy lives in other countries, people who hardly knew there was a war on. No one could ever be happy if they felt guilty because somewhere else other people were in misery. I expect we'll get our turn.'

A breeze cooled the evening, blowing up the Rhône delta with the faintest perceptible taste of salt on it. The Mediterranean lay only twenty miles away. The breeze stirred the dust and scraps of paper in the small square where we shopped and sat idly over apéritifs. Outside the Roman arena the bright banners, hung out for tomorrow's bull-fight, lifted before it like sails in deep graceful curves. By the time that we made our way back to the boat the moon was up. The surface of the Rhône was the colour and texture of hand-beaten silver.

Sitting in the cockpit we ate steaks with a garlic-and-butter sauce, and drank a bottle of local wine. It was so cold it made one's teeth ache and had the faint rusty tang of old iron pipes. Above our heads children wandered along the town ramparts, too tired after the day's heat to run or shout. Lovers, arm-in-arm, passed under the trees, stopping now and again to blend into a dark sculptured mass—arms, breasts and heads linked in long-drawn kisses.

'Tired?'

She shook her head. 'I could sit all night and just watch.'

We were three days in Arles getting *Mother Goose* ready for sea. All the standing-rigging of the mast had to be set up and checked; sheets and running-rigging rove; and the hundred-and-one details attended to which convert a canal craft into a sea-going boat. While I and a local engineer stripped and decoked the engine, Janet was busy on the upper deck, or bobbing round the ship's side in the dinghy, sand-papering and touching up the paintwork. We started work early in the morning, for by noon it was too hot to move. The cypresses, the fields, the river and the bridges danced. The sun was a blinding wheel. At noon the engineer would shake the sweat out of his eyes.

'See you at four,' he would say. We would down tools as silence fell over the barges and the town slept. Siesta. At four o'clock we started working again and carried on until seven. Then Janet and I took a stroll through the evening streets, and watched the shadows lengthen in the old town.

South! And we would find the emblems of this new world in the lizards on the hot walls, their throats pulsating; and in the cockchafers that droned drunkenly through the dusk and fell like fat black priests on the café tables. By day the cicadas were like a fever in the blood, and at night we went to sleep to the sound of bullfrogs booming along the damp banks.

We motored out into the stream again on a blinding day. The edge of thunder was rumbling over the Camargue and the flat Rhône delta-land of bulls and rice-fields was hazy, and seemed alien to the ordered world of France. It might have been Central Africa.

This feeling was strengthened by our first sight of Port St. Louis where we made fast to a steamy, crumbling quay in a town that was apparently deserted. Leaving Janet to wield a flit-gun in the cabin I went ashore to make arrangements for raising our mast next morning—Port St. Louis was our port of departure. To-morrow, if all went well, *Mother Goose*'s Dutch hull and leeboards would feel, for the first time in all their forty years, a warm and tideless sea beneath them.

After settling with a crane-driver to lift our mast, I bought some bread and fruit in a steamy shanty-shop and then found a bar. The roof was corrugated iron and the bare room shook with heat. Some of the *mariniers* whom we had met in Arles were sitting about drinking wine or pastis. Overhead a naked light bulb, speckled with fly dirt, swayed under the attacks of hundreds of large hairy moths. Round an acetylene lamp on the bar their shrivelled bodies lay in a tired circle. Occasionally the patron would sweep them from the counter to the floor with a dark hand.

'A large pastis,' I said.

He brought the glass and leant over the bar, his forearms making oval sweat marks on the surface.

'You just came in on the little boat?'

I nodded. His voice was like old sand-paper from drink and Gaulloise.

'You have mosquito-nets on board? Good. I should use them, m'sieu. It's not only the mosquito that we suffer from here. There is also a small black fly that stings like hell.' I thanked him for the tip, but it was a little late. I had come ashore in shorts, and my knees were already a mass of bites. My skin felt as if dozens of hot needles had been driven into it.

'My God, I'll be glad to get out of here!' Janet looked up as I jumped on board. 'I've emptied gallons of stuff over these damn flies, but they seem immune.'

We slept uncomfortably under mosquito-nets, half choked with DDT and insecticide. The thermometers recorded almost as much humidity as centigrade heat.

By noon next day we were ready to go. The mast was up; the standing rigging adjusted; the mainsail bent on; and the staysail and jib ready for hoisting. We were a mass of mosquito and fly bites, but our tempers were salved by the knowledge that within an hour we would be at sea.

'Just one thing more to do.' I said. 'I'll go and clear the ship's papers with the Customs. We leave the area of the Inland Waterways control here.'

'Clear for the High Seas?'

'And all ports beyond!'

There was a small hitch with my papers.

'But where is your *Laissez-passer*, m'sieu?' The senior Customs officer looked up. He had already stamped our passports, examined my ship's papers, and given me *Pratique*.

'My what?' I asked blankly. It turned out that I had come all the way through France without the one document that technically allowed me to do so. Officialdom was slightly rattled.

'Surely you were informed in Paris that you would require a *Laissez-passer*?'

'No. I showed all my documents, and my certificate of navigation to the Touring Club de France,' I said. 'They told me everything was in order.'

He accepted my word in the end, registering an oath or two at the stupidity of the officials in Paris. Then suddenly his eyes began to twinkle.

'Do you know that it would have cost you a thousand francs? Yes, it would have! And you've got all the way through France without it! Ah, that's good—that's good—that's GOOD!'

He called the other officials over, and told them the story. They looked at me with admiration in their eyes. Here was a cunning Englishman (they never believed in my innocence) who had got away with something. Here was an admirable fellow who had managed to defraud those much-disliked officials with 'soft' jobs in Paris—while they, for their part, sweated it out in Port St. Louis! I left the Customs office with a pat on the back, and surrounded by a glow of Gallic approval.

Halfway down the short canal which leads from St. Louis to the sea Janet climbed on to the coachroof and gazed ahead.

'Do you see it?' she cried. 'We're there!' About a quarter of a mile ahead of us the concrete banks opened out in a soft blue haze. The horizon was invisible. The sky and sea seemed to run up together in a lilac curve.

We had entered the Tancarville Canal at Le Havre on the 14th of May. Behind us the grey Channel was still heaving with the swell of a gale, and now, on July the 9th, we were out into the Mediterranean, into a sea shining as though freshly varnished, and stirred by a fair sailing breeze. We spread out the first of the new charts in the cockpit.

'Run over to Marseilles for the night?'

'Bouillabaisse for dinner!'

The wind was off-shore, broad on the beam for our new course—a real soldier's wind. We set the light-weather jib, then the staysail and, lastly, the main. The curved Dutch gaff slid smoothly up the tallowed mast; the loose-footed mainsail swelled, shook for a moment, and took its shape.

'Down starboard leeboard!'

The broad oak fan slid into the water, eased itself with a sigh against the cheek-block, and then began to purr as the sea thrummed against it.

We streamed the log, took a cross-bearing (as much for fun as anything else), and felt the salt wind on our faces. *Mother Goose* shook her head slightly and settled down with a bone of white between her teeth.

The land came up ahead of us, Cap Mejean, lion-coloured in the afternoon sunlight and the sails of yachts spread like gull's wings over the sea beyond Marseilles. On the horizon a lonely cargo-boat was smoking a cigarette.

5

GETTING our sea legs, adjusting ourselves to the world of wind and weather, we spent a fortnight idling between Port St. Louis and Italy. But we were both eager to be off to lonely beaches and still coves, and a fortnight was enough. The Riviera is a lovely, but tired, coastline. The whole land, as it runs down to meet the sea, seems to have become blurred and out-of-focus; as though the millions of cameras which have been trained on it have rubbed away the edges. The tideless sea laps against the thousands of brown bodies, and all along the shore the waves roll in heavily, their crests weighted down with *Ambre Soleil.* Like a ship discharging oil to calm the sea, the land spread out around it a soft film of sun-tan oil.

'Ready to go?' Janet asked on our second morning in Marseilles.

'All ready. I'll start the engine. You think we'll get any wind?'

'There'll be a land breeze, I think.'

We cast off from a friendly fishing-boat; took one look round at the hot, surging life of the Vieux Port; and set course for the Château d'If.

As we neared the island we felt a breeze coming off the land astern of us, no more than a cat's-paw at first, then light footsteps on the water; and at last a fine sailing breeze. We slid swiftly between the Isle Tiboulen and the Isle de Maire; a narrow passage where the waves slapped angrily on the rocks and the sun-baked cliffs seemed to close in on us, menacingly like a dungeon's moving walls.

'There's Bandol!' Janet pointed over on our port bow. The entrance to the harbour was flickering with white sails. Behind the town the summer green of trees and shrubs ran up to a hard blue sky. Streaks of cirrus cloud were visible coming up over the land. I looked at the barometer. It was falling slightly, and there was an almost imperceptible change in the quality of the wind.

'I'm not very keen on the look of that sky,' I said. 'What do you think?'

'Mistral?'

'It could be. Let's run in for the night, just in case.'

We were right. Somewhere north in the Rhône valley, a Mistral—the gale-force north-west wind—was starting to pour down off the hot land towards the sea. When the Mistral is blowing, or due to blow, the sky is usually very clear with an oversharp clarity. Sometimes there will be a little high cirrus cloud or mares' tails. There is scant warning of its approach and the small boat sailor needs to keep alert; the Mistral can raise a heavy sea within a few hours, and the wind speed may be seventy to eighty miles an hour.

We dropped anchor near a small quay inside Bandol breakwater, and took double warps ashore to hold our stern secure. Already we could hear the wind, and the sky was diamond-bright and hard. It had been a wonderful day's sailing and there was satisfaction in having one's judgement confirmed. As we flaked down ropes and made up the sails, treading with bare feet on the hot coachroof, we took pleasure in our calloused hands and bleached heads. The salt glistened on our arms and legs in a fine white powder.

The lights were coming on ashore by the time that we had finished; red and green eyes from cafés and bars, and a pearl thread of traffic glittering along the main road. Overhead, against a sky which seemed to glow from within—the sun had already set—the thin fingers of cirrus were becoming more and more frequent. Behind the houses the trees seemed to have divined the wind. They had caught it, as it were, in advance, and were twisting and turning their summer leaves in a sound that was like an echo of the sea.

Throughout the night, as we lay snug in our bunks, we could hear the wind tearing over the hills behind us and jumping with a wild splash into the sea beyond. Further out, by the breakwater, the waves were running high. Where we lay, there was only a ripple on the surface, and back-eddies of wind that made us sidle and swing between our cable and stern warps.

By the morning the sea beyond the harbour wall was scarred

with white foam splinters. Half a mile out, the waves had gathered momentum and a heavy swell was running. I watched a coastal steamer pounding into it.

'*Sale temps!*' said a fisherman. 'Is that your little boat, m'sieu?' He jerked his head towards *Mother Goose*. 'I'd advise you to let out more cable. Lay another anchor out, as far from your boat as you can. After the Mistral the wind often switches quickly to the south. Unless your cable is laid a long way ahead, you'll find you're back on the harbour wall before you know what's happened.'

I thanked him and took his advice. Twenty-four hours later I was glad that I had. The Mistral fell away, and then, within half an hour, a hard blow came out of the south. Several yachts and small boats dragged back against the quayside. I saw my fisherman friend sculling past.

'Thanks for the warning,' I said. 'Come aboard and have a drink.'

He was a genuine sailor, not one of the 'musical comedy' figures who masquerade for tourists.

'What other local winds are there along this coast?' I asked him.

'Well, you've seen a Mistral now, Captain. A strong one like that usually blows itself out in a day during summer. Then there's the Marin. It blows from the south-east. It's what the Italians call a Sirocco. You know that one?'

'Thick damp cloud,' I said, 'stifling hot.'

'Yes. It hardly ever blows very strong in summer. A good beam wind for getting along the coast. But you'll find that the day breeze, the Brise Soleil, is the best for your little boat. In the war, when the Germans would allow us no petrol for our fishing-boats, I and my father used to hoist sail in the morning, and go out to sea with the Brise Soleil from the east. Then we'd come back with it again in the evening, when it had gone round to west.'

Hardly a wind, a light air rather, the Brise Soleil is a solar air current that comes up with the sun in the morning, and changes direction with the sun during the day. Coasting along the French and Italian rivieras we often worked it, but one needs light weather sails and it is rarely strong enough to help a yacht of any size.

A few days later we were in Villefranche. 'Yankee Navy go

Home' shouted the breakwater. The bars and dives were full of large friendly sailors.

'Dis place is nothin' but a goddam clip joint,' a red-faced leading-seaman informed me over a drink. 'France is strictly for the birds! You think you can find yourself a bit of French —— here?'

'I'm married,' I pointed out.

'Yeah. Well, suppose you wasn't. Mac, you couldn't get yourself a bit of French tail unless you had a hundred bucks. At least!'

Moored next to *Mother Goose* was a well-kept little French sloop. Although no longer than *Mother Goose* she had two paid hands to look after her. I asked them if they often went out. They smiled wryly.

'Sometimes on Saturdays, m'sieu,' said one of them.

'You will see our owner when he comes down tomorrow.' He grinned. 'He isn't a real sailor, you understand. He has a boat because it is *chic* to do so.'

Next morning a Citroën drove down to the jetty, and a middle-aged man, immaculate in white flannels, blue reefer and yachting cap, got out. He was followed by a slim, honey-brown girl in white shorts, a dress designer's reefer—and a yachting cap. The paid hand gave me a wink. A few minutes later I heard him confirming that the ice-box was full, the cocktail cabinet replenished, and fresh flowers on the table.

They motored out to the breakwater and the two hands lethargically hoisted the sails. By five in the evening they were back again. The owner and the girl emerged from the cabin, and a few seconds later drove off in their car. The two hands busied themselves wiping down the topsides with fresh water, and coiling the ropes in hard, neat 'cheeses' on the decks. Later that night there were giggles, music, and the clink of glasses from next door. Their week's work finished, the hands were entertaining their own girls.

'You know,' said a Yorkshire yacht-dealer whom I met ashore, 'I make quite a good living along the Riviera in summer, what with charter work and selling on commission. I could sell your little boat in a flash—she's pretty enough. There's one thing lacking though.'

'What's that?' I said, on the defensive. 'She's in fine shape—good sails. Good engine. Good hull. Comfortable below.'

'Oh yes, I know all that. But they don't count. Very few of

these Riviera yachtsmen know a good sail from an old one. And if you could see the condition of some of their rigging, you'd faint. No—but you've got to have a double bed. You'll never sell a boat to a Frenchman unless you have. You think that sounds like the foreigner's idea of the French—Gay Paree and all that? Well, it's true, old boy. Every time I handle a boat, if it hasn't got a double bed, well, I get space for one somehow—even if it means doing away with the fo'c'sle, or cutting out the sail locker. A double bed, then a cocktail cabinet, or a full-sized bar if the boat's big enough. And then there's got to be a really good cupboard where a woman can hang up dresses and put hats out of harm's way. Now, if I had your boat to sell, I'd cut out that forward bulkhead, raise the foredeck to the same height as the coachroof and put a bedroom in up forward.'

'You'd ruin the boat. Why, she'd look terrible if you did that!'

'You're not dealing with people, old boy, who know how a boat should look in any case. All they want from a boat is a certain cachet with their friends, and a different ambiance in which to drink and you-know-what!'

On the 29th of July we cleared from St. Jean Cap Ferrat for Italy and all ports east and south. We knew we had crossed the invisible line between the two countries when, on the morning of the 30th, an open boat under a large lateen sail glided across our bows. Her crew were darker-skinned than the French fishermen, their clothes shabbier, their smiles more brilliant.

'*Buon giorno, signore!*' the helmsman shouted across. A youth in faded blue jeans whistled at Janet.

'*Che bella! Che bella la senorita!*'

One can forgive the Italians every weakness and insincerity for their looks and their operatic charm. But they have more than that. Among their working people we found a spontaneous kindness and a warmth of feeling that is rare in the modern world. Muzzi in Genoa was a case in point. He came aboard to take the fuel injectors ashore for cleaning and retiming, and within five minutes had become a friend.

Captured in the Desert during the war, he had spent most of it in a camp in South Africa. Far from regarding the Australians who had 'put him in the bag' with any malice, Muzzi was of the opinion that they had done him the greatest possible service.

'But look, Ernlé.' We were on Christian name terms at once.

61

'That most brutal war! If I had not been captured I might have been killed. Then I should never have seen my wife again! In South Africa life was good, the sunshine was like Italy—and I found myself a girl on the farm where I worked!'

Muzzi was a good engineer. He was happy with his wife and their one child. He wanted little more from life except a slight increase in pay. His socialism was out on the left flank, but unlike most of his fellow workmen he was not a Communist.

'How about the Church?' I asked.

He winked and put his finger to his nose.

'It's good for the women. But not for rationalists like you and I. Have you ever seen a thin priest? The first time you do, send me a postcard! I go to Church though—not often, but I'm no atheist. My God! How often I prayed during the war! My wife now, she goes to Church more than I. It does her no harm. And she will bring up the boy all the better for it. We've been married ten years, you know, and we only have the one son. One day the priest came to our house and asked me why we had no more children. I told him my marriage was my affair—but if he could secure a rise in wages for me then I would like to have more. You're not a Catholic?'

I shook my head. 'Protestant.'

'Ah yes. Your priests are allowed to get married. Much more sensible. If they are married they have other things to occupy their spare time. Here, in Italy, the priests spend all their energies on intrigue, on seeking for money and better positions. You'll see—when you get down south—what a country's like when the priests are in control. The southerners are poor, uneducated peasants. Only think of it—in Sicily the man hasn't even enough food for two people, so he and his wife have sixteen children! That's the Church for you.'

On the day we left Muzzi brought along a three-litre can of engine-oil in his tool bag.

'A little gift,' he said. 'Here you are. My firm won't miss it.'

'I can't take that, Muzzi.'

'Sure you can. Tell you what I'll do. I'll leave it behind in your engine-room—just as if I had forgotten it. Then you needn't worry about having taken it!'

I was embarrassed about trying to tip him but felt it was the least I could do. He pushed away the notes with a firm hand.

'You're not a rich man, Ernlé. Keep it. Buy something nice for your lady when you go to Rome.'

It was a problem which Janet solved—as we often had to elsewhere in Italy—by giving Muzzi some tins of coffee, as a present for his wife. In France one knew that one could always buy service and attention by a pourboire. In Italy it was difficult. In Greece and Spain, as we found out later, it was practically impossible. The poorer a country, the less easy it is to give money away. I have never known a tip refused in London or New York.

How we rolled on our way to Portofino! A Dutch boat, with a beam swell and no wind, is a pig to roll. Lacking a keel she has no grip on the water, and you cannot lower a leeboard to stabilize yourself unless you have got the pressure of the wind on the sails to keep the boat heeled. The swell was long, running up from the south. Somewhere down in the region of Corsica it must have been blowing hard. The Gulf of Genoa is nearly always bad for this southerly swell. Nelson refers to it in one or two of his letters, always with the same despondent irritation. I can imagine how the Mediterranean Fleet must have rolled in those days, with their great hulls high out of the water, and their heavy masts and spars towering above them. The bo'sun, looking at his depleted stores, must have cursed.

The Mediterranean is hard on canvas and rigging. In a summer's cruise the sails are hoisted, lowered and rehoisted to catch errant puffs of wind many more times than in Northern waters. Apart from this wear and tear, there is the sun's scorching heat which can turn a wet sail into a miniature salt-pan within minutes. After a time, Janet and I learned never to hoist the sails until we were sure of a reasonable sailing breeze. In this way we saved ourselves a lot of work, and the sails much useless slatting and banging. Once the wind did come, though, as often as not it came with a bang, out of a clear sky.

Portofino was lovely but spoiled; its atmosphere too like a stage set; a whimsical backcloth for the display of smart dresses and the 'click click' of cameras taking pictures for the glossy magazines. Motor-boats, with cynical disregard for the warps and cables of boats at anchor, streaked in and out of the harbour. The cafés and bars exploded in a bright confetti of shorts and shirts, bikinis, cocktail dresses and jeans.

63

'Let's climb the headland,' Janet said. 'We're rolling too much to eat in peace here.'

We took wine, sandwiches, and a green salad with us, and found ourselves a hidden shelf high above Portofino, on the seaward face of the headland. Night was coming on. We could see the wind's footsteps on the mild sea and wrinkled lines trailed over the surface like the whorl marks of a sea shell. A coaster, outward bound, grooved a cool vee across the darkening water. Above our heads a breath of south wind stirred the vines, and a lizard scuttled along a warm boulder.

From somewhere hundreds of feet below us came the soft chug-chug of diesel engines. The fishing-boats were putting out for the night.

'Look!' She pointed. 'You can see their lights. They're fishing with flares.'

They came out from Portofino, from Santa Margherita, from Rapallo and Sestri Levante, and soon the dark arms of the bay beneath us were braceleted by lights. Innumerable small moons swam up out of the still surface as the fishermen turned on their acetylene lamps. The night was so still that occasionally a voice would detach itself from one of the boats and come floating up past us, like a feather mounting in an air-current.

Next day we left for Sestri Levante. The swell was worse than ever, and any hopes we had had of making a passage south soon faded. The barometer had fallen slightly, yet there was no sign of approaching wind save the ominously long swell.

'Bad weather coming tonight, signore,' said a fisherman rowing past. 'When the swell rolls up as high as this, we always know we're in for a South-Easter.'

I went ashore and desposited my papers with the harbour-master.

'I'll be leaving tomorrow,' I said.

He smiled and looked at his immaculate fingernails.

'I think not, signore, bad weather coming.'

By nine in the evening, dust and sand were whirling off the foreshore. The barometer had fallen ten millibars since the morning. The swell in the harbour was increasing. We let out more cable and prepared for the blow.

The great advantage of *Mother Goose*'s shallow draught was that we were able to tuck ourselves away almost anywhere that a rowing-boat could go. Now, from our quiet anchorage right under the lee of the island on which the village of Sestri stands, I could see that further out in the harbour the fishing-boats were having an uncomfortable time. Their masts described great sweeping arcs against the darkening sky and the fixed yards of their lateen sails were yawing wildly. The sky was threaded with cirro-stratus, and the sunset was ugly.

'I think I'll keep an anchor watch,' I said. We had finished dinner and were both working at odd chores in the cabin.

'Call me when you want me then,' Janet looked up. 'I'm going to turn in soon.'

I took a blanket out into the cockpit, rigged a light on a wandering lead and sat back with a book. It was that kind of night when the landsman turns in his bed and remarks, 'A bit windy tonight.' How little he knows of the joy of being in a safe anchorage, in your small floating home, conscious of the wild wind and sea, yet safe from them by a few hundred yards.

It was cold so I put a heavy watch-coat over my clothes and wrapped the blanket round my feet. Above my head the electric light bulb, suspended from the boom, swayed to and fro with the boat's movement. I could hear the hiss of the stove boiling a saucepan of soup, and I could see through the half-open hatch the flicker of the blue primus flames reflected in the polished galley door. Janet lay asleep in her bunk, her arm curled behind her head.

With every roll our home spoke softly with her many voices; the creak of the gaff jaws against the mast; a groan from one of the leeboards as it dipped into the water; a rattle from the cable; and the soft tap-tapping of some halyard that had escaped my notice when I had lashed the others away from the mast. Every now and then I went forward and looked at the cable, then checked our bearings against lights ashore. The anchor held firm, and the wind was still in the same quarter.

Round about three I fell asleep. When I woke again there was that faint, clean smell in the air which comes with the dawn. Dew had fallen, and my coat and blanket were beaded with moisture. Eastward, over the village, the light was beginning to stir; more like a movement than an appearance of light; a faint rustle along the dim roofs of the houses. I started the stove, put on some

65

coffee, fried myself an egg with slices of aubergine, put a drop of brandy in my coffee, and had breakfast.

The barometer was steady at 1010 millibars, and we were clearly in for another twelve hours' blow. Further out in the harbour, where the fishing-boats lay, the crests of the waves were flying headlong like smoke. Beyond the breakwater I could see the iron-grey waves rolling down the coast, and bursting with a sound like gunfire to throw their barrage of spray over the coast road.

Six o'clock. My night vigil had left me with a curious feeling of lightheadedness. The sound of the wind and the waves, the movement of the boat, and the feel of the dew and the spray had made me a part of that clean, dawn world. I finished a cigarette, stripped off, and plunged over the side.

The water was strangely warm, and, swimming around, one could feel the lift and scend of the sea. I grabbed the cable and hung on, looking up at *Mother Goose*'s full-cheeked bows as they rose and fell a few feet above my head. I swam down the side. There were a few flakes of weed growing on the paintwork above the anti-fouling, but otherwise she was as clean as a bird. Janet came out on the upper deck and dipped a bucket over the side.

'Oh, there you are! I thought you'd probably rowed inshore. Did you stay up all night? You should have called me.'

An old fisherman, his face misted with three or four days' white stubble, rowed up and rested on his oars looking at me.

'*Buon giorno.* Isn't it cold?'

'Warm,' I said. 'Warm.'

He shook his head, and pointed to the sky.

'*Tempo cattivo, signore. Tempo bruto.*'

Tempo bello, I thought. You're wrong, you don't know how good it is. I swam slowly back to *Mother Goose*, one minute submerged by the swell, and the next looking out from a crest over the whole wild harbour.

It took three days for that gale to blow itself out. On the third night, when all but the swell was over, Janet and I went ashore. There was a fiesta in the small town, and rockets were winging over the harbour. The cafés were bright with faces, and squibs crackled underfoot. We went to the dark cavern of a wineshop that we had discovered in the old part of the town. Large barrels glowed in the light of a paraffin lamp, and the glasses on the stone counter were purple or greenish-white with local wine. We filled four bottles to take back with us to *Mother Goose*, and then sat down with the owner and his wife on rough benches near the door.

'You're leaving tomorrow?' he asked.

I nodded. 'Yes, we must get on. We've a long way to go. I want to be in Malta by September.'

'I was there once. Not nice people, signore. Neither Italians nor English. They are Moors.'

'When he was young,' said his wife, 'he was often away for many weeks.'

'My sons are taking over from me now,' he said. 'I am getting too old to go to sea. They transport the wine in our schooner nowadays. I just sit and look after the shop.'

'Do you remember just after we were married?' she said.

He smiled at her.

'There were no engines in those days. Often we would have to wait for the wind. Ten days once I had to stay in Livorno. And when I came back, there was my wife with a son for me!'

She shifted her heavy hips on the bench and her eyes were quite young.

'We had four sons,' she said to Janet. 'Now there are only three. We lost one during the war.'

'He was in a schooner off North Africa,' said the old man.

'They should never have sent schooners down there. He was my youngest son.'

I remembered a destroyer 'sweep' off that coastline, and I remembered how we had come up with a schooner convoy on a soft summer evening, with no moon. The Italian destroyer had fought well, but she had no chance. After she had blown up we had picked off the schooners at our leisure.

Before we left the old man insisted on standing us a glass of wine. His wife went into the back of the shop and returned with a handful of raisins wrapped in a piece of paper. She gave them to Janet.

'They are good to eat. If you live a man's life at sea you must eat well.'

They shook our hands, bowed and wished us 'Much happiness'. As we rowed back to the boat the sky was brilliant with rockets, and the sound of guitar and accordion music echoed over the harbour. A light rain was falling and the wind was in the west.

67

6

LONG passages with only two to work the ship are tiring, especially when the winds are as variable as they are in the mid-summer Mediterranean. Usually we managed to make daylight runs of forty or fifty miles; leaving one small harbour at dawn and idling into another at the soft evening hour when the first lights begin to shine along the quaysides.

Day would begin with the two of us taking a wash in a bucket on the foredeck. The whistling kettle would announce simultaneously our early morning tea and my shaving water. Then, while I scrubbed down the deck or attended to engine routines, Janet would get the breakfast going. Our life revolved round the cockpit, for we could not leave *Mother Goose* to sail herself for any but the briefest of periods. Her long, barge-type rudder made her more sensitive on the helm than a conventional yacht. Steering, working the boat, navigating, and maintaining her kept us busy. We slept well to the sound of the sea against her iron sides.

Waking was easy, for the morning air was always cool and fresh, and the prospect of an unfamiliar coastline with always an unknown harbour at the end of it drove us from our bunks. Still drowsy with sleep I would crawl out into the cockpit and feel the night-dew heavy on woodwork and ropes. The first bucketful of water over my head and shoulders never failed to startle me into a vivid awareness of the morning world: the dawn mist veiling the port, and the cloaked figure of a *carabiniere* half asleep in an old doorway.

The night fishermen would be coming in, extinguishing their carbide lamps and treading gently with their wet spongy feet among the heaps of squid, crayfish, flying fish, and dappled mullet that twitched under seaweed in their boat's wet bilges. Sometimes I would buy a few for breakfast, and the men would tell me what kind of a night they had had. They were fine people and the simplicity of their lives acquired great beauty in the soft Italian tongue. There were many fine sailing days as we coasted down to Naples.

Sometimes the 'Tramontana', the 'Cross-the-Mountains' wind, would blow steadily on our beam. The sky would be clear, though that faint Italian mist would linger over the land like a painter's tinted glaze. It was on just such a day that we left Piombino, a dull port on the mainlaind north of Elba, and set course for Santo Stefano some fifty miles away down the gulf.

'No wind,' I said to Janet.

We were motoring over an oily sea. Fishing-boats passed us, plugging out under their heavy diesels towards the grounds off the nearby islands.

'Maybe it will come later.'

I finished washing down the decks, hung the canvas bucket over the stern, with a bottle of wine in it to keep cool, and took the tiller.

It was about eleven o'clock when the sea began to sidle and murmur round the boat, twisting its crest towards us and setting us off-shore.

'Here it comes,' I said. 'Soon we can switch off the engine.'

We turned into the wind and hoisted the light-weather jib, the staysail and the main.

'Down starboard leeboard!'

The sea came up quickly as the wind increased. After half an hour we passed two of the fishing-boats which earlier had shown us their heels. They were labouring along under power, with crudely patched staysails set to counteract their rolling.

By one o'clock the wind was quite strong and we were a little over-canvassed. The sea was coming up with the wind, so we took a reef in the mainsail.

'She's easier now.' Janet took the tiller from me while I had lunch.

Already a short, steep swell was running off the land. *Mother Goose* rose to it, lifting over and sliding down the crests with an easy motion. She was a dry boat in all weathers, and mocked my friends who had said that a Boeier was unsuited for the open sea. Although we were sailing on a broad reach—with the wind full on the beam—our angle of heel was slight, compared with that

69

of a conventional yacht, and the scuppers were always free of water. A Dutch sailor had earlier given me some good advice: 'The moment your boat begins to take water in her scuppers she's over-canvassed. If you bear that in mind you won't go far wrong.'

The wire to the leeboard sang as the sea foamed against it—a plaintive wind-and-water music. Every now and again, as a large wave heaved under our keel, the leeboard would roll outwards on its pivot-bar, hesitate for a second, and then swing back into place again. Against the clear bright sky the sails took up their deep, full-bellied curves. The long masthead wimpel—the Dutchman's weathervane—streamed out to windward.

'It's getting a bit hard on the arms!'

I came out and gave Janet a hand to rig the tiller lines so that most of the strain was taken by their purchase.

'She's going like a bird, isn't she?' There is nothing better than to feel your boat going sweetly before a good breeze. And when you are sitting in the sun, with every mile taking you towards a new port, and when you know that in the evening you will lounge in some small café and watch the harbour lights, why then, there is no one in the world you can envy.

> 'The fair breeze blew, the white foam flew;
> The furrow followed free. . . .'

She completed it for me:

> 'We were the first that ever burst
> Into that silent sea.'

All round us the waves were breaking in long-crested wigs of green and blue. They seemed to reflect the trailing mares' tails which spun overhead. The barometer stayed high and steady; the wind had a clean taste and cooled our shoulders; we drank our wine and lit cigarettes. The wake spread out in a calm line astern, and flying fish were leaping in front of the bows. They soared away and formed part of the rainbow which flickered in the spray of our bow-wave. The land behind faded in a mist of blue, and then the land ahead ran up; first no more than a faded, imperfect transfer, and then, clarifying, to become the cape we sought.

70

During the day's run we had averaged six and a half knots—
no mean achievement for an old boat with one reef down. We
were still glowing from the wind and the sun as we rounded the
breakwater and came into Santo Stefano. It was dusk, and the
Tramontana was still blowing. A number of fishing-boats were
swinging to their anchors inside the harbour, and smaller
ones clustered like mussels along the jetty and the quayside
walls.

Next morning, as we were shopping, we met the local pilot.
An Italian-American, he had spent ten years in Brooklyn. He
had been on a holiday in Italy at the moment when Mussolini
called in the passports of all Italian citizens.

'No, I've never been back,' he said. We were sitting in a small
café drinking Camparis. 'Hell, I don't really regret it. I like it
here, and my wife wouldn't go back. There ain't no electric
wash-machine here, maybe, but the climate's better and they're
our own people. There's another thing.' He scratched his stubbly
chin thoughtfully. 'People are more honest here. Maybe they're
poorer, but they're more honest. I'll tell you something. I was
handling building work just outside New York. Another Italian
had got me the contract—he was in a big way of business. Well,
we got those buildings up in half the time expected. So—I see
my men paid and then I go along to collect myself. Nearly two
thousand bucks, it was. This boss-man says to me: "Come back
later this evening. I haven't got the money yet." So I go back
in the evening and pick it up. It's late and all the banks is shut
and I'm not happy having all these dollars on me. But I go back
to my lodging and put it under the pillow and lock the bedroom
door. About an hour later there's a knock outside. "Who's
there?" I calls out. Fellow answers me in good Italian, tells me
to open up, he's got news for me. I open the door a crack and
he gets his foot inside it. There are two guys there with pistols.
"Where's the dough?" they say. "Come on, hand it over. We
know you got it." '

He paused and sipped his Campari. The dusty jetty outside
was bright with vegetable stalls. Dark-eyed urchins were fighting around the fish market. The sky looked very blue over the
hot land.

'I let them have it,' he went on. 'All that dough, all them
weeks of work—finished! Not long after that, I say to the wife:

71

"Let's take a trip to Italy. Maybe it's not so bad there." So, here we are, just when Mussolini calls in all the passports. Been here ever since.' He looked down at the table. 'Sure, you make more dough in the States—but there's too many robbers. Our own people too, Italian people.'

'Why didn't you go to the police?' I asked.

The pilot laughed.

'Yeah, I could too. And wake up next day like this——' He swept his forefinger across his throat. 'Those guys are tough. And if they don't do that to me, you know what they do? Find out where my home is and beat hell out of the wife and kids.'

'How did they know for certain that you had the money?'

His slow wink comprehended all the cruelty and avarice of the world.

'Why, listen, Captain, of course they knew. The boss-man arranged not to pay me until the banks were shut. It was him who had me followed back home. That was how he got all his work done for nothing—or for just a few dollars handed out to his musclemen.'

On our way back to the boat we lingered along the jetty and watched the sprawling, bustling life of the fishing-boats.

'They come up from the Ponza Islands,' said the pilot. 'Every summer they come up to the north of Italy and fish and sell to the local markets. Down there they are very poor. They've got no trade except fishing.'

The boats were no larger than *Mother Goose*, but about half her beam, most of them open, though a few were half-decked. About eight men, mostly in their early twenties, lived aboard each one, cooking their meals on small primus or brazier stoves in the open air. Illiterate, unable to speak Italian comprehensible to the natives of the north, they preserved their own strange and remote life; living almost entirely on board their boats, eating pasta and oil, and the less marketable fish that they caught. Barefooted, tanned and lean, they had an untamed air about them. They laughed a lot and spat the pips of water-melons over the sides of their boats.

'They ask me about the States,' said the pilot. 'They all want to go. But there ain't much chance nowadays, now the quota's restricted.'

They all thought they would be happier if they had a city suit and three square meals a day. It is a common illusion.

I noticed that nearly all the boats were gaff-rigged cutters. They were keel-less and must have made a lot of leeway. Later, when I lived down in Sicily, I was often to go sailing in such boats. They are fast off the wind, but the lack of keel means that they cannot work well to windward. Usually, when beating to windward in boats of this type, one or two of the hands row so as to keep the boat from 'crabbing' sideways. Another unusual feature in these West Italian boats is their fixed, or standing, gaff. The mainsail is suspended along this fixed gaff on hoops—rather like a curtain on a rail. In order to reef or to furl the sail it is pulled back along the gaff towards the mast.

We were under way by four next morning. It was wonderfully fresh at that hour. The water splashed around my feet as I washed down the cable and anchor. It was as soft and as tepid as if the sun was still in it. I remembered the unemployed fisherman we had spoken to on the jetty the night before.

'It's not bad in the summer, signore,' he said. 'There are many things to do, even if one is not working. I manage to catch a few fish off the breakwater for the evening meal. And then the sun is good. I go down to the sea and swim, or lie in the shade and watch the boats passing. The sea is good.'

'*Il mare é buono*,' he had repeated the phrase in a soft, dreamlike tone, as if it were an incantation.

There was a light air off the land as we hoisted the sails to clear the point south of Santo Stefano. The bow-wave began to chuckle—that meant three knots—and the sun came up and the shadows lifted from the land. Coves, capes and headlands were uncovered as though a giant hand was sliding away a transfer. The morning mist poured off the terraced hillsides and ran like liquid smoke down the small valleys. When we had set out we had been wearing pullovers and long seaman's trousers, but within an hour we were in shorts and thin shirts.

So the days went by, mostly without great incident. There were two occasions when we left the boat in safe hands to take time for visits to Florence and Rome. We never had anything stolen anywhere at any time.

We revisited Anzio, which I had last seen under bombardment, anchored and rested a night in the volcanic crater that forms the harbour of Ischia; and spent a night reliving old wartime memories in Naples.

Although it was mid-August we rarely felt the lack of a refrigerator in our coastwise travelling. Most of our provisions were tinned and stowed in the coolness of the bilges. Our bread, fruit, wine and vegetables we bought from day to day. With a few exceptions the tinned butter that we had bought in England was still fresh when we reached Malta over five months later. One or two tins of corned beef and meat 'blew' through the heat, but they were the only casualties we suffered. Pasta of all kinds and its essential companion—salsa—we bought whenever necessary ashore. We did not eat like kings, but I have eaten worse in many 'Grand' Hotels. Fresh fish, vegetables, fruit, wine, olives, olive oil and good rough bread—a man can keep healthy on these. We drank cheap red or white wines with our meals, and an occasional glass of vermouth or brandy.

Naples, Torre Annunziata, Sorrento, Capri, and Salerno were behind us. There was a breath of autumn in the air. We were at sea southward bound between Capri and Amalfi. Since leaving Marina Grande the previous night we had had only three hours' sleep; yet we were as awake and untired as children for whom the first light round the bedroom curtain means the unfolding of another summer day. There was no wind and we were motoring over a sea that undulated softly and slowly, like a field that has once been ploughed and then left fallow. The kettle sang. The sun came up. The land unveiled on our left, high mountains and scorched grass. Astern of us the grey, whale-back of Capri loomed out of the mist. We were motoring through the Galli, the Siren Islands. I know now what songs they sang.

'They were good, weren't they, the fishermen?' I said.

'The ones at Salerno?'

'Yes. The simplest people always seem to be the best.'

'I expect they beat their wives though.'

'I'm sure they do. It's one sure proof of affection.'

I made a few idle cuts with the end of the mainsheet. Janet laughed. The morning air was very still. One could feel it on the skin, like silk that has been left lying in the sun.

We had arrived at Salerno one evening at dusk. We dropped anchor and were just finishing our evening meal when a boat bumped alongside and there was a gentle knock on the hatch. I opened it and looked out. There were four of them alongside in a rough fisherman's dinghy, their smiles caught in the light that fell from the lantern swinging on our forestay.

'Good evening, Captain. We thought we should tell you that there's likely to be a strong wind off the hills before the night is out.'

Raimondo, their spokesman, clambered aboard at our invitation. His companions sat diffidently in their boat. Finally, after a lot of persuasion, they all climbed into the cockpit and accepted a glass of wine.

'The wind will come off the mountains over there.' Raimondo pointed. 'In about an hour's time. You'd be wise to put out another anchor.'

'Bad weather?'

'No, signore. Just the nightly Tramontana. But sometimes it is very fierce in the gusts. Quite a sea gets up in the harbour. One needs to be careful.'

Janet and I deliberated. We were lying at a single anchor with our stern secured to the jetty. The best thing would be to take out the kedge anchor in our dinghy and lay it at the full extent of our long three-inch warp in the direction from which the wind was expected. The fishermen seemed to anticipate our thoughts.

'Give us your other anchor!' They scrambled back into their boat and pulled away while we paid out the warp from our bows.

Already the wind was getting up, and the dark water was beginning to flicker with small waves. By the time that they came back the night was sighing round us with cold voices off the hills. Salerno is a poor holding-ground and several times that night we had to stand by, with the engine running, ready to get under way if things worsened. That was the first time we met the fishermen.

On our second night in harbour—we were held up by an engine repair—Raimondo and his friend Pietro came back again. Raimondo was tall and handsome, Pietro short and craggy like a wind-stunted olive. They told us about the harbours and anchorages of Calabria, and about the fish they caught in those parts, repeating the names slowly for us so we would know what to ask for in future.

'We've brought one for you.' Shyly Raimondo held out a folded newspaper. He was awkward about his gift, as if he knew he was too poor to be able to give us anything worthwhile. By now I had a good knowledge of the Italian fisherman's life and wages. Raimondo would make about four shillings a day, on which he had to keep a wife and two children.

'I'll find something for his wife,' Janet murmured in English.

Pietro uncovered the fish and he and Raimondo looked at it with pride. It was one of the ugliest fish I have ever seen, nearly all head and jaws and weighing about six pounds. Janet and I looked suitably grateful and I prodded it appreciatively with my finger. It was an 'angler' fish—'St. Peter's fish' Raimondo called it—with a long antenna like a fishing-rod between its eyes.

'What's the best way to gut it and cook it?' Janet asked a little nervously.

'Here.' Raimondo pulled out his clasp-knife. 'I'll do it for you.'

For a few seconds we listened to the tearing sound of scales and skin, then he hooked it neatly along the belly and shook it out over the water.

'There, signora.' He held it up for Janet's inspection. He had cut away most of the head, leaving only the fat lumps of flesh that lie on each side of the jaws.

'Now we must wash it!' He dipped the bucket over the side, filled it and threw in the fish. Janet and I looked at each other. Salerno Harbour!

'There!' Raimondo laid the fish on the newspaper. 'Now, all you have to do is to boil it in salt water with some onions.'

After they had gone we gazed at it thoughtfully.

'Permanganate of potash,' I said. We washed it in a strong solution, rewashed it in fresh water, and then boiled it with onions and bay leaves. It was good, a bit coarse, but with a flavour not unlike tunny, and it went down well with the local wine.

Raimondo came back next night just before we sailed. We thanked him and Janet managed to get him to accept some coffee and tinned meat as a present for his wife. We sat in the cockpit and drank a glass of red wine together.

'I bought it here today,' I said. 'Eighty lire a litre.'

'That's a good wine.' Raimondo wiped his mouth.

'Only "Nazionali",' I'm afraid.' I held out the pack of

cigarettes. 'We've run out of English. Shan't get any more until we get to Malta.'

'Take care, you and the signora,' he said, 'going down the coast. There aren't many harbours. And the weather is beginning to break.'

He took out some wax matches and we lit our cigarettes and raised our glasses.

'Until we meet again!' We shook hands.

'And thanks! Thanks a million for everything!' I said.

Raimondo looked back over his shoulder as he rowed away.

'Don't forget,' he called out, 'Porto Palinuro and Santa Nicola! They're your best harbours in the next hundred miles.'

He waved and went away down the harbour, standing up at the oars in the Mediterranean way and bending in slow, easy strokes over the rough wooden looms. For a long time after he had gone we could hear the splash of his oars as he pulled towards the schooner where he worked as a deckhand.

'They're good people all right,' Janet said. 'I wonder why, in richer countries where people can afford to be generous and kind, they're only more selfish and grasping?'

'The more we have the more we want.'

'I wouldn't want anything except what we've got.'

'Nor I.'

Capri faded astern of us. Under a sky empty of cloud we ran on towards Porto Palinuro over an empty sea. In the course of the whole day we saw no ship, no hull, not even a sail. It was as if the wind which drove us southward had swept the world clean, and hurled the rubbish out of sight, somewhere way below the horizon's rim.

'There's the lighthouse!'

Janet had the binoculars up on the foredeck. The small headland was just visible to the naked eye, a pale cloud fine on the port bow.

'You can just see it,' she said. 'That's Palinuro for sure. There's no other lighthouse along this bit of coast.'

Soon I, too, could make out the white tower on the cliff, and the ruins of a fort lower down, overhanging the sea. The small natural harbour was surrounded by terraced green slopes at whose foot a few poor houses straggled down to the water. Under the lee of the point the water was calm. We motored in

77

and dropped anchor a hundred yards from the shore close to a fishing-boat. Her crew rowed over, and soon we were explaining for the thousandth time the mysteries of our leeboards, while they fingered our ropes and varnish-work, murmuring '*Bello! Bello!*'

After they had gone I jumped over for a swim. The water was soft and blue and warm. Five fathoms beneath me I could see the line of our cable trailing away towards the anchor and I swam slowly along its length until the anchor itself was in sight. I could make out the furrowed bed where the ploughshare-head had bitten deep into the bottom. A shoal of fishes feathered past me and dived to disappear into the waving arms of weed that covered the bottom.

'Supper's ready!'

We ate spaghetti with chopped basil and pine nuts, and drank a half-litre each of our Salerno wine. Afterwards we sat smoking in the cockpit and felt the day's sun and salt good on our skins. It grew dark quickly, for we were under the shadow of the westward-facing headland.

Small yellow lights came on in the windows of the cottages as we lit our own riding light and secured it to the forestay.

We were under way again just before dawn, the boat wet with dew, and the land hushed, and so deep in its sleep that it might have been the centuries and not the night which enfolded it. The hatch of the schooner slid open as we motored past.

'Good fortune! Good voyage in your little boat!'

'Good fishing!' I shouted back.

That day a fresh Tramontana surprised us, just as we were tacking in towards the coast. We were slow in securing the jib sheets as we went about and for a split second the sail took charge. In a quick, blind flurry the sheets wrapped themselves round the starboard lamp-bracket and whipped it over the side. The lead-block to the sheets lashed back and broke one of the forward scuttles to the saloon. The jib itself was torn in three small places.

The sea is no place for fools or slow wits. Too many fine days had made us casual, and hours of lazing at the tiller had made us forget that two people in a thirty-foot boat need all their wits about them. The sea has a poker face, and like all good poker players, can lull one into a false sense of security. I reminded myself that the Cape disappearing astern of us was named after Aeneas' helmsman. He, too, had grown careless off this same stretch of coast. But he was drowned.

'My fault,' I said. 'I should have got that sheet in quicker.'

'Mine too. I shouldn't have put her about until you were ready.'

If Palinuro had been our first experience of a remote Calabrian anchorage Santa Nicola was the quintessence of them all. There were no other vessels at anchor. Only a line of small fishing-boats drawn up on the beach showed that the harbour was still in use. The evening tasted of flowers and rich earth, and the land was cultivated, right down to the tideless water's edge.

'We need fresh vegetables.' Janet looked up from the locker.

'And wine,' I said.

'Yes. And get some bread too. If you can find a shop.'

There were no houses along the foreshore but, from where we lay, I could see the edge of a small village jutting out from the terraced slopes. I rowed in, drew the dinghy up on the beach and looked round for a path. I found a dusty goat track, overshadowed by shrubs and grasses, and scored everywhere by the thin tramlines of lizards. The cicadas were noisy in the scented thyme clumps and the whole hill was heavy with summer.

From the summit I looked down on *Mother Goose*, a dark blue shape like a beetle on the surface of the still bay. Small as an ant, and equally busy, I could see Janet on the fo'c'sle, bending with palm and needle over the torn jib.

There were white pillars and ruined slabs of marble among the rocks and scrub through which I walked, the remains, perhaps, of one of the many Greek trading-station posts which were once scattered along this coast. No Greek could ever have ignored so perfect a natural harbour. Perhaps I shall go back one day, an old man, and become its solitary historian. I shall be a crazy old man digging among the ruins in the violet evening hours, and spending my few lire on getting the fishermen to search the harbour bed for the ruins of trading ships lost when the wind was in the north. Santa Nicola is only open to the north.

The village lay over on the far side of the hill. As I neared it I saw that I could easily have saved myself the walk, for the houses trickled down to a small inlet that was invisible from the yacht. Goats were wandering through the dusty streets, children were everywhere, and women's agitated faces at the windows told me that strangers were unknown.

A burly man, standing in front of the church, hailed me.

'*Tedesco?*'

'*Inglese!*' I replied. I was tired of being taken for a German in Italy. The Italian has a simple, caricatural sense of race, and my fair hair and clean-shaven chin meant 'German' to them. To be recognizably English I needed a moustache and a pipe.

'Ah!' His face changed. He came over and took my arm. '*Inglese!*'

We made straight for the only tavern in the village. The entrance was jangling with one of those bead curtains that are known as 'fly-scarers' in the south. The interior was shadowed and cool, deep-girthed barrels buttressing the walls. Quite soon our table was violet-ringed with the stains of our wine-glasses.

7

A FORTNIGHT later the snow had come. The flanks of Aetna were white with it and leaden clouds hung over the mainland of Sicily. The wind had a sharp tooth and even when the sun was out we needed pullovers; warm trousers and heavy coats at night.

Calabria was behind us; its lost villages and its remote anchorages hugging the stark coastline. The fishermen were hauling their boats higher up the beaches; the women were buying charcoal for their braziers. Soon it would be winter. We were sad to leave Calabria for we had found great kindness there and many good people. We had found small fishing villages where we had been the first foreigners since the Allies stormed up the coast in 1944.

The Straits of Messina, running with ugly cross-currents, were also behind us; the Straits and Messina itself; and Riposto nestling at the foot of Aetna; and the lovely lake-like harbour of Syracuse. Time was pressing and the weather was breaking. It was October and, by the end of the month, I must have *Mother Goose* laid up at winter moorings in Malta. Our first sailing year was drawing to an end.

It was the morning of October the 8th and the low hog's back of Cape Murro di Porco, the peninsula south of Syracuse, was fading into the distance over our quarter. The barometer was falling. I entered the log: '1014 millibars. Wind north-east, Force 4. Occasional squalls, Force 5.' The wind was scudding all the way down from Greece, a cold north-easter that slammed into our canvas with angry grunts, like a heavyweight boxer trying for a kill.

I poured out two mugs of coffee, and added a liberal tot of Sicilian brandy, and joined Janet in the cockpit. *Mother Goose* was going well, with a sigh of wind in her rigging, and her wake drawing astern like a bright sword.

'I don't think we need reef yet,' I said.

She shook her head. 'No. We're going fine.'

'Let's get the best out of it,' I gave her her cup, 'and run off as much as we can. If it blows up, there are a couple of small anchorages where we can shelter—just off Cape Passaro.'

Cape Passaro is the southernmost point of Sicily, then there is a seventy-mile jump across the Channel to Malta, and then there is nothing but sea all the way to Africa.

I looked over to starboard where the long bare beaches glowed under the sun. The last time I had seen them they had been swarming with men and machinery. Out here at sea, where *Mother Goose* stumbled and swayed, the great invasion fleet had rocked in the swell. Then there had been gunfire north of Syracuse. It was strange how the beaches seemed the same. The sea was the same too, and so was the distant peak of Aetna, almost lost in her slatey snow-cloud. The Allied invasion of Sicily had receded, leaving nothing behind it but a page in history-books. Already it seemed as remote as the Athenian siege of Syracuse. I felt like a ghost come back. And so many who had been here with me had been dead a long time now.

The wind was rising and the sea lengthening. Inland, the mountains were silhouetted against the sky as the sun went down. Here and there their outlines were broken by the roofs and church-spires of villages. The houses of Noto, caught in the last glow, seemed to bristle like dragon's teeth, and streaks of green light were playing along the night clouds that had started to build up over the land.

It was just on six o'clock when the staysail fired a warning shot and the sky gleamed through a rent in the sailcloth. Before we could get it down the split had widened, another two tears had opened like dark wounds, and the sail was in shreds. We wore round into the wind and lowered it.

I took over from Janet at the tiller as she went below to enter the log and check the barometer.

'Still falling,' she called out. 'It's down to 1010 now.' A drop of four millibars in as many horus.

The light on Cape Passaro came on ahead of us, and a second later another light on the mainland, just inshore of it.

'Group flashing two every ten seconds—that's Cape Passaro all right. I'll give you the other.' I waited and timed the flashes. 'Group flashing three every fifteen.'

'Cozzo Spadaro.' She had the Admiralty light lists open on the saloon table in front of her. The wind was still freshening. If we were going to carry on, we ought to reef now—before nightfall.

'What do you think?' She came up and handed me a cigarette.

'I think we'll go in for the night. Take her for a second while I go and have a look at the chart.'

When you first go below it takes a few seconds for your eyes to become accustomed to the light. Then the friendly world of your home envelops you: the bright colours of book jackets: the wireless purring out dance music from Rome; and the paraffin stove spreading its circle of yellow warmth and its faint, all-pervasive odour.

I lay the chart out on the table, get pencil and dividers from the rack, and the *Admiralty Pilot* from the bookshelf. There is a bottle of Vecchio Alkamak in the wine locker—the best wine we have found in Sicily. Not so heavy as Marsala, it is scented like autumn. I pour myself a tumblerful, light a cigarette, and study the chart.

Few books have such eloquence or such eternal fascination as charts. Spread one out on a winter's evening in London when the cold rain is falling . . .

Even the tools of the trade—compass, dividers, and parallel rules—have a strange, almost ritual air about them. Few pleasures can exceed that simple one of spreading out a chart in the saloon on a dark night with the wind rising, studying it for a minute or two—and deciding to put into harbour for a good night's sleep.

There it is! I look again at the chart, and then back at the pilot manual. Porto Palo—no more than a small indentation in the coast, half a mile westward from the point of Cape Passaro. It will be a fine shelter from all northerly winds—and there is no sign at the moment of the wind shifting. I finish my drink, light a cigarette for Janet and go up top.

'How's Cape Passaro bearing?'

She squints along the compass. 'Just a little ahead of the beam.'

'Let's wait till she's abaft the beam, then gybe round and steer due west.'

Five minutes later we haul in the mainsheet, wait until there is a lull in the wind, and come over to our new course, taking the wind on our other quarter.

'We're pretty close to the point,' she says.

'It's okay. Steep, too. I hope!'

We round the point in a smother of spray so close that we can hear the boom of the surf on the shore. In the flashes from the lighthouse we can see the whole tower outlined against the darkness of Sicily, and the spume lifting like lace off the black rocks.

As we shot through the entrance of Porto Palo we came into a great stillness. The wind mysteriously died away, and the water was calm and oily, moving only with a slow, unhurried swell, like a sleeper's deep breathing. There were eight or nine fishing-boats lying at anchor. It was good to come out of that wild night into so peaceful a place.

Half an hour later, just as we had finished making up the sails, an old man sculled over.

'How is it outside?' he asked.

'Much wind,' I said. 'And more to come.'

'You're better off in here. Would you like some prawns, signore?'

I gave him the largest of our saucepans, and he filled it to the brim, scooping the prawns out of a wicket basket covered with a layer of seaweed.

'How much?' Janet asked.

'Nothing, signora. Cigarettes, if you have them . . .'

I held out a packet of 'Nazionali' and he diffidently took two.

'Take some more,' I said. 'That isn't enough. Take the lot. How about some lire as well?'

He stuffed the cigarette packet inside his shirt.

'That's plenty. Thank you, signore. They're more use than lire. Lire are no use. We've run out of cigarettes on board and we won't be able to buy any more until we get back to Syracuse. But thank you, that's more than enough.'

'Come and have a drink,' I said.

'Grazie, but not now. I must take back the cigarettes to my companions. Perhaps tomorrow.'

He paddled off towards the distant glow-worm of a schooner's light.

We dined that night off fat fresh prawns washed down with the Alkamak. We were tired when we turned in, our arms and faces burning from the day's wind and the sun. I could just hear the wind in the rigging as I lay in my bunk: a steady purr. But outside the anchorage it was blowing hard and a big sea was running.

The dawn was sullen with red-faced clouds, their cheeks full-blown like angry cherubs. The wind was still high but the barometer had steadied. We would wait until nightfall and then, if the weather was no worse, we would leave.

The day went by uneventfully, with high cirrus clouds coming over from the north and a scent of burning wood off the land. All the time there was a sparkle in the air that seemed like re-flected light from the snows of Aetna.

The Italian radio was noncommittal about the weather in the Malta Channel.

'Well, at least there's no gale warning.' Janet switched off. 'We'll go then?'

'Let's get out and take a look at it. If it's too bad we can always come back.'

A sailor on one of the fishing-boats waved as we motored past towards the entrance. He pointed to the sky and shook his head.

'Let's try it anyway.'

We took a deep reef in the mainsail, looked carefully to the stowage of everything on board, and left Porto Palo. Everywhere the waves were pronounced and fairly long. Their foaming crests slid past with a soft sigh and the sea was darkening at the ap-proach of night. At night the sea is always a little frightening, even if the weather is good.

We were setting the reefed mainsail and the heavy weather staysail as a fishing-boat, plunging heavily into the sea, crossed our bows. She was headed for Porto Palo. We looked at each other with the same thought—how pleasant it would be to put back, buy some more prawns, and take another easy night at anchor. After supper, with a cup of coffee and a tot of brandy, we could sit back in the warm and read. Far overhead we would hear the wind and, beyond the comforting arm of the land, the surge and swallow of the sea would be deep as a dream.

85

The squall came down on us a minute later. Janet had gone below and I was just settling myself into a comfortable position at the tiller. It was dark by now and I never saw the sudden whitening of the sea over my shoulder, though I heard—almost as it hit us—the sudden rise in the wind's note and a flurrying sound as if the leaves of a thousand autumns were whirling about me.

Mother Goose reeled as if it were a solid blow. The whole boat shuddered and there was a crash that made me think the mast had gone over the side. It was still standing though: something had fallen over in the galley. I ran her off before the squall, easing the mainsheet as I did so, and praying to God that the boom would not gybe over with all that weight of wind in the sail.

Mother Goose's stern dug down, her bows lifted, and for one wild moment we were riding the crest of a long roller; there was a thundering hiss in my ears as though a madman with a pressure-hose was spraying down the ship's side. I could feel the tiller quivering and straining against my arms, pitting against them all the dark strength of the sea.

'Okay?' Janet shouted above the thunder and the whine and the crackling spray.

I nodded, for I could feel the squall's strength dying.

It sped away into the night, leaving us with a last flicker from its coat-tails that sounded like the crack of a lion-tamer's whip. I eased *Mother Goose* gently back on to her course and cast a glance astern. The light on the island of Correnti loomed up and waved its white finger against the sky. We took our departure bearing and laid our course for Malta.

'I've filled it with coffee. Here!' Janet passed up the thermos flask. 'What do you make of the wind?'

'Five to six. Increasing a bit, I'm afraid.'

Half an hour later it was a steady Force six and there was a long, unpleasant sea running that took the boat just abaft the beam and lifted her with a nonchalant hand before throwing her away in a slow corkscrew. Steering was difficult even with tiller lines rigged. Every twenty minutes or so I shifted my position and moved from one side of the cockpit to the other to relieve the strain on arm and leg muscles. Janet was catching an uneasy sleep until midnight. I hoped I could avoid calling her until then. She needed the sleep, but we were carrying more sail than was good for us, and our wake was beginning to catch the following seas in an ugly way.

At midnight, wet, bruised and exhausted, we sat together in the cockpit and grasped tin mugs in cold wet hands. Ahead of us the furled mainsail humped itself along the coachroof like a dead whale.

'My God, I'm glad that's off her!' Janet cradled the tiller under her arm while I leant back and lit cigarettes.

'She's all right now, though. I don't think you'll find steering too hard.'

Only the arched wing of the staysail soared over the boat. We could see it curved high ahead of us, a small sail—all that we needed in the wind and the night. We were driving hard in a smother of foam. The noise of *Mother Goose*'s passing was like an express train through a tunnel, and the drum of the sea against her iron sides was thunder in distant hills.

Janet had put up a stew in our large flask and we ate it together at quarter past midnight on the morning of October the tenth. The sky was low and there were no stars, only the pale glimmer from the compass bowl to light our hands and faces.

How good that stew tasted—corned beef and tinned beans, cooked rice and three or four fresh tomatoes, the last of the prawns, and some cubes of beef extract. I think I never tasted better food. When one is hungry and alert, and tired and yet at the same time exhilarated, all food is good. Afterwards a cupful of brandy was more warming and more invigorating than anything I ever drank before or since.

'Go and turn in for a bit,' she said. 'I've got her. I'll call you at four, or later if I'm not tired.'

A second after I had pulled off my shoes and fallen into my bunk there was a tap on my arm. I came up groggy, with a foul taste in my mouth and my eyes half-sealed.

'Sorry I had to wake you, but it's five o'clock.'

It was just making a pale light over the water. The sky was two-thirds covered with cirrus, long, ugly-looking mares' tails.

> 'Hen's scarts and filly tails
> Make lofty ships carry low sails.'

And ours was no lofty ship, just a small thirty-foot Boeier that some people had said was only suitable for canal work. She was still going well, and the staysail was set in so firm a curve that it looked as though carved out of metal.

'There's a little coffee left. I'll put some more on as I go below.'

'No. Put on a kettle and put some tea-leaves in the pot and lodge it in the sink.'

'O.K. 'Night.'

I could lean forward quite easily and, without leaving the cockpit, reach the kettle when it boiled and pour it in the teapot. I had drunk too much coffee last night.

A flicker of spray came over and cleaned my face and opened my eyes. Now I could smell the morning; the clean salty taste of it with never a touch of earth or ordure or corruption—the clean original morning as it was in the first days. Grey and bleak, perhaps; a hard planet to live on, but always with some compensation or other tucked away. A good life if you don't weaken, but no welfare state; not then, not now, nor at any time to come.

I loved the old boat. She was sweet and easy, even in the big seas that were running. Rubbing my hand along the carved tiller, as a groom will over a horse's neck, I felt her great, good qualities. She was our horse, our house, our ship, and our shelter from all the winds of heaven.

The sea was still long and high, and we were logging about five knots. I wiped the salt away from the glass on the log face, took the reading and jotted it down. Six o'clock. Another five miles in the past hour.

When I made my tea I looked at the barometer. It had risen two millibars. A bit too quick. This was probably no more than a ridge of high pressure between two 'lows'. The wind, which had taken off a little, would come back with renewed strength in an hour or so.

We were only about twelve miles north of Gozo, the smaller of the two Maltese islands, but there was still no sight nor sign of it. In the troughs of the sea there was nothing but a world of moving water. Green and black pennants swirled past, and the wind-blown foam was like lace before the advancing crests. A merchant ship broke into my private world and jogged slowly across our bows, headed westwards through the Channel. She was making heavy weather of it, and every now and then she would come down with a clump! that must have made her shiver from stem to stern. I don't suppose anyone on board her ever realized that there was another boat in the neighbourhood. They would never have seen us in that world of low-flying scud and grey sea.

And then I saw the first pale headland lift up ahead of us— Gozo! A few minutes later the Cathedral was pricked out against the horizon. The dome caught some distant gleam of sunshine and held it for me like a bubble while I took a bearing.

'Gozo?' A sleepy voice at my elbow.

The swell increased as we neared the land, and the wind came back stronger then ever—a good Force seven, reaching eight as the occasional cloud leant over us. The shadowy outline of Malta lifted beyond its sister island, and churches and towers and spires and sandstone houses crept out towards us over the sea.

'Where's the quarantine flag?' Janet was fumbling in the locker under the seat.

'Don't you remember? We lost it in France.'

'I've got a clean yellow duster—that'll do.'

We boomed through the breakwater, past Ricasoli lighthouse, with a long swell beating and breaking against the old lion-skin walls. A bugle was sounding-off from some anchored ship, and a bosun's call trilled over a loud-hailer.

Our blue jerseys were wet and stained. My trousers bore the traces of cigarette-ash and food. Janet's hair was a sad nest of serpents, and our eyes were rimmed with salt.

An immaculate Maltese Customs officer gazed at us with some distaste.

'Where from?'

'England,' I said. He looked startled. I could explain later that there had been a few stops on the way.

'What was the signal flying from St. Angelo when we came in?' Janet asked. 'The blue flag? My husband and I were having a slight argument about it.'

'The blue flag? Oh, that means small boats are not to proceed to sea because it is too rough.' He thawed and gave us a smile. 'I would classify yours as a small boat. There now . . .' a signature on a document. 'You can take down your quarantine flag. Everything is in order. Stay anchored here off the Customs House until you find a permanent mooring. Congratulations on your voyage.'

The official had become a human being. 'Have a whisky,' I said.

After he had left we came up on deck and looked about us. I had last seen Malta during the war.

'What do they call those boats?' Janet asked.

'Dghaisas. We'll get one later and go ashore.'

'When we've had a few hours' sleep.'

The clouds were lifting slightly; the north-easter had blown itself out. There was a shaft of sunlight falling over Valetta and lighting up the dun houses until they became a soft matt gold. On the ramparts of St. Angelo a few figures were moving, dark blue against the increasing brightness of the sky.

8

A WARM, still night. The patter of rain on the deck over my head. There is a liquid xylophone music alongside my ear as the water runs from the scuppers into the sea.

I look at my watch—three o'clock—and hoist myself out of my bunk. One sleeps too much in Malta, lives life a little too easily, and then suddenly one wakes in the middle of the night, and feels restless.

It is three steps from my bunk to the galley. I open the doors quietly, pour some methylated spirits into the left-hand burner, light them and wait a few seconds. When the small cone of fire is beginning to flicker and go out I turn on the tap from the paraffin tank. The jet lights with a plop and a hiss and I look carefully over my shoulder towards the other bunk. Still asleep. I get water from the small fresh-water pump at the side of the sink and fill the kettle. In five minutes' time I will have a pot of tea.

Outside lies a white world of moonlight. The rain has stopped—it was only the drift from a passing cloud—and the night is breathless, with a gentle steam lifting off the island. Such stillness! The sleep of centuries holds the quiet quarter where we lie, and there is nothing but the sound of my own small life, as I wipe dry a seat in the cockpit, to break the heaviness that lies at the heart of silence.

Mother Goose, her leeboards and her mast removed, rests in the boat pound of Fort St. Angelo. We live in her as we would in a miniature flat or caravan, almost forgetting that she is water-borne, so secure are we in our winter berth. All round us lie the trim barges of admirals and flag-captains; their brass dolphins shining in the moonlight; their bright work and their shark-skin-scrubbed decks as luminous as ghosts.

Some fifty yards away a sentry pauses on his round of inspection, climbs into one of the boats to test its warps, and gives me good night. He walks slowly back the way he came, past the dark, tunnelled entrance into the sandstone mound where once the galley-slaves had their quarters. He taps with his stick on the door to make sure that it is closed, then mounts a ladder to the ramparts and is gone.

The tea tastes good and freshens me up. I light a cigarette and dream. It is a spring night and there is a new warmth in the air. I can smell the flowers on the rampart gardens—a heady southern scent of freesias and something else I cannot quite place. Earlier on, in one of the island villages, they were holding a fiesta, and the distant crackle of fireworks and a church bell, monotonous and slightly out of tune, were the last sounds I heard before falling asleep. Fiestas are as much a part of Malta as the dghaisas gliding through Grand Harbour; their oil-lamps blinking like glow-worms as the dghaisa men bend and dip over the long-loomed oars.

Five months have gone by since *Mother Goose* folded her wings in the still waters of Grand Harbour. Christmas and New Year are over, and already the island is beginning to come alive with spring. Yellow flowers like primroses, known locally as the 'English weed', are growing round the base of the bomb-scarred buildings. The minute fields, each enclosed by its low sandstone wall, are darkening with the purple clover. By day the sky has a kindlier light, and the sea beyond St. Elmo lighthouse is beginning to forget its winter mood. Small fishing-boats, which have been laid up since the autumn, are already poking their bows outside the breakwater. They are a little hesitant, for the season of the 'Gregale' (the gale-force north wind) is not yet over. The island is full of birds waiting, on this last staging-post beyond Europe, for a hint that spring has come to the countries of the north.

I remember the first day that we arrived, how tired we were; and how we slept late into the afternoon, undisturbed by the swell of passing barges or the rumble and thunder of the dockyard.

No sooner had we opened the hatch, blinking at the bright sunshine and trying to remember what harbour we were in, than a reporter from the local paper jumped from an idling dghaisa and scrambled aboard. He looked about him uneasily and then held out his hand.

'Mr. Bradford? We've been expecting you. Some friends of yours said you should have been here last week.'

'Bad weather,' I said.

'So? But how small your boat is!'

I showed him round while he dutifully admired the right things. But only one aspect of the boat had really impressed him.

'How small she is!' he repeated, and then: 'All the way from England? You've really come all the way from England in her?'

'Why not?' I said. 'Smaller boats than this have crossed the Atlantic.' I hoped that this drop of water from a cold ocean would tone down his Mediterranean viewpoint.

'Ah, the Atlantic . . .' He dismissed it with a shrug. He was a young Maltese journalist, and rightly eager not to have his story spoiled. 'The Atlantic, perhaps. But not from England to Malta. Do you know yours is the smallest vessel to have come here from so far?'

I filled in the details of our voyage, and read an alarming account in his paper next morning.

Our daily life quickly took up its pattern. Shortly before eight, when the thunder of the exhausts of the admirals' and captains' barges beat against the ship's side, we made breakfast. At eight, when the bugles and bosuns' calls sounded out all over the harbour, I dutifully hoisted our blue ensign. We ate breakfast while the ripples in the pound subsided and the barges went off for their morning's work. Then we smoked a cigarette on the upper deck, and cleaned the boat.

By ten o'clock I was seated at my typewriter and worked without a break until lunch. The life of a writer is uninteresting; he is a grub spinning a cocoon, and if in the warm days something good comes out of it he is lucky. I wonder why so many novelists choose writers as protagonists in their books—a form of self-esteem, perhaps, for most of them live dull lives.

Janet would shop and then carry on with the routine. Work on a boat is endless, especially if you live in it all the time. Batteries must be charged, bilges kept clean, rust prevented, paintwork washed, and brightwork polished. One need never stop, for the eternal enemies, water, and salt air, and decay, are attacking every hour of the day. Friends would often call in about lunch-time, and then—unless we were strong-minded— the day was lost. People in the Services seem to have more time on their hands than they know what to do with. How easy it was to spend a winter's afternoon in a club, or idling from bar to bar, or dreaming life away in a foggy siesta, waiting for the evening's amusements to begin.

Only the necessity for work saved us from drifting into an idle dream where time would have a stop. The Mediterranean has its own special brand of ennui. A resignation, a *'mañana, mañana'* philosophy rises like a mist off the tideless waters. The rhythm of life is unhurried. The ruins of so many civilizations that litter its shores—their crumbling towers and walls visible on many a cape and headland—induce a mood of nostalgia for the cradle and a weary acceptance of the unimportance of one small life. Passion flickers over this surface like a wind across a pool, and love assumes a strange fiery mask. It is the rocket which lights the night sky for a brief moment and then leaves all velvety dark again. Here, as elsewhere, alcohol remains the great antidote for all unachieved ambitions and disappointed passions.

It is curious how the English, wherever they are in the world, take with them an atmosphere of tea-shops, floral print dresses, saloon bars, beer, and an indifference to the refinements of cooking. Only seventy miles from Sicily, a sandstone garrison exiled in the heart of the Mediterranean, and surrounded by many nations and cultures, Malta retains the architecture and the atmosphere of a Victorian seaside town. It does this despite the palaces and fortresses of the knights, and despite a Baroque Catholic Church, which remembers the Middle Ages with affection. Yet even the British are not unaffected by the climate. Even the conventionally minded soldiers and sailors, and their wives, turn more readily to the drugs of drink and love than they would do at home.

After months in Italy and France you sail into Grand Harbour and go ashore looking for a cheerful café, a bright restaurant, or the cool, barrel-shadowed cave of a working man's bar. There are none of these—only row upon row of 'pubs' that might have come out of the back streets of Plymouth or Portsmouth. You suddenly become aware that your coloured shirt and your canvas trousers—which looked normal elsewhere in the Mediterranean— are sadly out of place. Shamefaced, you hurry back, put on grey flannels, a reefer, a white shirt, and an old school tie.

'Have you been invited to the Governor's party?' 'Aren't you going to the dance aboard ——?' Reinforced against the insidious attacks of the climate and of Mediterranean morals, the tabus of middle-class England are as plainly displayed as the coloured photographs of Her Majesty which gaze at you with a certain forced cheerfulness from every bar or barber's shop.

On a normal day we lunched aboard and then worked through the afternoon. After five months my book was finished. It seemed curious to be completing a history of European jewellery in a small boat, alongside a jetty, in the boat pound of the old Knights of Malta. Most of our acquaintances were convinced that the book was a 'blind' and that really I was completing some secret report for M.I.5. I only found this out by accident, when some sharp-featured matron at a cocktail party asked for my opinions on the political issue in Greece. I said that I knew very little about it and that I hardly ever read a daily paper. She gave me a slow wink and a twist of her lips over her glass.

'But you should know something about it—I mean, shouldn't you?'

'Why? I'm going to Greece in the spring, of course. But I don't think its politics will affect me.'

Again the wink.

'Oh come! . . . I'm an N.O.'s wife, you know. All Serviec people here. Everyone knows that you're M.I.5.'

'Personally?'

'My dear——'

A Maltese steward refilled our drinks.

'My dear chap, Captain T—— would never have let you lay up your boat in St. Angelo if you'd been just a plain civilian.'

'I *was* in the Navy during the war, perhaps that's why?'

She raised her glass. 'Cheers! Well, of course, I mustn't press you. And you've certainly got a very convincing manner. But then you should have, shouldn't you?'

We might have gone on like this for ever but a sudden surge through the party drove us apart. I saw her dart into a group of wives in the far corner and their heads turned for a second in my direction. So that was it! I was a British agent quietly mooching through the Mediterranean, keeping an eye on things. It accounted for one or two odd remarks which had been made to me, and which I had dismissed as being due to some mental lapse on the speaker's part.

'You know I'm supposed to be Secret Service?' I said to Janet as we were wandering back to the boat.

'Oh yes. They keep trying to pump me about you. They think it's so romantic—and how brave I must be to share your strange life.'

'Well, well.'

'Besides, you might be. I wouldn't know, would I?'

'It would be damn difficult to keep a fact like that secret in a small boat. Can you imagine my swarming up ropes after dark and prowling through other people's houses with a gun in my pocket?'

'Secret Service characters don't behave like that—as you well know. They just listen to gossip and send it back to H.Q.'

'Well, there's enough of that—gossip, I mean—in this island.'

Strangers like us were welcome in Malta because they added a new ingredient to a society which must die of boredom but for the arrival of 'visiting firemen', or the automatic replacement of people who had served their time on the station.

The island had a certain attraction, though less than anywhere else I knew in the Mediterranean. It was too small for one thing, and too unsure of itself for another. It embarrassed me that the average Maltese should try so hard to be English, and it embarrassed me far more that so many nondescript young Englishmen and their wives should feel that they were superior to 'the natives'. That was why, despite all the good that we might have done them, our foreign colonies were always glad to see us go.

I imagine one of the reasons for the success of the Roman Empire was that the conquerors intermarried and absorbed the customs of the conquered. Britain has taken Wimbledon with her throughout the world, and set up a tennis club and an exclusive bar. She has administered her territories more justly and honestly than any race in history, but because of that one small vice of snobbishness she has never been loved.

At a cocktail party one evening after I had been talking to ——, a Maltese doctor and a most interesting and erudite man on the antiquities of the island, Peter, a pleasant young naval lieutenant, said to me:

'Interesting chap, isn't he? Pity he's a Malt. Mary wanted to go to him when she was sick last week. But I wouldn't let her. Wouldn't like having a Malt look at her.'

But the strange sandstone appeal of Malta lay far away from the cocktail-party world and the bar of the Phoenicia Hotel. It lay in the small side-streets remote from fashionable Sliema; in the fisherman's bar at the head of Pieta Creek; and in the narrow alleys and village shops of Vittoriosa. The people, though, did not have the same friendly charm as the Italians, nor the northern integrity of the British. They were touchy, somewhat uneasy about themselves and their race, over-sensitive to criticism, and deriving the strengths and the weaknesses of their response to life from an autocratic Church which bore little relation to the more liberal Catholicism of the West.

Even in Sicily—often reckoned by the Northern Italians to be the last bastion of the Middle Ages—Malta was something of a byword for the intolerance of its priesthood. In Syracuse I had met a rapier-like Jesuit who had come aboard *Mother Goose*, sat over a bottle of wine with us, and borrowed a copy of *Pride and Prejudice*.

'So you are going to Malta,' he had said. 'Holy Malta. I am afraid that what you see of our Church there won't impress you. Ever since the days when the Church had to stamp out Mohamedanism in the island it has kept the people in a somewhat despotic grip. The liberal attitude of the British, the establishment of Protestant churches and clergymen in the island has made the Maltese Church close its ranks even more firmly.'

He gave a wry smile.

'I am afraid that more British have been driven into thinking our Church a mediaeval, reactionary relic by a visit to Malta than by anything else.'

But sometimes, inside the great Cathedral of Valetta, or slipping quietly into one of the small churches in the dockyard area or in one of the villages, I would be absorbed as I had been in Southern Italy into the deep dream of the Faith. It was rather like picking up *Cellini's Life* and feeling one's way back into Renaissance Italy. I had the wish to believe and not the ability. (It would be pleasant again to go to bed on Christmas Eve and know that Father Christmas would have come down the chimney by the morning.) But at sea, alone at the tiller, on a clear night with the stars in their millions and oneself alone, a pinpoint to the moon, I felt nearer to the cool abstract heart of the universe. Whether it cared for us or not was another question.

The moon dipped into a bank of clouds and lay there smouldering. The night was suddenly touched with a cold wind and I shivered and came out of my reverie. There were biscuits in a tin inside the galley and some cheese. I topped up the tea-pot again, lit a cigarette, and began to go through the notebook which lay on the saloon table. There, under various headings, were listed all the things that had to be done before we left Malta; the stores and supplies to be brought; the mechanical fittings to be overhauled; and the sails, rigging and gear to be checked over. Most of the items bore a tick against them; there were few major things remaining. Next week we would move from the boat-pound and go round to the slip. Weed was heavy on the bottom after so many months in the warm, still water. Cans of anti-fouling compound, enamel paint, and varnish were stacked in the fo'c'sle. As soon as *Mother Goose* had her new spring sheen there only remained to step the mast, replace the leeboards, bend on the sails, and go.

The new charts gleamed in the rack above my head; chart after chart; an expensive bundle exuding the clean, exciting smell of paper and print. I slid down a folder and opened it in front of me. There lay the whole bright Aegean: Poros and Seriphos, Delos and Cos, Santorin, Melos and Rhodes; their names like a lisp of water and their coastlines and small harbours as exciting as a spring morning. They held the promise of many coves and inlets, of marble gleaming on forgotten headlands, and small villages where there was no radio, and where the sea would slide up to the houses and the open doorways be caverns of coolness against the midday sun. In the rustle of turning charts I could hear the clamour of island waterfronts and smell fish-soup steaming in bowls on scrubbed wooden tables.

I wonder what prompted the memory? Suddenly I was back at the Round Pond in Kensington Gardens on a grey February morning in 1930. There was a light mist over the water and just enough sailing breeze to keep my small boat moving. I could see her from where I stood—*The Bird of Dawning*—as she cut through her familiar sea. I could just make out the blue figure of the helmsman where I had lashed him by the tiller. There were grey-white clouds banked behind Kensington Palace; heavy, motionless clouds with lower edges that seemed carved out of clay. To-morrow it would snow.

I stamped my feet and tapped my stick on the dry ground—my stick with its special hook at one end for grabbing the rigging if the *Bird* sidled near the shore and then tried to tack out again on some unauthorized course. She was slipping away now out into the mist, headed for the far end where, just visible against the cold sky, the statue of the horse and rider ramped between the winter trees.

'How is it this morning, young man?'

It was the old captain, my great hero—a retired Merchant Navy officer who took his walk every morning past the pond. He was a great spinner of yarns, and his breath smelled of beer. Sometimes he brought me small carvings—the wooden helmsman in his neat blue coat and white cap was a gift from him.

'Very well, sir. Is it going to snow, do you think?'

'It'll snow before nightfall—that's my guess. Time you went back to school, isn't it?'

'I'm going back next week. I've had 'flu.'

'Well, I must be going now. It's too cold for an old man like me. My blood's got thin.'

He stumped away towards some bar with a warm fire and I was left wondering about his thin blood, and whether that was why his eyes watered and his nose was shiny blue. It was then that I heard them—the sudden wild thunder of the swans against that strange sky. They circled the pond and went out past me heading for the river. Their wings soughing startled the frozen air. The sound dwindled away and faded in the mist until there was nothing but a faint sigh over the trees. A sigh and then nothing more. I strained to hear them, and then, for the first time, I realized that the silence of my world was not silence, but the dull rumour-like beat of London's traffic.

The sound of their wings was in my ears as I sat there in the small cabin and turned over the charts. I looked again at the notebook. Most of our stores were already aboard. The new injectors for the engine were due by air tomorrow. It was tomorrow —no today—that the sailmaker would deliver the new staysail and a large light-weather jib. I had looked at them both in his sail-loft (a silver-bright room smelling of tarred ropes, canvas, chalk and dust, with huge dirty windows at the far end giving out on the untidy world of Dockyard Creek).

'Hello. Are you awake? What's the time?'

'Quarter to five,' I said.

'Ugh! Call me with a cup of tea at seven. Are you feeling all right?'

'Yes, fine. Couldn't sleep that was all.'

I could not sleep because I was like an eight-year-old a night or two before Christmas. (Soon I would unwrap all the presents.) We had bought a new dinghy—a collapsible one—which meant that there would be more room on the coachroof. Then there were the new leads to the leeboards. And the ice-box which a shipwright friend had made in his spare time. We would be able to keep meat and fish fresh for longer—and wine cool. Then there were all the minor improvements which we ourselves had done over the winter: the alteration of wiring and switches; the re-siting of cleats and leads; innumerable small things which would make life easier and sailing more efficient.

We would have six months' stores of food when we left and enough spare gear and replacements so that we should need to buy nothing except fuel, fresh vegetables and meat, local wine and bread. This year the gods who ordered the lives of modern man had decreed that no more than fifty pounds' worth of foreign currency per head should be taken abroad.

'Do you think four dozen tins of coffee will be enough?' Janet was still awake and had caught the drift of my thoughts.

'Of those one-pound tins? Plenty.'

I go out on deck and walk quietly forward and stand in the bows. It is getting light already and the great bastion of St. Angelo looms up against the sky, shadowing the small pool where we lie. The water is turning from black to violet. The moon is down and this new light is the dawn. The silent boats around us keep up an idle slapping sound in the gently moving water: a sound that reminds me of our first night on board in Birdham Pool. So many months ago, another life almost.

Through the arched causeway that rises above my head a sudden eddy of wind scatters *Mother Goose* with fine particles of sand. The rudder groans faintly as we sidle out from the quay, and the ropes whisper over the deck as they take the strain.

It is time that we were going. . . . Tomorrow!

9

WE HAD a gentle sail from Malta to Sicily. The spring was fine that year, the winds light, and the sky cloudless. There was snow on Aetna still, but the island was bright with wild flowers. We moored against the main quay at Syracuse, a few yards away from Arethusa's fountain. At night we could hear the splash of water and by day we idled round the stone rim and watched the carp glide among the reeds.

I had first seen Syracuse during the war. I remembered one vivid noon when two German fighters screamed in low over the land, their cannons blazing, to skid their fragmentation bombs among the gathered shipping. It seemed a long time ago; more remote than Nicias and the Athenians. The old city was mellow under the new sun, and the narrow alleys pulsed with life. We made expeditions to the theatre, the catacombs and the new excavations. Once or twice we picnicked in the rock quarries whose harsh depths were softened by almond trees in blossom.

We needed the engine a great deal that spring for the winds had died away, and day after day the surface of the sea was only stirred by errant cats'-paws. From Syracuse we crossed to the foot of Italy and coasted along its low shores, touching at fabled Croton on the sole and Santa Maria di Leuca on the heel. We hurried through Corfu, Paxos, and the Ionian islands: we would see them on our return, and our aim was to reach the Aegean as quickly as possible. The western coast of Greece, save for the islands, has always been a barren, sad area, and I was eager to dive through the neck of the Corinth Canal and swim out into the haunted Aegean.

On May 17th we turned eastwards into the Gulf of Patras. Ithaca was astern of us, blotted out by driving rainclouds, and there was thunder echoing around the hero's hills. The glass was falling and the wind began to pipe up. We had planned to sail through the night and reach the small port of Parga in the morning.

'What do you think?' Janet handed up my oilskins as the wind and the rain began to reach us. 'Looks as if we're in for a blow.'

'Let's have a look at the chart and see if there's anywhere we could lay up for the night.'

She took the tiller while I scrambled below. It was warm and friendly in the saloon after the bleak world outside. The chart gleamed on the table, a small dagger of cross-bearings marking our position twenty minutes before at the mouth of the Gulf. We had better get another fix while the land was still visible. I called up to Janet who took three bearings and shouted them down to me. I noted the time on the clock above the bookshelf and put them down on the chart: they placed us somewhere inside a half-mile triangle just to port of the main channel.

I looked at the chart and then at the pilot. Curious! I had always wanted to go there, and I had hardly realized we were so close. It looked as if we would not have too much trouble in negotiating the channel that stretched through the mud-flats to the town. I worked out a course and went up on deck. The horizon had disappeared and the rainclouds were all around us, low on the water.

'Missolonghi,' I said. 'It's a bare ten miles away. Come to port about twenty degrees. There's a buoy at the mouth of the channel. Unlit. But we ought to pick it up before the light goes.'

The rain was coming down hard now and we sailed for a little over an hour with the visibility down to a few hundred yards. I was beginning to worry because the coast about there is flat; mudbanks and sloping sandshelves running out into the sea. I would look a fool running ashore at some five knots in the Gulf of Patras—with no tide to lift me off twelve hours later. If you run ashore in the Mediterranean you are apt to make a good job of it.

'Down sail?' said Janet, voicing my thought. We spun *Mother Goose* up head to wind, lowered the mainsail and the jib, but left the staysail flying. Then we started the engine and motored cautiously ahead. I got out my old German binoculars and peered ahead. The rain was easing a little.

'There!' shouted Janet. She was pointing off our port bow;

we had been set down by the wind and sea more than I had expected.

Out of the lifting rain-mist an old iron buoy sighed and sagged on the crested water. We passed it with a few yards to spare and held the course down the channel. Soon the mudbanks began to sidle up on either side of us and we lowered the staysail. Janet took the tiller while I went up in the bows with lead and line. It was a cold world of swamp and flatland, with no sign as yet of the town or the hills behind it.

The wind had increased and the blown spray from the lagoons on either side was like a white mist. Swaying heads of bulrushes and reeds marked hidden mudbanks and gravel patches. I was gazing ahead, motioning to Janet to ease down the engine, when suddenly the channel widened out into a small basin. We had arrived.

It was a lifeless, dreary scene. A few buildings straggled back from the water, as if seeking shelter for themselves, and what appeared to be a deserted fishing-boat swayed against the quay. I was wondering what to do when, all of a sudden, the place came alive. Four fishermen sprang out of the boat and, with shouts and arm-waving, showed us where to moor.

A one-eyed man, who looked like a bedraggled wolf, took our ropes and helped secure the boat. Within a few minutes we were comfortably berthed and then, with all the friendly vitality of the Greeks, he and his helpers squatted on the quayside in the pouring rain and began to ask me questions. My knowledge of Greek was sketchy at the best of times, but the dialect they spoke had me completely beaten. I made signs to them to come aboard out of the rain, but with one accord they pointed to their muddy shoes and said they did not want to mess up my little *Lordiko*. It's a curious word for a yacht, meaning literally 'Little Lord', and dates back to the days when the only private yachts seen in Greece belonged to wandering English 'milords' in search of the fountain-head of classical culture. Hence any private boat became known as a 'Little Lord'.

A swarthy Customs official loped along the jetty to collect the ship's papers. For the first and only time in Greece I found that there was no one present who spoke a word of any other language: that is, if one excludes the bearded ancient from the fishing-boat's crew who had a phrase of French which he repeated over and over again—'*Bon appetit, mes enfants*'. This did not seem to get us very far, so I took the Customs officer below and, over a glass of whisky—which he pronounced '*pollee kala*' (very good) —I explained where I had come from and why. I was visiting Missolonghi, I said, to see where Lord Byron had given his life for Greece. It seemed easier than to say that I didn't like the look of the weather outside, and I felt my words might possibly help Anglo-Greek relations.

The name Byron—pronounced 'Veron' in Greek—was like an open sesame. The Customs officer's face lit up with a broad smile. He clasped my hand in friendship and we raised our glasses to the immortal memory. I could see that I had made a friend. Five minutes later he and I, together with all the fishing-boat's crew, were sitting in the local bar cementing our friendship in glasses of ouzo. Ouzo is the Greek version of the many anis drinks which flourish in the Mediterranean. It turns white when you pour water in it and is fine provided you like the taste of aniseed.

It was a primitive bar: a rough wooden table; huge wine-casks throwing their shadows on the ceiling; a few bottles stacked on a rickety shelf; a cat with a litter of kittens; and a hen seated in the only chair. The woman who served us, smiling broadly at my bastard Greek, called out to her husband: 'Come and meet a strange Englishman! He's sailed to Missolonghi just to see where Milor Veron died!'

Sleepy and unshaven, her husband finally emerged from behind a partition that must have screened their bedroom—for the head of an old camp-bed protruded from it and a child slept in a cradle at the entrance.

'You've given the Englishman no mezé,' he remarked as he searched under the counter. A few seconds later he brought up a handful of olives and some pieces of salted fish which he laid carefully on a plate and offered to me. His hands were dirty but, despite the hen in the chair, the bar seemed clean, and I accepted. One must occasionally risk stomach trouble rather than hurt people's feelings.

I ate the salted fish—it was rather good—and we all talked. Or rather, in snatches of broken Greek, hand-shakings and smiles of friendship and mutual incomprehension we exchanged a few remarks about Byron, the high price of food in Greece, the dangers of the sea, and the hard life of fishermen.

It was nearly dark by the time that I got back to the boat—with a bottle of wine to excuse my absence. The light from the small cabin spread a comfortable yellow glow all around. As I went below I took a last look at the lonely scene. Grass grew on the deck of a deserted schooner moored a few yards away. Old forgotten ropes slapped against its unvarnished mast, and a pile of cable rusted sullenly on the foredeck. Beyond the harbour basin I could just make out the stork-like houses of the fishermen, rising on piles out of the muddy, windswept lagoon. They were strange houses, reminiscent of Africa, perched some four or five feet above the water, with ladders leading down from them to a causeway. They were roughly thatched with reeds and their sides were plaited like peasant basket-work. The grey sky streamed with rain and the wind was increasing as the day died. The channel wound away towards the invisible sea, lonely and cold.

It was on a night just like this that Byron lay dying in a small house up the road. The year was 1824, and the poet who had come to Greece filled with a generous enthusiasm for their cause had lived long enough to be disillusioned by the interminable bickering and treachery of Greek politics. And here in Missolonghi, lonely and frustrated, he died of fever, caught through being out in an open boat, in the rain, on this same lagoon.

Who could have foreseen that so brilliant a life would end in so strange and so desolate a place? I wondered whether Byron in his delirium had not roamed far away from here. Perhaps he had recalled the brief season of his London fame, days when the stanzas of 'Childe Harold' were on everybody's lips, and when the talk of the salons was all of 'Byron'. Or was it the ghost of a waltz that haunted him? Down in the cabin there was a copy of the diary Byron kept when he lived in Venice. 'Oh! There is an organ playing in the street,' he had written. 'A waltz too! I must leave off to listen. . . . Music is a strange thing.'

A storm burst over Missolonghi just as we sat down to eat. There was a storm, too, on the night of Byron's death—such thunder, lightning, wind and rain that the Greek soldiers said that a god was dying.

After we had washed-up I went out on the upper deck to check that the moorings were secure for the night. The lagoon was misted with cloud and the hills echoed with thunder. I was glad we had decided to make harbour instead of remaining at sea. Lightning scissored the darkness. The moon was hidden, but every now and then the edges of the clouds would catch a pale glow—their blackness intensified by those wandering patches of moonlight. Otherwise—nothing but the wind and the rain.

Next morning we woke to a pale bright sky and the smell of the earth, clean and fresh. But the night-time impressions did not fade—even though the modern Missolonghi is a far call from the primitive village that Byron knew. After we had shopped we wandered through the town park, and there, among other heroes of the War of Independence, we discovered the poet's statue. A melancholy figure, he brooded over the dark-eyed Greek children, who scampered bowling their hoops through the shining wet grass, for all the world as if sorrow had never existed. Moss was growing on the poet's stone waistcoat, and his cheeks were bearded with a spider's web.

The town has few other memories of Byron, though the site of the house in which he died has been carefully preserved. In the centre there is a small flower-garden and a bust. As we lingered there in the sunshine, a wedding group arrived, and a photographer with one of the world's first cameras proceeded to pose them in front of the lonely poet.

But the real Missolonghi, not the modern market town, but the fishing village, cannot be greatly different from the place that Byron knew. It begins where the modern town ends. The fishermen's houses march out on spindly legs into the water and brown-skinned children run up and down the rickety ladders with the nonchalance of those who are native to the sea. Nets and eel-traps hang from the walls to dry and patchwork clothing sways in the morning breeze.

I collected my papers from the Customs officer, had a last drink with him and my friends in the bar, and went back to the boat. Ceremoniously the fishing-boat's crew shook us by the hand and wished us *bon voyage*, then they cast off our moorings and we stood out for sea down the Missolonghi channel. The wind was favourable, and the water chuckled against the ship's side. As I looked back and waved, a verse of Byron's came into my head. It should be cut in stone and erected somewhere on that bleak shore.

So, we'll go no more a-roving,
So late into the night
Though the heart be still as loving,
And the moon be still as bright. . . .

Though the night was made for loving
And the day returns too soon,
Yet we'll go no more a-roving
By the light of the moon.

The sun came out as we tacked at the head of the channel. Janet spread out the next chart and determined our course for the narrows by Patras.

'Due east,' she said. The wind was off the land. We freed the sheets and listened to the chuckle of our wake as we headed down the sun's path on the water.

10

Every island is a revelation. You leave one behind and the sea enfolds you, deep as a dream. The next island is a fresh awakening. It swims up out of the Aegean, pearled with cloud in the early morning, or shining like a hard gem at noon, or pulling the night over it like an old cloak and twinkling with lights along its sea-worn quay.

I think of Hydra first because its burnt, barren beauty represented that aspect of Greece and the Aegean which fascinated me most. It held the secret of that intellectual light which makes Greece different from anywhere else in the world. We came to the island at dawn, after a night's leisurely sail with a beam wind. It was July, and the wind would freshen as the sun rose, for the Northerlies—which the Greeks call *Meltemi*—are nearly as reliable as the Trades. They blow hard during the day in summer, and fade at sunset, leaving only a working breeze for a small boat. They leave, too, a long slopping swell that makes one stagger from crest to crest, while the boom scoops the water and an undiscovered tin of food clanks from side to side in the bilges.

I had taken over the tiller at four o'clock and was enjoying those quiet morning hours when one smokes a cigarette and has time to think. The wind died on me, so I hardened in the mainsail, ran forward to lower the jib, and then started the engine. It caught at once and settled down to the contented low mutter, which I knew so well that it had become a part of my silence. We had been three months in the Aegean and there were many days before the Meltemi settled down when we had been forced to motor. As I eased myself into a corner of the cockpit Janet looked out.

'No wind,' I said.

She nodded and went back to her bunk. The light began to lift along the water and there were small cumulus clouds dozing around the horizon. Every cloud represented an island. Soon they would rise up like bubbles and make a pattern of soft round shapes, and glow as the sun caught them.

Even if you smoke, your sense of smell becomes more acute at sea. You lose it in big cities—a form of self-protection, I suppose—but after months of living the sea life it comes back to you, and when it does, it is another sense restored. I could smell the decks damp with dew and the hemp of the new main-sheet and the dry-wheat smell of my sandwich, made from bread bought yesterday in Syra. I had laid a fried egg inside two thick slices. A cup of tea rested in the coil of the mainsheet at my elbow.

I could smell the sea—clean as if the land never was—not heavy as it sometimes is on hot days, nor rinsed and sparkling as it is when the big winds blow, but simple-fresh—holding the promise of a fair day and a wind that would come later.

Suddenly I remembered the navigation lights and went forward to take them down. The dimming glow went out at a puff as soon as I had opened the backs of the metal boxes, and then there was the fat curl of their death on the air—the smell of old hot lamps that reminds me of childhood. Quite often I would sing while on watch at sea, or pass the time remembering poems. When the irritating halt of a forgotten word checked me I would go below to the bookshelf and free the stream of memory. Some poems were no good at sea. They belonged to the land and to cities. Others stood up well: old ballads were the best; Housman; some of Tennyson; Rimbaud; Wilfred Owen; and the later Yeats.

When I came back and took the tiller again—we had swung off course in a big easy curve—the dawn was quite clear. The sea had a different face now, and the phosphorescence that had trailed with us all night had turned into a stream of bubbles round the stern. A dolphin jumped way out on the starboard beam, easy and graceful with his belly clear of the water. There was a school of them. When one of them came up alongside the cockpit I could hear his throaty gasp for air, before he plunged back and ran like a deep torpedo, down under the boat and then out on the other side.

For some time the sea was still, and then a cat's-paw crept out over the water towards me; a breath of air from ahead. Now I could smell the land. There was a brisk touch of pine; it must be off the mainland, for Hydra was almost treeless. And then—yes, perhaps it was the island after all—there was a warm smell of baking bread and narrow streets, and human beings, and charcoal fires, and the first cups of coffee circulating in the tavernas.

It was six o'clock when I sighted Hydra. It came up ahead of me like a wind-washed sail so that at first I thought it was a trading schooner. Then the sail hardened and began to shine under the morning sun. A low bone of rock, crested by one tall peak, it lifted out of the sea's haze and made its sharp statement against a sky that was already holding the deep summer.

We were lowering the mainsail and making ready to enter harbour when the caique came out towards us. She was deep-laden, with the sea running free across her decks, and her bows were pointed eastward. There were three or four men on board, and a boy sitting up forward in the bows chewing a slice of water-melon. He took his face out of the red half-moon and spat some pips over the side. The caique's skipper gave us a wave and altered course.

'Where from?' he shouted.

'Syra,' I called back.

'I'm going there.' He pointed to his mainsail and I caught the word 'Meltemi'. Yes, it would blow hard later today and he would drive through at fine speed—as long as his canvas lasted. The sail was a Dutchman's trousers of patches, with the head formed by an American flour bag. But the Greeks are great sailors; they will put to sea in any beaten-up old craft and in almost any weather. They are the true seamen of the Mediter-ranean, and they carry the virtues of a dying race—men who use sail instead of machinery. But even in the islands the diesel engine is triumphing. A few years more, and sail will be only a memory, or the toy of yachtsmen.

Janet took the helm while I got ready the anchor. The seventy-five-pound C.Q.R. anchor was about the only piece of gear on board that was difficult for a woman to handle.

'I'll ease her down,' she shouted as we came up to the break-water. 'Sing out if you spot a good berth.'

There were fishermen lounging on the warm stones above our heads. Their lines and floats were out for the day. They would stay there contentedly until it was time for the siesta, then they would reel in and leave their fishing until the cool of the evening. One or two of them waved, and a barefoot boy pointed to our ensign and shouted 'English!' They still didn't hate us, despite the politicians in Athens and London.

The first sight of Hydra is startling—a clash of swords and a clangour of trumpets. White as wedding cake, the houses mount the deep basin in which the harbour lies. Impeccable in line and form, they have a classic severity, and yet there is something feminine about the atmosphere. Perhaps it is the Italianate campanile that gives you at once the feeling that this is an island with a rare history. The pavements are whitewashed; the air shines and crackles; and you have a sense of expectancy.

I pointed to the end of the mole by the inner basin. It was deserted except for one small open boat. We ran in slowly, dropped the anchor, went astern on the cable, and then got our warps over to the jetty. It was so bright a morning that the light was already dancing along the stones.

We had just done our shopping: some bread, a cucumber (one of the few vegetables to be found in the islands) and a melon, when Theodore found us. He came weaving through the crowded market stalls, tall and dark, with the head of a Byronic Corsair.

'You should have been here last week!'

'We stayed longer than we meant to in Santorin,' I said.

'Ach, Santorin!' He made a wry face. 'Nothing but old pumice stone.'

'Very good wine,' I said.

'But we have better here. And look at Hydra! Isn't it beautiful? Admit now, it's the most beautiful of all the islands.'

Although Theodore lives and works in Athens his family comes from Hydra. He has the islander's passionate love for his own small strip of rock and soil and herb. It is this sensual love for one particular place that sets the Greek apart from other men. Once you have understood this passion for an island, a valley, or a village, you can understand the whole of Greek history—the bitterness of the old city-state strife, and the fire and love that created the noblest world of the human heart.

Theodore dragged us into a bar and ordered two ouzos, a glass of white wine for Janet, and several plates of mezé.

'*Zeeto Ee Ellas!*' We clinked glasses. Theodore gripped my elbow.

'I'm not going to talk politics—but what is your Government doing?'

No true Greek ever talks anything but politics—or ever has. I was not to be drawn.

'I don't know,' I said. 'I don't read the papers. I'm working on a book.'

'I don't understand it,' he said. 'Your Prime Minister has a reputation for loving freedom and justice. He's a handsome man,' he added inconsequently.

'He's got the face of a St. James's Street club that's seen better days.'

Theodore began to laugh. 'I must tell that to the General.'

Make a Greek laugh and he is soon diverted from his fiery preoccupation with politics and personalities, and with justice, freedom, liberty and all the big words that men die for.

'Tell us about Hydra,' said Janet.

He was off then like a blue streak, painting a poem of his island, which was not just a small rock in the Aegean, but the still centre round which the world and the universe, even, revolved. It was a place where the sun was best, the wine incomparable, the ship-builders superb, the women beautiful as goddesses, chaste yet passionate, and the children not sired in ordinary beds but products of fire and sea. Cyprus and Enosis were gone through the window, dark birds blown clear away over the dappled harbour water.

The mezé arrived. They are the snacks served with drinks which, as a schooner skipper explained to me in Santorin, 'Prolong the pleasure of drinking by saving one from getting drunk too soon.' Half a dozen plates were placed on the wooden table-top: goat's cheese, cucumber slices, potato chips, fried octopus tentacles, small pieces of lamb (cut from a joint that turned on a clockwork spit in the corner of the room) and rock-fish seasoned with onions. The landlord, a black-jowled bear of a man with a sagging paunch, beamed approvingly, shook Janet's hand and slapped me on the shoulder.

'In a little boat?' he said. 'Mr. Theodore tells me you came all the way from England in a little boat?'

'He is like Ulysses,' said Theodore, 'only he has a wife on board.'

'Not so wily,' I said.

'Oh no. Ulysses was a Greek!'

The landlord laughed and laid his finger to his nose. He went back to the bar, rinsed out some glasses, wiped them round with lemon rind and threw the water outside on to the pavement. A puff of steam lifted in the sunlight and within a minute the dark stain of water was gone.

The taverna began to fill as noontime approached. A white-haired man with three days' growth of beard and circles of tiredness round his eyes joined us. The owner and skipper of a trading caique, he had just come in from Rhodes. Tomorrow he was northward bound for Athens to unload a cargo of sponges. He sat heavily in his chair, leaning back as if he were bracing himself against the swing of the sea. As he sipped his wine he kept revolving a necklet of beads in his rough hands. Their soft click-click! punctuated our talk. Everywhere in Greece I had seen men sitting in bars or cafés or outside their houses, sliding these beads between their fingers. They were usually made of fine honey-coloured amber.

'What's their origin?'

'It's not Christian,' Theodore said. 'Though it looks a little like a Catholic rosary. The Turks brought them to Greece. Each bead represents one of the names of Allah. We Greeks adopted the habit, and it still holds with us. It's a cure for nerves and restlessness.'

'Better for you than tobacco,' said the skipper.

'The Greek has a lot of nervous energy,' said Theodore. 'Not like you phlegmatic English! We must have something to absorb our vitality—even when we sit and drink.'

The beads clicked, the talk around us swelled, the door-curtain jangled as more men came in. Outside, a great stillness had fallen. The quay was deserted, the fishermen on the break-water had gone home, the boats were lifeless, slapping idly at their moorings in the hot water. The sun seemed to lean down and touch the earth.

You wake after a siesta on such an afternoon with the deck-head above you hot to the touch, and a dry mouth, and a tiredness in all your limbs that seems as if an eternity of sleep could not relieve it. There is a damp patch underneath your body where you have been lying, and your eyes are weighted and feverish. There is only one thing to do, and that is to dive over the side, before your eyes have properly opened. Even though the water is warm there is a brief shock, and the stretch of muscle and deep gasp for air clear away the lassitude of the afternoon hours. The boat shines above you, rising and dipping slightly in the swell that the Meltemi is sending into the harbour.

'There's a touch of weed already,' I say as our two heads lift and rise over the water. I have been down looking around the propeller and the rudder.

'Thank God she's built of iron and not wood—at least we don't have to worry about worm.'

We scramble back on board and dry ourselves on towels that are rough-tongued from salt and sand. The sun is setting behind the island, the shadows are growing longer on the quayside and the town is beginning to stir again. A caique comes slanting into the harbour, the wind strong in her sails as she slides past the end of the mole. The sails come down with a run and the anchor goes overboard with a splash. She settles back on her cable and two dark-skinned sailors—barefoot and wearing only faded khaki trousers—jump ashore with her stern ropes.

'Neatly done.'

We watch other boats, ships, and yachts nowadays with the eye of people who live permanently on the sea. Our lives have become conditioned to its rhythms. We know now, without question, on what nights we shall have to keep an anchor watch; at what moment the large jib must come down and make way for the smaller; which saucepans are best to use when she's rolling in a seaway; and how to plunge deep into sleep the moment one has come off watch, yet still keep a sense of the boat's movement so that any interruption or change in it will wake us immediately. Ashore in Athens we were hesitant among the traffic, worried by the noise and smells of a big city, and depressed by the sense-lessness of newspapers, and the cupidity which governs the land life. Here we are brown and well-muscled; healthy and feeding well on simple things; drinking our wine and living close to the sun and the sea. They lived like this in the old days—before life changed.

Fishermen and sailors in the islands would often ask us if they could come with us as crew, but *Mother Goose* was too small. If I had wanted a hand there is no one I would rather have had than one of those Greeks. They were real seamen, quietly mannered; with a strong sense of keeping their boats as well as they could afford; and they would not have let you down if things were bad.

The old man who came aboard us in desolate Levkas in the Ionian islands was a good example. He spoke a little English, for at one period of his life he had served on a collier running out of Newcastle. It seemed strange to hear the 'Geordie' accent in that bleak island with the earthquake-ridden houses tilting back from the quayside and the sense of old defeats heavy on the air.

He would come with us anywhere, he said, and I believed him. He was a gaunt old hawk, with a fine head and massive shoulders. His hands were scarred, and knotted with veins like tarred hemp. He would come with us only for his food and shelter—if we could not afford to pay him.

'I must get away,' he said, 'before I am too old. I can't make any money here. And I must make money.'

'Are you married?' I asked.

'Yes, John is married,' said the harbour master, and his eyes twinkled. They were sitting with us round the saloon table.

I asked the question one must always ask. 'How many sons?'

The old man shook his head. 'I have no children.'

We had another drink. There is no greater tragedy for a peasant or fisherman than to be childless.

'But he has children,' said the harbour master with a feline smile. 'You have three girls, John?'

'Yes, I have three girls. But I don't count them.' He turned to me. 'Let me come with you, Captain. Look, I can splice, I can steer a compass course, I know about sailing. I have been a sailor all my life—a real sailor, not just a coal-and-shovel man. I could make more money there.'

'I'm sorry,' I said. 'You see how it is. There's only room for myself and my wife.'

'I'd sleep on deck. It's summer now.'

'There isn't room, John,' said the harbour master.

The old man got up. 'Well, good night, Captain. I'll come along in the morning. Maybe you'll change your mind. Anyway, I can show you where to get fresh bread and wine. I must get home now—to a house full of women!'

'What happens now women have got the vote?' I asked the harbour master.

The old man overheard me and stopped at the foot of the ladder. 'I get two votes—that's all,' he said.

'Never mind, John,' said the harbour master. 'They're fine girls, your daughters——'

'Girls!' said the old man. 'And they even eat bread—like men!'

He went out soft-footed across the deck. The harbour master laughed—he had two sons. 'Poor John!' he said. 'And so he has to find dowries for three daughters. That's not easy for him. And in Greece, as you may know, Captain, if a man hasn't a dowry he can't get rid of a daughter. It doesn't matter how handsome she is. After all, as the peasants say, a woman's beauty is gone as quickly as a bottle of retsina. When it's gone, the dowry remains. And then you hope for sons to take over your fishing-boat or your land when you are an old man and want to sit by the taverna door.'

The old man was back next morning. He stood silently on the jetty watching us hoist the mainsail to let it dry out. The sail flapped gently in the light morning wind and spattered the decks with dew.

'It's good, isn't it, Captain? The sail is better than the engine. Still, you have an engine?'

'A small diesel. Would you like to see?'

'Later perhaps. Now I'll show you where we get the best bread. Wine, too, if you need it. But it's not very good here in Levkas.'

We had a drink together after I had done the shopping. He would take no tip.

'You are a stranger here. One day, perhaps, I will be a stranger in your country.' He repeated his few English phrases:

'Good morning. 'Ow about a cuppa tea? Bloody bad weather——'

'It always is there,' I said.

When the time came for us to leave he stood on the quayside and handed the ends of the warps over to me. I pushed a packet of cigarettes in his hand as the gap between the boat and the stone wall widened and the bows began to fall away south.

'Thank you so much,' he said. 'Good voyage. I'd come with you—even as far as the next island.'

But the current running through the straits had drawn us away and out into the stream. There was an anchored caique ahead of us to negotiate, and I had the tiller in one hand and was trying to coil down the stern warp with the other. He was still standing there looking after us as Janet went forward and began to hoist the light-weather jib. It ballooned up and shone in the bright morning. By the time that it was set and sheeted in, Levkas was disappearing into the mist of the sea.

The people whom we met in Greece, whether they were educated and multilingual like Theodore or poor and ignorant like the old sailor, were individuals first of all, and all the time. They did not subdivide easily as do our people into income groups, social classes, and union or non-union men. Greece is the last home of the individual man in Europe. Everywhere else that one looks, the eccentric and the original personality is being stamped upon and eliminated.

I know it because, some years later, when I came back to England and tried to explain why my National Health cards were four or five years out of date, I was treated as a criminal. Finally, in a sour voice, the verdict was given against me.

'We don't have a system that fits people like you. Why can't you stay put like everyone else?' I was branded, I knew, because the herd hates the solitary. But in Greece I had the feeling that every man or woman I met was standing alone in a private landscape. He existed first and foremost as an individual soul, and only secondly as part of a community.

The bleak violet mountains and the barren burnt-out air, washed always by the sea wind, add to this feeling. Greece is poor and patched, shabby, bitter and passionate, yet in some curious way she seems to guard the last dignity of Western man —the dignity that the rest of us have sold.

The night we left Hydra I tried to convey something of this to Theodore, yet always keeping my love for his country and countrymen within bounds of criticism. (Theodore needed no foreign friend to tell him what to admire, or what to boast about.)

'And when you go back to London,' he said, 'what will you do and say then? There you'll have to look like the others, or they'll hate you and give you no work.'

'I'm never going back,' Janet cut in.

I looked at her, but said nothing.

'What will you do then?' Theodore repeated.

'I don't know,' I said. 'But I have to go back. Another year or two, and then I must. If I lose all my contacts there, then I can't earn a living any longer.'

Another bottle of resinated wine appeared on the table.

'You'll never be a success,' said Theodore. 'How does it go?

> 'Weave a circle round him thrice,
> And close your eyes with holy dread,
> For he on honey-dew hath fed,
> And drunk the milk of paradise.

And you know what happened to poor Coleridge!'

There was a full moon the night we left Hydra and set course northward; a full moon, and the voices singing in the tavernas, and the timeless feeling of old defeats, and the steady continuance of life at a level where poverty was met with dignity. In those warm lands it is still possible to be poor and dignified. Success has not entirely been equated with the size of one's bank balance.

Theodore was swaying on the jetty. He had two or three other friends with him. We had all had plenty to drink, and the night seemed luminous with boundless possibilities. It was like Youth—wine had charged our hopes, and cut us free from the narrow limits within which life is normally lived.

'Come back again!' they shouted as we slanted out down the bright moon track, and ran up the sails.

'We will!' I answered. But deep down I knew that we never would.

Weeks later—it was the night before we left Corfu and set our bows westward for Malta—I was sitting in the saloon trying to sort out my impressions of Greece. They were so vivid that I felt as if all my life had been meaningless in comparison with those past few months.

Sometimes, even nowadays several years later, I wake at nights—no matter what part of the world I am in—and I come out of a deep dream of Greece. I think I must dream of that sea and those islands more often even than I remember. Sometimes, when the alarm clock sounds and the thunder of a big city calls me back to the hard task that we all must face of living life as we must—sometimes it seems as if I have left reality behind me and that this 'real' world in which I live is more insubstantial than any dream.

I was sitting in the saloon then, that night in Corfu, and sorting through my diary and notebooks. Janet was busy in the galley. There was a lot of laughter and noise on the quayside; two British destroyers were in harbour on a courtesy visit.

There was the dawn over Delos that I remembered so vividly, the morning when we had climbed Mount Cynthus and watched the sun rise over the Aegean. We had seen the water change from pewter to lilac until the sun touched our feet in the temple where we stood.

There were the winnowers of Santorin—the figures of the women on a golden evening, sifting the chaff from the grain with long, flail-like scoops. I remember the chaff drifting away down-wind to powder the small green vines. There was the night we slept out under the stars at Delphi and heard the oracle tell us that things must get far worse in the world before they would ever get better—and that we should never live to see the better days.

At Mycenae in Agamemnon's tomb the bearded face under the golden helmet had spoken of war, and had laughed at welfare states. The sound of the bees under the dark dome had been like a memory of the sea.

In Seriphos I had exchanged an old pair of trousers for two pounds of goat's cheese, and the old woman who sold us the cheese told us that drachmai were of no value to her. Year in, year out, she and her husband never left their cove or went near a shop. The only time that they bought anything was when a wandering caique came in to shelter from the weather. Ours was the first yacht that either of them had ever seen. They had brown, leathery faces and white hair, though neither was more than fifty. The man had surprising light blue eyes, and his goats came running up like dogs when he called them.

At Naxos we had drunk the island liqueur, *citron*, which is the distilled essence of lemon and has a flavour and fragrance like a lemon orchard at dawn. In a cove on the southern end of the island, slipping in silently at nightfall, we had surprised ancient Greece—two naked youths skipping stones along the still water, and racing each other up and down the lone, sandy shore.

All the memories were too vivid then for me to put them into any kind of shape. Later, when I could see the pattern of our life there and of our voyage, I wrote to a publisher in London and suggested that I might write a book about the islands for him.

'Greece has been done,' he wrote back. '*Everybody* is there. Why don't you move over to Turkey before the rest of them do?'

It was our last evening in Corfu and we were singling up our lines and taking a final look round at the Venetian houses, which were butter-yellow in the late sunlight. A Greek friend and his Scottish wife came down to say good-bye, and gave us a bottle of ouzo.

'Something to remember us by!'

We left at dusk when the eastern slopes of the island were blue with shadow.

'South-west and a half south,' Janet called from the cockpit. I checked the steering compass against the standard.

'Steady on that!'

The mountains of Albania were catching the last light. They seemed to be burning and the sky behind them was like folds of velvet. Janet uncorked the bottle and we took a long drink. To Greece!

'Let's not forget the old gods.'

'No. They looked after us while we were in their waters.' She tilted her glass and let a few drops splash into our wake. The night wind was beginning to come down from the north, from Italy and the Adriatic. I checked away the mainsheet. It looked as if we should have it steady on the beam all night. Already the log was clicking away merrily. We were making a good four and a half knots. Janet held up her hand.

'Listen!'

Now I could hear them—splashing and playing about the boat. There were three of them, maybe more, tumbling in our wake or dancing like children under a hose, just in front of the bows.

'Dolphins!'

'Do you remember,' I said, 'the morning we came to Greece? The dove that landed on deck? We said then it was a good omen. Now we have dolphins to see us off.'

'We should never have left.'

All the night through, as we drove westward under our fair wind, they stayed with us. Shortly after dawn, when the air was full of the scent of the night sea, they circled the boat in farewell. They turned and went back towards the sunrise while we, having made our choice, held our course westward.

11

SOMETIMES, in the late hours with a big city blinking outside the windows, people ask, 'But, out of all the places you've been to, which would you prefer to live in?' Always I am about to say 'Greece,' then something checks me, and I answer, 'Sicily.'

Greece is the dream world, the girl one first loved, the garden one played in as a child. I should be afraid to live there in case the dull giants of Bread and Butter dissolved Cloud-Cuckoo-Land and turned it into just another jungle where we all fight for our crust. Sicily, though, is a jungle that I know and have lived and worked in. It is the familiar face on the pillow which I love despite its weaknesses.

I know Sicily better, perhaps, than anywhere else in the world —better certainly than I know my own country. During the war, as a navigating officer, I had learnt its coastline, had studied it over and over again; long before the days when we landed on the sun-dried beaches. Now, in the course of the next year, I was to circumnavigate the island twice, and in those two voyages and more I was to visit every port and harbour, every inlet almost, where a small boat like *Mother Goose* could anchor or take shelter from the sea.

I know the changeable face of the island from the long, fruitful plains of Catania to the barren burnt-out south by Agrigento and Porto Empedocle. I know Erice when the clouds blow through the streets, and the foothills behind Trapani when the spring flowers are so thick that one seems to be walking over an embroidered counterpane. It is an island with many faces, and starred with the ruined columns of all the civilizations which have lingered there and drowned.

We had hardly arrived in Malta before we decided to leave again. We stayed only long enough to load the boat with a further six months' provisions; to refuel and water; to write a series of articles that put a few pounds back into the bank; and to have one or two minor repairs done which elsewhere would have cost us foreign currency. Malta was too dear for our light pockets, and a week there was more expensive than a month in Greece. Both of us preferred the silence and the peace of forgotten coves to the clamour of Valetta and Grand Harbour. Both of us preferred the cheap, wine-stained bars where the fishermen sat talking together like old trees creaking in the wind to the gossip of cocktail parties. In Malta, on that return visit, something went dead inside us. The newspapers—which we had not seen for months—were there to give us their unrelenting news that man was a sick animal; with their sad dopes of urbanized sex; and their tales of success, where success meant money, meant power, and then again money. When you go into a madhouse there are only three choices open to you: either you must go mad yourself; or you must escape as quickly as possible; or you must become a healer and try to aid your fellows. Neither of us was big enough to attempt the third. We took ship again 'for happiness is somewhere to be had', *n'importe ou hors du monde,* and we did not feel the peace come back again until we had been twenty-four hours at sea, and until we saw the low lion-skin hills of summer Sicily rising out of the water dead ahead.

'Have you come far?' asked the fishermen lounging on the walls of Sciacca. 'All the way from Malta! And in so small a craft!'

'Take me on as a hand,' said one of them. 'If you want to sail round the world, who better could you have as a guide?'

I mistrust local guides, and have a well-founded suspicion of fishermen's capabilities once they are taken outside the few square miles that form their normal 'beat'. But I was saved from making my excuses by the arrival of the harbour master, who examined the ship's papers, welcomed us to Sicily, and accepted a glass of whisky.

'Fierce and strong—but not unpleasant,' was his comment. He was from the north of Italy. Had I tasted Grappa? I had? Well now, there was a man's drink. He had once—at a wedding —emptied his glass of Grappa into a bowl of flowers. In the morning all the flowers were dead. *Si, é vero, signore.*

He had an engaging smile and quick black eyes the colour of

sloes. While he talked he gestured lazily with his right hand, the little finger cocked in the air to show the inch-long finger-nail that set him apart from common men who toil with their hands.

He was just about to leave, having complimented Janet on her beauty, myself on my boat, and both of us on our Italian—so that we were sitting in a trance of flattery—when he hesitated and rapped with his knuckles on his forehead. 'Oh, just one thing, signore. I'd advise you to get a sailor to look after your boat. That is, if you're going to be ashore very much. I wouldn't leave her unattended if I were you.'

I explained that I always locked up the boat when I went ashore.

'Anyway,' I added, 'in your so beautiful harbour I am sure she will be quite safe.'

He smiled, shrugged, and left.

'What was all that about?' Janet asked.

'Don't you remember, last year in Syracuse,' I said. 'The English-speaking Jesuit who told us to watch out for thieves? Let's leave it for tonight, anyway. If we decide to stay for more than a day we can always get a watchman.'

Janet went ashore to shop while I tidied up the boat and had a shave. There are few things quite so good as a shave when you have two or three days' growth of beard, and your skin is leathery and salty from the sun and the sea. The hot fresh water, the lather, and the cool action of a new blade seem to give you back the face of a twenty-year-old. Afterwards I changed and walked out along the jetty. Sciacca is a small fishing port, with a depth of only six or seven foot in the harbour. The open lateen-sailboats with the eyes painted on their bows, and their bright colours, had a real beauty. They were roughly finished, but they were cared for, and ornamented with simple art. In their roughness, their timelessness (any one of them might have come off a Greek vase) and in their bright primary colours, they seemed an embodiment of the island.

The sun was sinking along the western coastline, catching the headlands in its final fire. Small open boats were putting out from every cove and harbour: the night fishing-fleet, going out with their flares and nets, to get what they could from the overworked coastal waters.

Janet was still away up in the town. The town and shops of

Sciacca are on a rock that hangs over the harbour, and at night, looking up at the lights and the sixteenth-century battlements, you get a lift of the heart. I thought I would find a bar, revive my Italian by catching the tune of the voices, and put myself back in touch with something I seemed to have lost since we left Greece.

It did not take me long to find my way. I could hear the voices and smell the vino and the cooking halfway along the quayside. The bar was brilliantly lit by four bare bulbs hanging from the rafters. There was a large fire in one corner and an iron pot hanging over it. Garlics, onions, red peppers, and salted cod were slung from hooks along the ceiling. The fishermen stopped talking for a second as I came in. Then I heard one of them whom I had seen on the quayside explaining who I was. I was just ordering a drink when he came over, and insisted on paying for my first glass of wine in Sicily. His name was Pietro. We clinked glasses and toasted one another.

'Would it be possible,' I asked, 'to watch or give a hand in the tunny fishing? I've been told that now is the season for it.'

Pietro stroked his dark jowl and gave me a keen look.

'Certainly, signore, I'm sure of it. I'll speak to the *Rais* and arrange everything. I think you'll not have to wait long—maybe two days at the most. The tunny are coming along the coast already.'

I ordered drinks for us both. Pietro leant towards me and said quietly:

'You'd do better, Captain, to get a man to look after your boat while you're ashore. It would cost very little. I would do it myself, signore, if you so wished.'

I had already summed him up as a good hand, but I was reluctant to start paying out lire for a service I did not really want.

'I'll think about it,' I said.

Half an hour later I left and made my way back to the boat. I was tired after the voyage and wanted nothing so much as some supper and a long sleep. I could see that Janet was back by the light from the saloon. Then I quickened my step—surely that was a figure leaning over the stern? As I came up the dark shadow straightened, became a man, and made off down the quayside and into the straggling line of cottages. I ran to the boat and looked about for signs of theft or damage. At first I could see nothing out of place; then suddenly I noticed that where one of my mooring warps should have been coiled on the quarter, there was nothing but a clean-cut tail-end. Someone had cut off about three fathoms of my best manila! Janet had never heard a sound.

Next morning, although I had already decided to engage a watchman, I thought I would report the matter to the harbour master. I found him in his small office at the end of the quay, offered him a cigarette, and told him the story. He listened, looked down at his desk, and said at the end:

'I'd advise you to get a watchman. You'll have little peace unless you do.'

It was not the theft which irritated me, so much as this complacent acceptance of it. Outside I could see two *carabinieri* lolling in the sun, smoking, and whistling after the passing girls.

'How about the *carabinieri*?' I said. 'What are they supposed to be doing?'

He shrugged his shoulders and looked at his nails.

'The signore has visited Sicily before,' he murmured. 'You speak good Italian—not the coarse dialect of these parts. As I told you, I'm an Italian—from Genoa—that is why I'm employed down here. Because they would not trust a Sicilian! You've surely heard of the *Mafia*? Do not imagine that it has ever been stamped out. Not even Il Duce—and he tried hard enough—could eradicate the *Mafia*.' He stopped as the skipper of a fishing-boat came in to collect his ship's papers. 'I should get a watch-man.'

I left and wandered back to the boat, arriving just in time to find a group of urchins throwing pebbles through the open sky-light. They were still running away when Pietro appeared on the scene.

'You're hired,' I said. 'Look after the boat as long as I stay here.'

He gave me a beautiful, ingenuous smile.

'I will protect the signore's interests with my life.'

There was no more trouble during our stay in Sciacca. Although Pietro would often be ashore in the town at the same time as us, nothing was taken from the boat when she was un-attended, and no damage was ever done to her.

The secret of our immunity during the rest of our stay in

Sciacca was explained by Pietro's presence. Without asking him (and if I *had* asked he would have denied all knowledge of what I was talking about) I knew that Pietro was a *Mafiusu*.

The operations of the *Mafia* are very simple, and my own experience was a case in point. Here I was, a stranger, arriving in a small Sicilian port. Although, by my standards, I was poor, by their standards I must be rich. Had I not my own boat? A rich man then. How can we make money out of this stranger? Why, of course, he must have a watchman for his boat. He doesn't want a watchman? Oh well, he soon will. We'll see that he gets no peace until he does.

The *Mafia* is the world's original 'protection racket'. It has other connections with Sicilian traditions; with the elimination of the foreigner, or the North Italian, from competitive business with the locals, and with the protection of the native islander. For the *Mafia* is, and always has been, an organized system whereby a man obtains protection for his business, his home, and his family, by the payment of certain dues and—if he is a member of the organization—by fulfilling certain obligations. The 'protection racket' which existed, and still exists, in many cities of the United States was taken across the Atlantic by Sicilian immigrants who found that the New World was wide open to a system that had learnt over centuries how to operate among the constrictions and difficulties of a small Mediterranean island.

The *Mafia* never bothered us again in Sicily. I think this was largely because we both learnt a little of the Sicilian dialect, and were quick to establish ourselves in the small shops and bars of the ports and fishing villages that we visited. The locals soon knew that we were not rich 'yachtsmen' but poor like themselves and with little, if anything, more to spend; people who worked hard, and just happened—by some curious quirk of character— to live on a boat in their country instead of in a house in our own.

There was only one other occasion when I came into contact with the *Mafia*, and that was many months later. It was in the winter, in Palermo, where we had moored the boat up until the spring. We lived on board, as in a caravan, in the strange slummy dockland of Sicily's capital, known to the fishermen, the *carabinieri* and the longshoremen as 'a couple of crazy English' but harmless, *simpatico* even, and good for a cup of coffee on a cold night. Gasperi was the name of our watchman—not our watchman, entirely, for he was paid by a film company to look after the barque that they were keeping in Palermo ready for their next blood-and-crossbones film.

Gasperi was a *mafiusu*, a member of the club. He never said so in so many words, but he knew too much about it to be anything else. He was kind, honest, generous as only the really poor can be, and a great wine drinker. At nights, when he had had a glass too many he would sit up on the poop of the barque and give forth to the moon in the tired scratched voice of an old tom-cat. '*Bedda Fontana*' was his favourite song—'*La Bella Fontana*' in Italian, but the L becomes a D in the dialect. One evening (it was autumn and the dockland of Palermo had a haunted, foggy look) I stopped work and went on deck. Janet had gone into town for drinks with some friends, and I thought that a warm bar with the light pooled on the tables, and the harsh clatter of Sicilian voices, would make a change from the loneliness of the private world in which I had spent my day. Gasperi, I noticed, had gone into town for a 'quick one': he was a reliable watchman after midnight but not before. I knew his favourite taverns, and I felt like listening to some of his reminiscences. One could learn more about the real Sicily from an hour of his conversation than by days spent in libraries.

The rough Sicilian wine—it takes the enamel off your teeth and leaves it on the roof of your mouth—is the only wine I know that gives you a glow like a spirit-drink when taken on an empty stomach. I had a couple of glasses in two different bars before I ran the old man to earth. He gave me a wink as I came in.

'Locked up?'

I nodded.

'Your lady ashore with friends? It's good for her to get off the little boat occasionally. Thanks, Captain, yes I'll have another. *Nero.*'

I ordered two *neros*—they call the red or *rosso* wine 'black' in Sicily. There is more iron in it than a mound of spinach, or a box of iron pills.

It was a typical Sicilian 'pub'—dark in the corners and lit only by one fly-speckled bulb. There was a statue of the Madonna above the bar; two or three wooden tables; trestle benches; and a dozen or more great wine-casks casting their shadows on the ceiling. I ordered a plate of cheese to go with our drinks and sat down to listen to the old man. The landlord was deep in conversation with some crony at the bar.

We had just filled our glasses when a shadow fell across the door and a stranger joined us. He was an ordinary Palermitan workman, in faded blue overalls with a day or two's growth of beard, and he, too, ordered a *vino nero*. It was not until he took it from the counter and made for a table in the corner that I noticed he was swaying on his feet.

'Drunk!' chuckled Gasperi. 'He's got a long start on us.'

Half an hour or so went by. The landlord's crony left. Gasperi croaked on about life as he had known it as a small boy in the Palermo of the 'nineties. The man in the corner drank slowly and quietly. Then another stranger made his appearance. I took a little more notice of him, for he gazed hard at Gasperi and myself before turning to the landlord. He was thin and sallow-faced, with a hard, searching look in his eyes. You could smell the hostility coming off him. I sat watching him while Gasperi talked about the puppet shows, the palazzi in their glories of candelabra and footmen, about sailing-boats and long-dead sailors.

The new arrival was just about to order a drink when some instinct told him there was someone else in the room. He swivelled quickly and peered across the dark space. Then he saw the drunkard and made straight for him. With one hand he raised the man up by his lapels, with the other he slapped him hard across the face. Gasperi and I tensed ourselves. You don't slap a man's face in Sicily without intending to take the quarrel a long way further.

The landlord heaved himself across the counter, bounced towards the two men, and, with an unexpected dexterity, hustled them both out into the dark. He came back and wiped his forehead. Gasperi looked at him.

'*Uomini cattivi!*' he muttered. 'Crooks! Scoundrels!'

At that moment from somewhere outside in the misty street there came a scream. It was followed by a wet bubbling noise that was all the more unpleasant for the way that it trailed off into silence. The landlord darted through the door. Gasperi grabbed me by the arm.

'Come on! Let's get out!'

As we passed through the door he steered me hard left.

'Shouldn't we——?' I began.

Gasperi shook his head. 'It never pays,' he muttered. 'Other people's business.'

As we turned away down the street we both looked back. Fifteen or twenty yards away a small crowd was already gathered. The landlord was shouting to high heaven in their midst. A woman was sobbing. One and all, they were gazing at the body that sprawled along the pavement.

Next morning in the local paper I read that a certain Vincenti P—— had been stabbed to death after an affray outside a tavern in the poorer quarters of Palermo.

'What was it all about?' I asked Gasperi. He gave me a troubled look.

'It would seem that the man we saw—the drunk one—had just left jail,' he said. 'It was he who was killed. He had been in jail for robbery, but the police had never found the jewels he'd stolen. Now'—he scratched his chin—'it would seem that "certain people" were interested in those jewels, and that they asked the thief to give them their percentage of the loot. He refused. That was unwise.' I could get nothing more out of him.

Some time later I was talking to a Sicilian journalist and asked him about the murder. He confirmed Gasperi's story.

'And who were the "certain people"?'

He smiled and laid a finger to his nose.

'The same who've been running this island for centuries. The murdered man was a renegade *Mafiusu* who was trying to keep more than his share from a jewel robbery. The *Mafia* asked for their share—he refused them. The fact that no one knows where the loot is now, doesn't matter. The murder was a matter of discipline. They'll never catch the man who did it. Who saw him? You and Gasperi and the landlord of the bar—and you couldn't recognize him again. And Gasperi *wouldn't*. Neither would the landlord. Simple, isn't it?'

But Sicily is not all *Mafia*. I know people who have lived there for years and are hardly aware of its existence. I knew about it, and came across references to its activities, only because I was living at the same level as the peasants and fishermen among whom it largely operates. The *Mafia* is only one of the curious strands in the island life which make the whole pattern unique and disturbingly interesting. There is one Sicily which is laid open for inspection by the tourist: the golden columns of Girgenti; the smoking foothills of Aetna; and the warm stonework of decaying palaces. But life is not all art, and the bedazzled eye behind the Leica which sees only a picturesque tramp on a noble staircase, or a handsome peasant girl among the vineyards above Riposto, sees only the powdered surface of a world. Sicily, like Aetna on an autumn evening, when the lazy smoke-spirals signal off the land, provides one of the most perfect backcloths in the world. But it takes lava and igneous fury to furnish that aesthete's dream of a smoke-plume against an opal sky. Sicily would hold less interest for her true lover were the island no more than the skin and patina which enraptures the transvestites of Taormina.

There was a real morning of fire and champagne-in-the-blood some few days after we had reached Sciacca. Pietro called me early and said: 'The *mattanza*, Capitano! Hurry or we'll be late.'

'Ready,' I said.

He looked dubiously at Janet. 'Does the lady come too?'

'Is it possible?'

'Oh yes, it's possible. It's only that—eh! It's not for the weak stomach, you understand? Still, if the lady sails about the world in a small boat, she must be of a strong nature.'

It was just before dawn as we rowed up the coastline. There were many other boats stirring through the early mists as well as ourselves. Most of the men from Sciacca would be busy round the nets today, for the *mattanza* is something that needs plenty of manpower. We had been rowing about twenty minutes, and I had just given Pietro a spell at the oars, when he touched my shoulder.

'Behold! The barges—the *camera della morte*!'

The 'chamber of death', the words in his husky voice, had a sinister ring even on so sweet a morning. We made our dinghy fast to the side of an old black-hulled barge and scrambled aboard.

The *mattanza*—the word itself is a relic of the Spanish occupation of Sicily and means 'the slaying'—is the climax to a special type of tunny fishing practised off the coasts of Sicily and North Africa. The technique is one which the Sicilians learned during the Moorish occupation of the island (Sicily must be the most ravished island in the world). It depends on two factors known to the old Arabs: first, that the tunny at a certain season of the

130

year closes the coast to spawn; and secondly that a tunny will not double back on his tracks once inside the net.

At certain points along the coast where the fishermen know that spawning tunny run, a long net is stretched out to block their path. The fish, on coming to this obstruction, turn along it and in doing so sail into the first of the nets—a square box-like net let down to the sea-bed. Looking for an escape route, they go further inside, only to find another opening and another net. By the time that they have reached the third and last net—the *camera della morte*—they have lost their sense of direction and will do nothing but swim aimlessly round and round until, as now, the moment comes for their death. The last net is unlike the others in that it has a bottom to it, and its four sides are supported by four barges. When the day comes that the foreman or *rais*, who has been keeping count of the fish in the net, decides to close the door the *mattanza* is proclaimed.

The *rais* (the word is Arabic in origin) was a broad-shouldered man in his fifties, with a stubble of white beard. He was gazing into the water through the glass-lined bottom of an old drum. He straightened up as Pietro deferentially wished him good morning and introduced us.

'Not very many,' he said; 'about twenty fish, I think.' He pulled a face. 'Let's hope this won't be a bad season.'

By now the men were assembling along all the barges. The dawn was very close. You could feel its stir in the air and a flicker of light was running along the water. I took out my flask and Pietro and I had a deep drink. We were only wearing thin shirts and the air was still damp. Janet had wisely come in a duffle coat.

The sun had only been up about ten minutes when the *rais* stepped forward on the central barge and the chatter of the men was stilled. Everything in Sicily must have its ritual. They are wise enough to know that even the actions by which we earn our daily bread acquire more meaning if they are invested with a little mystery. The *rais* said a short prayer, invoking the blessing of the Virgin on our activities and beseeching her to prosper the catch. No sooner had he finished than a crackle of blasphemy broke out as the gathered men stooped to the long ropes and began to haul up the net. The door to the net was already closed and now, as with cracking joints and sinews we heaved it up from the bottom, the fishes' watery world began to contract. Inexorably, to the sound of our grunts and curses, the dark folds began to lift from the bottom. The frightened fish started to circle inside it, swimming always a little nearer towards the surface as the net constrained them.

It came up slowly. The sun was quite bright now. The mist had lifted and we were all sweating. Leaning over and looking down into the water I could see the great fish circling and circling. They plunged past each other, bright and silver, as their world receded. But never—so faultless were their instincts—did they seem to jostle or touch each other.

When the bottom of the net was only a few feet below the water the *rais* shouted to us to stop hauling. The net was secured and the ropes turped up round wooden sampson posts on the barges. When we turned back to the square patch of water, it had gone mad. The fish were leaping and splashing as they felt the harsh folds beneath them. They were frightened when they saw the sun, and when they felt against their flanks the solidity of the black barges hemming them in.

Row after row, black against the sunlit water, the men poised themselves for a brief second and then—as if with one accord—struck downward. I can see them still on that bright morning: the gaffs rising and falling; the huge floundering fish spouting blood and the men hauling them up the barges' sides and turning them with a twist of the gaff so that they fell into the holds. As the great tunny came over the side of a barge one of the men would place his hand over its eyes—it struggles less when blind. Sometimes, and the gesture had a curious touch of pity about it, they would give the fish a gentle pat on its shining side as they threw it down to die in the hold. So I have heard Litri talk to the bull on a hot summer day in Barcelona, speaking to him of their common world while he sighted along the *estoque* and prepared his death.

In that brief half-hour, with the sun up and the sweat on our bodies and the spray flying and the blood on our arms and faces, one came very close to the ancient mysteries. I know now how the maenads went mad along the violet hills, and what it was that crackled in their veins so that with all their cruelty they were very close to the heart of the world.

We took twenty-seven tunny that morning, a giant ray, and

innumerable smaller fish who had followed the lords of the sea to their death.

'Not enough,' said Pietro, as we had a last drink out of the flask. 'Last year at this time we took fifty.' He wiped his hand across his forehead, leaving a bloody streak, then patted my shouder.

'Eh, Capitano! We ought to pay you like the rest!'

The *rais* came over and lit a cigarette with us.

'Stay for the next one,' he said. 'I thought you were just a tourist at first.'

'He is a sailor,' said Pietro.

'And your lady?' asked the *rais*.

Janet smiled. Afterwards she said: 'That was rather grim. The fish were so beautiful. I don't think I want to see it again.'

The net was being lowered in readiness for the next shoal of tunny. The sun was high now, and as far as the eye could see the Mediterranean rolled lazily away, a brilliant almost artificial blue: except in one place, where a deep sheet of scarlet blood drifted lazily before the waves, rising and falling. The sweating bronze bodies of the men, the blue sea, the bright blood, and the shining saffron cliffs seemed to lift the veil of the ancient world. Like a golden bead of oil, the moment held compressed the whole history of this sea; it hung for a second in the sunlight and then fell. When I turned and looked again, the mantle of scarlet had dissolved.

There was other fishing, though, which had a cool nobility about it, a kind of precision and a sure purpose which removed from it all the sad undertones of death. We were trying to live on two pounds a week. We had all our stores on board, cigarettes for several months, and a locker of spirits. But two pounds was our ration for bread and fresh meat, fruit, vegetables, and any entertainment. It was not easy, so I would help things out by making sure of one fish meal a day. In Malta I had bought flippers, snorkel mask and steel-spring gun, and I used them much as a countryman may use his twelve-bore in a daily walk over the fields.

It might be any afternoon of that golden Sicilian autumn when I would pull on my gear and slip silently over the side. As often as not *Mother Goose* was lying in a deserted cove, or a small roadstead off a beach, where only a distant farmhouse, maybe, signalled human life from a lone chimney. Janet would be busy about the boat; occupied with paint-brush, or varnish, or sailmaker's needle; and I would slide into the warm silky water, take a deep breath and go down to the new world.

Fish slime and moving weeds and mackerel-light patterned the bottom of one remembered cove. It was within sight of the golden ruins of Selinunte, where in a whole day's wandering we had seen no other human being. (In Selinunte a heavy, interrupted world waited for our departure and took up its conversation again, with a sigh, after we had gone.) I had dived over after tea —the one English custom that everywhere stayed with us—and the green glow of the surface had become my sky. Lines of small wavelets were shadowed on the sandy floor, like marbling.

I cruised leisurely along the surface watching for the flicker of fish. Most of the small coves and bays were well stocked and the fish, unlike the ones who have seen underwater men before, were unafraid. Sometimes I felt a mild pity as I took on my spear a cool body and innocent eye that only a few seconds before had been sharing a peaceful world with me. But we are all constrained to eat—and I was not the architect of the universe.

There! Spinning their fat rudders through the silver water a shoal of *dendici*, grey ambling fish with a good flavour, slid into a patch of groundweed. A deep breath, I jacknifed and dived after them. My mask was misting up (I must rub some vaseline on it when I got back to the boat) and I lost them. With a switch of their tails and an effortless undulation of their bodies, they vanished into deeper water. I had gone down about twenty feet and my lungs were bursting and my ears thundering as I sprang up towards the daylight world again. The sun poured over my shoulders like a warm liquid as I rested panting on the surface. I made slowly for the rocks that fringed the shore.

Looking down I could see the green-fringed holes and crannies where the rockfish lie in wait. The ugly head of one of them flickered into view, like an old woman peering between the bead-curtain of a doorway. The spear took him clean through the gills, he quivered for a few seconds, and then I threaded him on the line round my waist. Within half an hour I had four more —enough for supper. They were not good table-fish by themselves, but along with the two flatfish and the small octopus that I had caught in the morning, seasoned with garlic, onion and red peppers, they would make us a fine stew. After we had eaten, we could lie back on the upper deck, light cigarettes, and watch the cove darken into night.

Sometimes if we ran into a fishing-boat I would barter with cigarettes or tinned meat for fresh sardines. Then we would have one of the best Sicilian dishes of all, *pasta alle sarde*. The first time I heard of it I thought the mixture sounded unattractive— spaghetti with fish, it could hardly be a happy combination! But, next to the coloured ices and the rum babas of a certain pastry-shop in Palermo, it is the best thing in the local cuisine. One needs fresh sardines, good quality spaghetti, pine nuts, fennel and raisins. The spaghetti is done in the ordinary way—not over-boiled as it usually is outside Italy but, as they say, 'To the tooth', with a light but definite consistency. The sardines and the other bits and pieces are fried in pure olive oil, which is drained off before the sardines are added to the steaming mound of spaghetti. Take a glass of rough white wine with it and you have as fine a dish as any in the world.

The autumn was turning into winter as we came up the iron-bound coast towards Palermo. We were worried about money. Despite our careful budget, our small pile of lire was getting very low, and we knew that we must lay up the boat for at least three months of the winter. The Mediterranean is no travel poster for the small-boat sailor from November until March; and I had work to do; and the boat itself needed a winter's overhaul and refit after the thousands of miles we had sailed during the year. Malta was too expensive; besides, we had spent one winter there and would rather stay in Sicily. But how?

The film company, whose two galleons plodded across the bright waters of Palermo Bay, provided an unexpected answer.

It was the morning of our first day in Palermo, and I was sitting in the pinchbeck autumn sunshine making up a coil of rope for winter stowage when someone hailed me from the jetty.

'What the hell are you doing here?'

I looked up and recognized a friend from Malta. He came aboard and sat in the cockpit.

'We thought you might have gone off to Greece again. Or anywhere!'

Over a cigarette he said: 'Would you like a job? Earn some lire?'

'Would I not!'

135

In half an hour I was signed on as assistant naval adviser to the film unit.

'You don't have to do anything except drive a high-powered motor-boat about—when required—with the director and cameramen on board.' He sighed. 'As for naval adviser, well—that's me. But I might as well not be here. Only yesterday I pointed out that you couldn't have the two galleons—they've got engines, of course—approaching each other, apparently under full sail, from exactly opposite courses! "What the hell!" was their comment. "No one will notice on the screen!"'

So for nearly a month, with Janet as paid deckhand, I drove a fast diesel-craft up and down the coastline, helped to film mock battles, rescued seasick pirates, and watched the weird world of the film-makers as they argued, hated, and loved each other with pendulum-like rapidity. They were stimulating people, enjoyable, like children, in small doses; one and all imbued with the idea that they were worldly-wise and astute. The simple peasantry and fisher-folk made rings round them.

There was a small fishing village close to Palermo which the film company had more or less taken over, converting its crumbling breakwater into a battlemented harbour, painting its fishing-boats to look like pirate craft, and redecorating the only tavern so that it lost its true piratical look but became what world audiences would prefer a pirate's hideout to look like. Nearly all the fishermen had some job or other connected with the film, while their wives sewed dresses, arranged flowers, and kept themselves and their daughters well out of the way of the immoral English and Americans.

Day by day, as we drove in and out of the small harbour, I would watch the locals at work. They were as busy as a hive of ants into which someone has upset a picnic basket. Never in all their days had they dreamed of such pickings, of such coils of rope, of so many cans of paint, electric light bulbs, diesel fuel, paraffin, fenders, cigarettes, and cast-off clothing. The richness seemed to them inexhaustible.

I had hired a genial rogue to look after *Mother Goose* while we were working during the day. From him I acquired the poor man's eyeview of a film company on location. He was full of admiration for the male lead, a film star the rumour of whose private life had reached even this quiet backwater.

'And is it true, signore,' he asked me one evening, 'that he has three women here with him—all at the same time?'

'Only two I believe.'

'Two! And yet Piero tells me that only the other night at the big hotel he tried to seduce one of the maidservants! As if two weren't enough—what a man!' He brooded in respectful wonder at such virility.

'I expect it is because they eat better than us,' was his final comment.

Some of the good-looking fishermen, however, confirmed that the female English and Americans were also without any standards of morality. One of them, who had had a great success with an attractive blonde, remarked: 'But what can you expect of a non-Christian?' (Only Catholics are termed Christians there.) 'I'm glad that my wife was properly trained to behave as a woman should.' I thought perhaps he was a little ungenerous to run down the lady who had been sharing her money and her evenings with him, but I understood his outlook.

'They drink so much!' old Gasperi said admiringly. '*Per Bacco!*' (The pagan expression came well from his lips.) '*Per Bacco!* How they drink! Your friend'—he went on, referring to the 'star'—'they tell me he drinks a bottle of whisky a day!'

When the film unit left, a strange quiet descended over our lives. I was sorry in one way to see them go, and they had certainly solved the problem of how we were to stay in Sicily over the winter. But, within a week, we had dropped into a pattern of living that was as satisfactory as any I have ever known.

Palermo is a wonderful city to live in, but you must stay several months in order to dive beneath its surface. You must savour the rich steamy life that exists behind the façades of the ruined palazzi and the squalling, bawling world that fumes like a dung-heap behind the leprous plaster housefronts of the poor. The casual visitor sees only Monreale and the Opera House and, perhaps, the swaying dried corpses in the crypt of the Cappucini. That is Palermo, too, but I think of it on a morning of early winter when there was snow on the mountain peaks behind the city and the orange groves were hung with gold lanterns and a wolf had been reported on the outskirts of the city.

'It's true, said Gasperi, blinking like an old barn owl in the early sunlight. He was just about to leave for his breakfast and his bed. I had a saucepan of hot water outside in the cockpit and was shaving myself, peering into a mirror propped against a coil of rope. He flapped the *Giornale di Sicilia* against the ship's side above me and handed down the paper. The wolf had been caught in a chicken-run by a farmer's dog; it had savaged the dog and escaped before the farmer could get his gun.

'There aren't so many of them as there used to be,' said Gasperi. 'In the old days, in winter, I often heard them in the hills. At night, in the hills.' He crossed the deck and went up the ladder to the quayside. 'Till this evening then.'

'My regards to your family,' I called after him.

These two sentences were our morning ritual. In the evening when he arrived he would say 'Good evening, Captain. How is it with yourself and your wife?' And I would reply: 'Well, thank you. How about a drink to keep the cold out?' He liked us, and nothing pleased me more than the day when he asked us both to come home with him and share his family's dinner. The Sicilian is reserved, and there is no greater honour than to be allowed into his home, to meet his womenfolk and children.

While Janet got up, made the bunks and folded them back into the saloon panelling, transforming our bedroom into the warm, mahogany-panelled study that it became during the day, I went ashore and bought fresh rolls. Most Italian bread is poor, because the best of the wheat goes into *pasta*, but there was a kind of rough brown peasant bread we bought in Palermo that was like Ceres' golden gift to man. It was brought into town every morning by an old man and his son in a painted Sicilian cart. All day the two of them sold these small loaves by the edge of the harbour to the dockyard workmen and the crews of the local boats. At breakfast-time the rolls were still warm from the oven. The workmen at midday would buy one, open it, pour in a small measure of olive oil, and add a tomato or an onion. That was their lunch.

The carts from the countryside were still trundling into town at that early hour, bringing goats and hens and eggs, green vegetables and fruit to the market. The fishing-boats were unloading their dappled catches along the fish quay and there was always a pleasant stir of life beginning. Half a dozen youths were booting an old football about in the open space by the bridge where the bread-seller's cart was drawn up. They did not bother me any more for lire which I didn't have, or pester me for cigarettes: they had seen me in the pubs with their fathers and had grown to accept me. 'The blond one' and the 'sailing lady' we were called.

'More snow in the hills,' said the old man. He gave me my usual four rolls.

'They're good today.' I knew that his wife had been up all night baking them. The son came over. 'Did you see the football results? You look in the *Giornale* then! We beat the English four goals to two!'

'How many did you cripple?' I asked.

He laughed. 'Only one.'

I went back, pausing along the main quay to watch the overnight boat from Naples come in. The bay was crisp and clear behind her, the wind in the north, and there were only a few high cirrus clouds in all the sky.

Sometimes if my work was checked and I wanted to let things settle—or sometimes just because I felt lazy—we would close the boat in the morning and go to the market. The old market in Palermo, tucked away down the narrow cobbled streets off the end of Via Roma, is an explosion of life, a firework display taking place in the sunlight. It has a mediaeval colour and feeling about it. Villon would have been at home here—in the street of fishmongers; the street of the toymakers; the street of the fruit and vegetable-sellers; the street of cheeses and butter; the street of wine; and the street of all-the-flowers. Everywhere there was the surge and the bright flow of human beings buying and selling.

We would linger among the stalls of mullet, pause among the octopus, the squid and dogfish, and hang entranced over gratings where coffee and bread-smells rose up on a cold morning like air from heaven. Noon would find us with our few purchases—parmesan, salsa, fresh sardines, anis-smelling roots of fennel, oranges and tomatoes—leaning back in some coffee or wine bar, content to sit wordless, mindless almost, watching the pattern of life as it swirled along the narrow streets.

March came on us unexpectedly with a stirring over the island, with spring flowers on the hills, and a gentle sky. We were lost in our deep dream of Sicily. The necessity to haul up *Mother Goose* for anti-fouling, to re-rig her, and make fresh plans, came like a clash of cymbals in the midst of a string quartet. Exploring the

139

island with Sicilian friends, dreaming in a friend's golden baroque house at Bagheria, speaking always in a foreign language—thinking even in its rhythms—we had forgotten that our life was somewhere else.

It was then that I realized, with a feeling almost of sickness, that within a year I should have to return to London. I was becoming forgotten among the sea and the islands, and the letters of friends and business acquaintances were becoming fewer, spiced often with an understandable envy. But once let an editor envy one of his contributors and he soon ceases to employ him. I was happy where I was, but where I was I could not earn a living. There, back there, more than two thousand miles away, I would be unhappy, but I would eat. I would wake in the morning to a grey northern sky and hear hard-by the rumour of the buses. The ugliness of Victorian houses and the strident shouts of posters and advertisements would meet my eye—instead of Monte Pellegrino and baroque fountains in old squares. But I would eat. There is no sadder figure than a man who has drifted so deep into a dream that he can no longer earn his living—except the man who earns a good living and does not know what life is.

I went to Santa Rosalia's shrine at the top of the mountain one noonday and prayed that I might stay in her city. The wax figure hung with jewels, the votive offerings on the walls, the long candles thick as a man's arm, the scented darkness at the head of the shrine heard me. There was no answer.

12

You never really leave a place or a person that you have loved. All emotion is a kind of wound, and the wounded carry in their hearts the encysted fragments. Sometimes, for no known reason, they work their way to the surface and are discharged for ever, but usually they stay there until the end. I have not seen Palermo since that winter, but sometimes in the streets of London or New York, a Sicilian accent or gesture has entranced the day. I have seen the sun spiral down the narrow alleys, caught in my nostrils the smell of ancient poverty (plain pasta and oranges in that land), and heard the crackling applause at the puppet show as Rinaldo vanquishes the Moor.

Remembering Sicily, I remember also some of the outlying islands. Little visited, off the traveller's beat (unless like us he comes by sea in his own boat), they are not unlike the islands of the Aegean except that, in place of the Greek sparkle and shrewdness, they have a sun-mellowed charm and an undercurrent of despair. In our wanderings we visited most of the Liparis to the north, and all of the Aegadian islands off the western coast of Sicily. Levanzo I remember best, for we went there twice, and the first time by accident. The island lies eight miles west of Trapani and is the smallest in the group.

It was August, not long after we had left Sciacca, and we were standing out on a long tack from the coast when a pale bubble loomed up on the bow. We looked at the chart, Levanzo.

'Shall we put in there for the night?'

'Let's see if there's an anchorage.'

There was a small open roadstead called Cala Dogana and a village at the head of the bay. We had no trains to catch, no time schedules to adhere to, so we freed the mainsheet a little and bore away towards it. That is the greatest happiness in life—to be able to do what one wants, unfettered by time, as if one had an eternity of free will.

> But at my back I always hear
> Time's winged chariot hurrying near—

Like the high cirrus which forewarns the seaman of an approaching depression, or the ground frost which hints at autumn, the sense of mortality is our warning and our excitement. It is the lemon to the oyster of the world. Somehow with chance-encountered islands one feels more deeply than usual the impermanence of our brief life and loves.

As the sun came up, the breeze freshened, and soon we were nearing the rocky shore. Already I could make out the green of vines to the right of the main headland, and a fishing village leaning over the waters of a small bay. The houses began to glint and twinkle under the rising sun. Windows opened and flashed messages of greeting. What at first had been no more than a huddle of buildings resolved itself into a cubist pattern of pink, pale-blue and white cottages.

An open fishing-boat skimmed out from the island, balancing herself like a gull under the wing of her lateen sail. We passed on opposite courses, within a few yards of each other. Her crew waved and gave me the heliograph of their smiles—their teeth brilliant in their mahogany faces.

'Is it a good anchorage?' I called out.

'*Si. Si. Buono ancoraggio!*' her helmsman shouted back, and then something which I didn't catch about 'going in close to the shore'.

For the next few minutes I was fully occupied. I sounded my way into the bay with lead and line and found that it was deep water right up to the village. Finally we dropped anchor at the head of the cove, within a few yards of the nearest house. Barefoot children were dancing up and down on the foreshore, and a woman was hanging out clothes in a small back garden.

We were busy washing down the decks, splashing happily about in the warm water, and breathing in the lovely smell of clean, wet teak, when a rowing-boat put out from the shore. It was perilously overcrowded. There were at least six people in it, one of whom—he was the *sindaco*, or mayor of the village as I found out later—must have weighed about twenty stone.

'*Buon giorno, signore!*' they shouted as they splashed alongside and made their boat fast.

A few seconds later they were all sitting round in the yacht's small cockpit, the mayor panting slightly with exertion, while his wife—a lady almost his equal in size—sympathetically fanned his face with the brim of a straw hat.

'Welcome to Levanzo!' A hawk-nosed man in the uniform of the *carabinieri* held out his hand. He introduced himself—Chief of the island's three-man police force. Our guests were a reception committee consisting of most of the island notables: the mayor and his wife, the chief of police, the owner of the village's one tavern (a handsome man with a head like an old Roman), the captain of one of the island's fishing-boats, and the *parroco*—the village priest. The latter was an old, white-haired man with a lean brown face in which was set—a most unusual sight in that part of the Mediterranean—a pair of faded blue eyes.

Within a few minutes we were all laughing and gossiping like old friends. I passed round some of my English cigarettes. The mayor's wife and the priest accepted a cup of coffee, and the chief of the *carabinieri*, after a brief scrutiny of the yacht's papers, had a glass of whisky. The mayor looked longingly at the bottle, then shook his head.

'Too hot, signore!' He pointed at the sky which, early though it was, was already taking on the deep purple hue of summer.

Within half an hour they had presented us with a complete portrait of the island. There were 310 inhabitants. One church. One priest. And this one village. Most of the men were fishermen, though the island's second activity was vine-growing. Looking over their heads as they talked, I could see the rich, cool green of vines splashed over the centre of the landscape.

'Today,' said the captain of the fishing-boat, 'is the first day of the harvest. You must come to the wine-pressing.'

'And this evening,' the tavern-keeper broke in, 'you must come with me and drink some of last year's wine. Last year was beautiful for the grape.' He smacked his lips.

In the middle of the afternoon, when the silver flanks of the mountain behind the village were shining like a looking-glass, I rowed ashore. Janet, who had a touch of one of the stomach upsets which are as inevitable in hot countries as headaches in big cities, had retired to bed.

The village was asleep under the hot August sun. A dusty black cat crossed the road in front of me carrying a fish-head, otherwise, there was no sign of life. I knocked at the door of the small bar-cum-general store, and a few seconds later two of my new friends—rubbing the siesta sleep from their eyes—had joined me.

We struck inland across the island, following a stone track that danced under the sun. It was a strange landscape. Prickly pear, trained to form the hedgerows, raised spiky heads on all sides.

'*Figghi d'India*,' said Pietro, the tavernkeeper. Figs of India! A more romantic name than prickly pear. I pointed to the mountain behind the village.

'What lies on the other side of that?' I asked.

'*Niente, el mare*. Nothing, the sea,' Pietro replied.

'*And* the Cave,' said my other companion. I was just about to ask 'What Cave?' when we turned off from the track and made our way towards a small farm building. A group of women were busy outside its doors, emptying baskets of grapes into great tubs. A dozen or more brown-skinned children ran among them, leaping and playing like bronze kittens in the sun.

'Here we are!' said Pietro. 'Here is the press.' Inside the building it was cool, and scented with a crushed-grape smell. Two large vats were being pressed—one by a simple, wooden screw system, the other by the traditional method of the human foot. It was strange to stand there—a visitor from the twentieth century—and watch the two bounding figures of the men chosen as pressers, as they plunged up and down, almost thigh-deep in the squelching, bursting, bundles of grapes.

Suddenly one of them leapt from the tub and ran across the stone floor, leaving behind him a trail of violet-coloured foot-steps. A fat, jovial man turned on a tap and hosed down the grape treader. The man spluttered under the icy-cold water, and then ran back to the vat. Pietro chuckled.

'It's not only to keep him clean and cool,' he explained. 'But also to clear his head! The fumes rise, you see, as they tread. And then—pouf!—your head begins to swell like a sponge!'

That night, with my imagination still stirred by this ancient ritual (it had been like watching a vase-painting come to life), I accepted the second of my invitations, and went to the local bar to try last year's wine.

There is no electric light on Levanzo, and the candlelit group that sat round the wooden tables might have been painted by Rembrandt. There were the same peasant faces with their deeply etched lines; the same hands that have known nothing but toil all their days. They were all caught and held in the soft, yellow candlelight.

I was just toasting the *parroco*, who had slipped in quietly to a corner seat, when I again heard a reference to 'the Cave'.

'Tomorrow morning, if the Englishman would care to see it,' Pietro was saying, 'I will go with him.'

The *parroco* looked up at me. 'Ah yes,' he said. 'You must see the Cave of Ghosts, my friend. You mustn't leave Levanzo without doing that.' Then he told me about the cave.

There had long been a rumour on the island that there was something strange on the far side of the mountain. Sixty or seventy years ago it would seem that one of the islanders had stumbled upon a cave overlooking the sea. It was dark inside but, by the light that filtered in through the entrance, he could just make out figures on the walls. They seemed to dance. Frightened, he returned to the village with a story about a 'Cave of Ghosts'.

Over the years people forgot about the Cave—or, if they remembered it, it was only as a tale told by old people over a winter's fire. Shortly after the last war, an Italian lady who was holidaying in Levanzo heard the local story of the haunted cave. Finally she managed to get some of the fishermen to take her round to the far side of the island and look for it.

'After a day's search,' the *parroco* went on, 'they chanced upon it. It was a huge rabbit warren—well, you will see for yourself. And there on the walls were the drawings made by our ancestors —oh! many, many years before the birth of Our Saviour.'

The cave in Levanzo—like the famous caves of Lascaux and Altamira—is yet another of those strange temples of pre-historic art. But what makes the Levanzo cave unique is the fact that it is the furthest south that any trace of this early European culture has been found. Even more fascinating is the revelation of bulls and antelope and cattle on the walls of a cave in a tiny island that nowadays can only support rabbits. Levanzo, we now know, was once joined to Sicily, and the island was surrounded by a large fertile plain.

145

Next morning I was woken early by the sound of Pietro and his friend coming alongside in their boat. We got up the anchor and motored over a tranquil sea round to the far side of the mountain. The sun was up and the island was beginning to steam with morning mist. We landed by rowing-boat and made our way up the steep cliff face over a harsh soil of granite chips, sparse sea bracken, and clumps of thyme.

'There is the Cave,' Pietro pointed. A dark shadow like a whale's mouth opened in front of us.

'I'll go first,' he said. We switched on our electric torches and one by one crawled through the narrow opening. The daylight faded behind us.

'Now you can stand up.' Pietro touched my shoulder.

We were in a huge, vaulted cavern—cathedral-like in its size and echoing space. This impression was further heightened by the pillars of stalactites and stalagmites which glittered all round under our torch beams. A bat whirred eerily past my head. And then—as Pietro flashed the light round the walls—a whole world sprang to life.

Huge bulls ramped and plunged; antelopes on delicate spindly legs ran in herds across a background peopled by tiny men—men with nets, and men with spears. Most of us have seen that world in reproductions of other cave paintings—but to me, that morning, suddenly to come upon it in this remote Sicilian island was one of those moments of revelation that haunt us all our lives. Some of the animals were painted, but others were incised. They were cut into the rock wall with infinite precision, and yet with a nonchalance, almost, that made one marvel at the skill of those first artists.

We went deeper into the cave, sliding on the damp floor, and the deeper we went the more we seemed to recede in time. I glanced at Pietro's dark, craggy jowl caught in the torch light. How much did he differ, I wondered, from those distant ancestors who seemed to stir around us in the dark? Twenty thousand years ago they had painted this wall. Suddenly Pietro gripped my arm.

'There she is,' he said. 'The white goddess!' Alone among the many figures of men, a woman's figure shone on the wall. Almost unique in prehistoric art, where the female body is rarely delineated, the goddess of Levanzo presides over her secret temple. She is a white woman—that one can tell from the white clay with which her body has been painted. But the mystery still remains. What did she symbolize? Was she, indeed, a goddess, or was she no more than the ancestress of all pin-up girls?

When we made our way back to the outside world, we did so in a curious, reflective silence. At the mouth of the cave I stopped and, pulling aside a fringe of green creeper that hung over the opening, gazed down on the Mediterranean Sea. It was wrinkled already by the first stirring of the day breeze. What other men before me had looked down from here, had looked and seen a long level green of plainland? And deer had roamed where *Mother Goose* lay rocking in the south-east swell!

My two friends stood beside me. 'Come,' said Pietro, 'there is a fair breeze. It will be astern of us all the way home.'

Leaving the cave of ghosts behind us, we stepped out into the bright Mediterranean morning.

13

IT WAS autumn again, and the wind was rising. The clouds were moon-dappled. Dark and torn, they flung themselves over our heads like wet linen flapping on a line. When the moon leaned for a minute or so through a cave in the sky it lit up a wild sea and shone greyly on our wet decks. We were taking a lot of water over, but the boat was going well, driving hard through the rising sea, and reeling off the miles. Even so I was not quite happy. I did not know her motion and I was unsure of my judgement. Perhaps we should have reefed at sunset? Certainly the sky, the barometer, and the warning advance of a swell had told me that we were in for a blow. I was unsure of myself because I was unfamiliar with the boat. We had bought her only three months ago, and this was the first time we had been out in anything like real weather.

We had sold *Mother Goose* in Malta that spring, soon after our return from Palermo. The offer had been a good one, and at the time I was planning to go straight back to England. I had been deeply sorry to see her go. A boat becomes part of your life in the way that a house or a car or anything else never does. A boat in which you have sailed thousands of miles, and in which you have lived for two years, becomes as close to you as a trusted friend. She is like the friend who has been beside you during a war (peacetime friends are never the same thing), who has been with you when things were bad, and whom you know will never let you down. If you fail, you fail together. But *Mother Goose* was growing old and I knew that I would never get as good a price for her in England. I knew, too, that she had a good home, suitable for her declining years, with a Maltese family who would never take her far from the island, and never take her out when the weather was bad. She would become a cocktail bar and a diving platform moored in one of the creeks—the tale of her long voyages told with something like amazement on golden summer evenings when the sandstone cliffs of Malta were hot as a baker's oven and the water was very blue and still.

It was curious, though, on the day when I had signed the final documents and the deed was done I had a feeling of unease, as if in some inexplicable way I had sold our luck along with the boat. And then—to be boatless! For a man who has once lived in a boat and who suddenly finds himself back again among the shore-dwellers is worse off than a homeless tramp who regrets the vanished security of childhood. The truth is that the seaman and the landsman speak different languages. In countries like Sicily and Greece I had seen the difference between them expressed in its simplest terms. The peasant was constrained to meanness; he was avaricious, and possessed by his possessions. But even the poorest fisherman was generous and had a spontaneous warmth of heart. (Even in big cities, down by the docks, I can tell the seamen from landsmen. One has a frank eye and an open-handed simplicity with his money. The other has an eye like a corkscrew and hands that are stretched towards the sailor's pockets.)

These were my feelings as I walked the hot streets of Valetta, a boatless man, nerving myself for London again. But *Mischief* was for sale—*Mischief*, the old Bristol pilot cutter who had been moored so long in Kalkara Creek that she had acquired the look of a permanent building! And it was in *Mischief* that I now sat, looking up at the curve of the mainsail and wishing that I had decided to reef at sunset instead of leaving it until after dark.

I took another turn on the tiller lines, for she was heavy to hold over-canvassed, and looked at my watch. Half past eleven. I would wait until the watches changed at midnight and then we would get the topsail off her and reef down a little. There were three of us aboard: Janet, Ted, and myself. Ted, who had two months' leave from the Navy, was choosing to spend it with us, cruising back as far towards England as we could get before his time was up. He was a good seaman, and a cheerful companion. He was strong—and we needed strength with *Mischief*'s heavy gear—and always good-humoured. That was more important than any other virtue in a small boat.

Mischief had a very different motion to *Mother Goose*. She heeled more, and she moved in a fast-driving hush that seemed

149

strange after the resonant bubble of water against an iron boat's sides. With *Mischief* there was nothing but a chuckle around the stern, and a soft sliding hiss like an iron running over velvet to lull you asleep in your bunk at nights.

I was a little afraid of the topsail. I had never handled one before, and ours was a big jib-headed sail that, I now knew, should have come down several hours ago.

Midnight. I called the watch below.

'Ted! Twelve o'clock.'

He murmured something, half asleep, and then with the seaman's instinct listened as he fumbled with his clothes.

'Going hard, aren't we?'

'Yes. I'm just going to get Janet up as well. We've got to reef. She can take the tiller while you and I do the job.'

I went back to the cockpit and waited while they had their coffee. Ted passed me up a cigarette. The wind seized the end and burnished it, sending off a shower of tiny sparks. For every puff of mine the wind took three or four, and even in my cupped hand the end glowed like a bright electric filament.

'I've got her.' Janet leaned against the tiller.

'We'll get the topsail off her first,' I said. 'Just give us a luff up into the wind when I shout. It'll only be for a second. Just as we start the halyard.'

Ted and I slipped on oilskin jackets. The spray was leaping up forward and it was going to be wet working round the mast.

'Okay?'

'Let's get it over and done with.'

It was dark, cold, and wet on the bouncing deck. The wind in her shrouds had a high angry sound. Everything I touched was taut and hard; the jib sheets were leaning up from the deck-blocks and crying a little as they moved; the staysail sheets, which I held on to as we went forward, were straining against the winches and hardly yielded even to the full weight of my body. Ted snapped on a light and shone it up the mast. The topsail looked like an aluminium wing in the glow; pale, sinister, and hard against the night sky.

'I'll take the halyard and the downhaul,' I said. 'You stand by the sheet. Sing out when you're ready and I'll get Janet to luff up.'

I undid the wet coils of rope hanging on the mast, left one

turn of the halyard on its cleat, and took the downhaul in my right hand. When Ted was ready and the boat had rounded up into the wind, I would ease the halyard with my left hand and pull on the other with my right.

'Okay,' came Ted's voice from the darkness by the shrouds. I called out to Janet and a second later I could feel the boat beginning to alter course. The topsail shook itself and started to slat as the wind drew ahead. I eased the halyard and heaved down. It began to render and then checked.

'Ease the sheet, Ted!'

'All slack!' he shouted back. I got both hands on the downhaul and bent my weight on it. It rendered another foot and then went taut again. The sail was firing shots like a revolver over our heads. The mainsail, too, had begun to shake by now, and the boom was lurching across the deck. *Mischief* had come almost head to wind and I could feel the way dying on her.

'Turn up! Tell Janet to get back on course!'

He ran aft, stumbling along the wet deck. *Mischief* paid off slowly before the wind and then began to gather way again.

Ted came back. 'What's up?'

'The bloody thing's jammed!' I said. 'I didn't want to try any more until we'd had a look at it. The way the sails were slatting just now I was afraid we'd have the mast out of her.'

With my ear close to the mast I had heard the thunder of the topsail as it shook in the wind, and I had felt the big stick quivering, giving ugly jerks as it felt the struggle of the wild sail.

'You're sure you had the sheet eased off?' I asked.

'Sure. It was quite slack. I expect the halyard's jammed.'

'I'll go up and have a look. Let's have the torch.'

I hung it round my neck on its lanyard and went across to the shrouds. I had renewed all the ratlines myself before we had left Malta and I had confidence in them. The wind was really high now—gale-force squalls off the edges of the low-flying clouds and a steady Force 6 all the time. I went up the shrouds on the weather side of the mast, feeling the wind hard in the small of my back like a giant hand. My serge trousers below the short oilskin were soaked through, and the cold wind wrapped them and moulded them against my legs.

The higher one goes the more a boat seems to swerve and

sway, and the more insecure seems the mast. In a gaff-rigged old-fashioned cutter like *Mischief* the mast is not a taut 'strut-in-suspension' like the modern Bermudan type. It is very much a moving, living thing. It sways gently like a tree and yields to the wind, or bows slightly as the boat swaggers over a large roller.

So now, as I climbed to the cross-trees some twenty foot above the deck, I found that the higher I got the more I had to hold on. I wedged my knees against the shrouds as the ratlines narrowed and curved beneath my weight.

'Okay?' Ted shouted up and switched on a torch to light up the crosstrees. How it seemed to thunder up there among the working world of the boat! The canvas and the halyards and the creaking mast-blocks, all spoke of strain. On deck one heard the wind and the rattle of the spray, but it was silence compared to twenty foot up where everything seemed to cry with effort, groaning like lashed slaves as they caught the wind to haul us northward, away from Sicily towards Sardinia.

A patch of sky opened and let the moon wander out. I hitched one arm firmly round the after-shroud and switched on my torch. The downhaul was quite clear at any rate. I leant over as far as I could and seized the straining luff of the topsail and pulled. Strange, it seemed to render slightly. Ah, that was because the sheet was still a bit slack.

I was gazing up along the torchbeam when *Mischief* rose to a big sea and for a second I seemed to be floating. I was floating! My body had been left behind as the boat dropped away below me, and my feet had slipped on the ratlines. Only my crooked arm held me firm. I came up on it with a jerk that frightened me, my feet dangling through the ratlines, my other hand fighting for a hold on the mast, on the shrouds, on anything that seemed secure.

'All right?' A voice from below.

I was too winded and shaken to answer. If you lose your head when you are aloft you are finished. The only thing to do is to wait coolly for as long as you can, gaze straight ahead at the mast, at anything that looks permanent, and hope that the trembling of your hands will stop. They knew I had slipped because my torch hung swaying from the lanyard round my neck and pooled the deck below me with light. I got a grip again, got the torch into my right hand and peered aloft. 'The sheet is free,'

I said slowly to myself. 'The down-haul is free. Then it must be the halyard itself.' Yes, the halyard had jammed in the sheave at the top of the mast—some twelve foot above my head. I had no intention of trying to climb the topmast on an angry night with the boat pitching and the sail snapping and twisting beside me.

'What's up?' Ted asked as I let myself down onto the deck. It was heaving as much as ever, but it seemed wonderfully firm after that wild bird's world twenty foot up.

'The halyard's jammed in the sheave,' I said. 'If I stood on the crosstrees I might just be able to reach the head of the sail and cut it free.'

'And then what?'

'Well, if you were to haul on the downhaul just as I cut the halyard I think it would come down in a flash.'

'And so might you, my son! Figure it out for yourself. If I'm a second late on that down-haul and the sail flaps, it's odds on it'll have you down too. Nothing doing. Let's leave the b—— up there.'

'We've got to get some canvas off her, Ted. It's really blowing up.'

She was beginning to stagger now, and the lee gunwale was awash. The water was boiling along the decks.

'We'll have to leave the b—— up there and reef the mainsail underneath it.'

It was unorthodox, but that was what we did. *Mischief* had the original old Appledore worm-gear roller reefing and without much trouble we got the mainsail rolled down to nearly half its size. There was a wide space of heaven above it and then, lone, proud, and somewhat mad, there was the topsail flying like a defiant banner against the night.

With the mainsail reefed well down, the next thing was to take the jib off her. She was tending to bury her bows, and the long, old-fashioned bowsprit was picking up water like a scoop and tossing it aft as far as the cockpit. While Janet looked after the sheets Ted and I fought with the sail. It was a big, heavy-canvas jib designed for all weathers—a sail that you really had to fight. You had to beat it into submission and bring it cringing and lifeless to the deck.

Ted got a crack over the ear from a swinging block that knocked him flat on his face. I could hear him swearing like a madman at the wind as he crawled along the foredeck to get another grip on the canvas. One of the spring clip-hooks caught my forefinger and opened an old cut that bled all over the sail before I knew what had happened.

'Stow it below?' Ted asked as we were bundling up the sail.

I shook my head. It was too wet to go below, and I was too tired and too wet myself to want to bother any further. There was one good thing though, about working on *Mischief*'s foredeck: her high, old-fashioned bulwarks always gave you a comfortable feeling of security, and you could afford to use both hands on the sail. A big, deep-draughted boat of her type, with all interior ballast, had an easy motion. You could anticipate the heave of her decks and, even on a bad night, I never got that rat-being-shaken-by-a-terrier feeling which most modern boats inspire.

We had been over an hour on the job by the time that we gathered aft again and lit cigarettes.

'What a crazy rig!' said Janet. 'Still, she's much easier now. Unless it blows up any more she should do for the night.'

Janet handed the tiller over to Ted. It was his watch, and she was due on again in only three hours.

'How about a drop of that Sicilian brandy, cock?' he asked.

'I was thinking the same thing.'

It was cheap rough stuff we had bought in Marsala just before taking our departure from Sicily twenty-four hours ago. I poured out two full measures in the big enamelled cups that we kept for cockpit use. You could feel the brandy going down your throat like sulphur and iron filings. A few seconds after it landed there was a steady burning sensation, and then the flames began to roar and the whole system caught alight.

'By God!' Ted sucked his moustache. (We were both growing beards for the trip.) 'That's an amazing drink. I'd hate to think what it's doing to the sensitive lining of our stomachs!'

It was dark again now. The moon had gone for the night and the sky was ten-tenths cloud, rain-bearers with squalls of wind tucked away in their folds, and hard showers that whipped the surface of the sea and then disappeared into the night like a rattle of shot.

I stayed there with him for half an hour, watching to see how the boat behaved. It was not my watch until seven in the morning, and I had reached that stage of tiredness when one's body seems dead although one's brain keeps clicking away like a calculating machine.

There was not a light on the sea nor a sign of anything except ourselves in the whole world—only our two faces and our gloved hands lit by the swaying circle of the compass bowl. At moments like that one recaptures the deep sense of companionship which most of us lost when the war ended. When I hear men of my generation talking nostalgically of the war I know that it is not only their youth that they are regretting, but that sense of common cause—of belonging to a band of brothers. In the jungle of the competitive industrialized world it is that lack of brotherhood which makes everything seem hollow. Seamen in the old days of sail knew what I am talking about, but the modern professional seaman no longer does; to him the sea is only the dull tramline over which his vessel runs its routine passage. Mountaineers and small-boat sailors are two of the last groups left who know that companionship in danger is one of the things that makes life worth living.

'How's the ear, Ted?' I asked.

He put his hand up and felt his head.

'Lump the size of an egg. I thought that sail was going to have us both in the drink. Caught your hand on something, didn't you?'

'Opened a knife-cut that I've had for weeks. Every time the thing starts to heal I catch it on some damn thing or other.'

'We must be crazy. I sometimes wonder why one does this. Wet through, beat about the lugs, only three hours' sleep—and another rainsquall coming up on the bow!'

I left him as it began to rattle on the deck, hearing him swear thinly into the driving cold as he pulled his sou'wester down over his ears.

Mischief was a lot bigger than *Mother Goose*. You could see that the minute you went down below. At the foot of the ladder on the port side was the engine, a powerful six-cylinder which could push her twenty tons along at a little over five knots. It was petrol, though, which I was afraid of; and, apart from that, the engine was American, so it ate petrol with a smug disregard for European prices. But it did work; that was the main thing, and I always knew that at the press of the button it would rumble into life. Its heavy bubbling exhaust note reminded me of an old

Bentley going through an English lane. On the other side of the gangway was the W.C., a comfortable W.C. with a book-rack and room to turn round, but spoiled for my pleasure because the proximity of the engine and the tank meant a strict 'No Smoking' rule.

Through a sliding door and you were in the saloon, with a big skylight over your head, a gimballed table in the centre, bench seats on either side, and behind them—tucked back against the ship's side—two bunks with book-shelves above them. Ted's bunk lay as he had left it, a tumbled mass of blankets and clothing, with books, socks, letters, and a passport all piled up around the foot. The table, balanced by the heavy lead weight under the centre, swayed gently with the boat.

I put down my drink, lit a cigarette and pulled an ashtray within reach. Down here you knew little of the blustering night outside. Occasionally a heavy spray of rain would hit the deck-house skylight with a cold splatter that almost made you duck. It was then that you knew the comfort of being below—the primus stove gleaming yellow in the corner, the warm mahogany of the table shifting with the lightest of sighs to the boat's move-ment, the colourful rows of book jackets, and the Greek peasant-weave curtain at the far end bulging and shifting almost imper-ceptibly as the boat wound on through the night. Beyond the curtain, where the mast—comfortable, strong and varnished—came through the deckhead, was the small cabin with Janet's bunk and mine. There was nothing else there except a Victorian chest of drawers with the radio on top, a Regency print of Mr. Thomas Cooke as 'William in Black-Eyed Susan', and a heap of sea-boots and cast-off wet clothing on the floor.

Janet had been reading Byron's letters. I picked up the book.

The great object of life is sensation—to feel that we exist, even though in pain. It is this 'craving void' which drives us to gaming—to battle—to travel—to intemperate, but keenly felt pursuits of any description, whose principal attraction is the agitation inseparable from their accomplishment.

There was a sudden slatting of the mainsail above me and the hull gave a lurch as we came up into the wind. I ran up on deck. Ted gestured with his free left hand.

'Suddenly came up on them out of that last rainsquall. I had to bear up to miss them. I don't think the bastards have seen me yet.'

We were whipping past the stern of a small coaster—about 200 tons—little more than fifty yards away. The thud of her diesel engine was quite loud and clear on the upper deck, though I had heard nothing below. She went away from us with a plock and gurgle, as her stern dipped into a deep trough. There was only the faintest glimmer of light from her wheelhouse. Her navigation lights shone softly, mysteriously even, over the moving sea.

'I'm just going to turn in, Ted. Blow that whistle if you need any help.' (We kept a policeman's whistle in the cockpit and we had all learnt, even in the depths of sleep, to recognize its shrill scream.)

'Hope we don't run across any more. The visibility's just about zero in the squalls.'

I switched out the light in the saloon, pushed the curtain aside and went into the cabin. Janet was asleep. An oilskin hanging on the base of the mast flopped to and fro with the boat's movement. Through the door leading to the fo'c'sle and the galley there came a glimmer of blue light from the stove. Good. She must have left the kettle on. The galley was sited in the old-fashioned way well forward in the boat, on the port side. I wanted to move it aft, but it would mean rearranging all the fuel supply.

It was pleasant and warm in there. I leaned against the ladder leading up to the forehatch and made myself a cup of tea. I noticed that, despite the canvas cover over the hatch, a thin trickle of water was finding its way below. It looked rather as if the caulking round the after-end was letting in the spray. I would have to look at that tomorrow.

We had recaulked all the decks in Malta. They needed it after years of blazing sun and no attention. What hadn't we done in Malta, during those three months of summer? Living on board in rough conditions, we had converted her from a half-forgotten hull into a boat that could really go to sea again. It was madness, of course. All and more than I had made in the sale of *Mother Goose* had gone back into *Mischief*. With the exception of the standing rigging and the hull itself, we had had to renew, replace, or strip down and clean, practically everything. I knew that she still wanted a lot of money spent on her, but I had neither got it, nor at this present moment did I mean to spend any more. We had not worried about fancy alterations or improvements, concentrating solely on the things which would make her a safe sea-going vessel. Later, some other day, if there was time and money, she would be worth more attention. But her hull was sound and, like all the old Bristol pilot-boats, she was a sweet ship for deep water. In *Mother Goose* I had often felt anxious when the big winds began to blow; she had not really been designed for the full strength of the sea. *Mischief* was: that was what I liked about her, and why I had bought her.

The cable was tapping up forward in the locker. I opened the door and lashed the loose end away from the ship's side, making a mental note to cut it before we dropped anchor next time. Right up in the bows there, one was really alone with the boat. The weedy smell of the cable—we had scrubbed it thoroughly but always a little dirt gets below—was in my nostrils, that and the tang of fresh paint from the cans ranged on shelves around the locker. She shook a little up in the bows, especially when we cut through a big sea and the water dropped with a crash above my head. There was no water coming through the deck at any rate: we had really got them tight. That was some compensation for the long hours under the blazing sun when my brains had seemed to boil and the sweat running down my chest had fallen into the hot pitch. It had taken three months' hard work, every day from seven in the morning until after dark, to get her fit for sea. It was good now to feel that we had done the best we could for her. She was standing up to her first real blow as well as any boat of her size.

I closed the door, went back to my bunk, and kicked off my boots. My trousers by now had dried on my legs: better to turn in fully dressed on a night like this, just in case there was a sudden call. They were full-sized bunks with a deep leeboard panel, so there was no danger of being thrown out. One lay in them safe and warm with the finality and security of being in a coffin—or a womb. That was part of the attraction of the bunk in a small boat: its warm, 'everything-found', secure embrace. I was deep in the dark, while outside all the noise and thunder of the world beat on the sides of the ribs that carried me. I knew down there in my drowsy, well-fed sleep, knew through the invisible cord that linked me with the man on deck, what the world was like outside, and how cold and harsh it was. I knew I would have to come out and face it, sometime; but not this hour, nor the next.

Janet shook me at dawn.

'You'd better come up and have a look. Wind's eased off a lot. The coast's in sight. We could set some more sail.'

It was strange how quickly one came awake at sea. There was none of that drugged half-hour which lies between sleep and waking, when one stumbles about a house waiting for the kettle to boil. No, once on deck and the dawn air was like a damp flannel drawn across the face. The sun was just fingering the rim of the horizon and setting fire to the base of a semi-circle of fat cumulus clouds. The wind was no more than a fair working breeze, the sky overhead was almost clear, and I could sense in the palms of my hands that it would be a soft day.

'The glass is going up slowly,' Janet said. 'You can see the coast ahead.'

'We've been making good time during the night.'

'Yes. We can't be more than twenty miles off.'

I went up to the bows. The deck was still wet but there was no spray coming over now. The air was damp, unbelievably clean, with just that faint taste of salt which makes it astringent. The mountains behind Cagliari were quite clear, their peaks catching the sunlight. We were too far off to make out any landmarks yet. I took the cover off the forehatch and opened it. The yacht inside smelt frowsty and warm like a mouse's cage, and there was condensation along the deckhead. I shook Ted.

'Sorry to wake you early. But we ought to get some more sail on. The topsail's still there, by the way.'

It looked better when we had got the full mainsail up again, and set the jib. The boat felt the extra canvas and began to pull ahead happily, leaning to the sails and going along with an easier motion. I timed the log over ten minutes. That was a good deal better, round about five knots. We should be in harbour before noon if the wind held.

Ted lowered a bucket over the side and we took off our shirts and had a good wash with salt-water soap. Janet was allowed the woman's privilege of washing in fresh.

'That feels better.' He towelled himself and skipped around the deck. 'How about that topsail now? Shall we get it down?'

159

'Let's wait till after breakfast. Keep it flying until we're nearly there. Then we'll do what I suggested last night.'

'Hey, you two!' Janet called from the cockpit. 'If one of you likes to give me a spell I'll get washed and start some breakfast.'

Ted sat in the sun putting a whipping on the tail of a rope. while I lolled at the tiller, feeling the sway and lift of the sea as it passed underneath us. The tiller moved slightly under my arm, but she was well balanced with all her sails set and with this fortunate wind that had eased back on to the beam instead of drawing ahead as I had been afraid it would. I could see the shimmer of heat and a faint blue smoke rising from the forward hatch. Ted put his nose down to it and strolled aft with a smile on his face.

'The cook's in good humour. Says we deserve a big breakfast —sausages, eggs, bacon and tomatoes. Tea's ready if you'd like a cup? I'll get one.'

It was going to be a warm day, the wind was just right, the swell had died quickly, the boat was going like a bird, and breakfast was on its way. The mountains ahead were coming up quite quickly, defining themselves as stark crenellated peaks and torn silver shoulders. In the far distance they were quite blue, and it looked as if there might be snow on some of them.

14

I T W A S a hard winter to come back to. There was a north-easter blowing, and England looked old and small and tired. It reminded me of the nursery to which one returns when grown-up. How small the windows have become! The walls have shrunk, the ocean of the floor is only a small pool of lino, and the fireplace—once a roaring cavern of dreams—is only a Victorian basket-grate after all. I remember gazing over the ship's side as we drew near to Dover. The white cliffs were grey and the sea was pewter and the people on board seemed sad.

'Home again!'

We had been away two and a half years. In all those months we had only slept ashore five nights. We had exiled ourselves more completely than any conventional expatriates, for we had adopted a way of life that was the far side of the moon compared with life in modern England. Our preoccupations had been with wind and weather and anchorages, and islands beyond the sea's rim. Time had been governed by the boat's needs, by the change of watches, and log readings every hour. Other than that, it had been only sidereal time that had concerned us as we waited for the sun and stars; watched the deck-watch and called out 'Now!' when the sun's lower limb dipped at noon, or at dawn or dusk when a star steadied on the mirrored horizon. We had forgotten city time. We remembered it as the grimy train pulled out for London.

'What time do we get in?'

'Will there be time to buy anything before the shops shut?'

'What time do the pubs open?'

'I must phone Henry tomorrow. What time does he get to his office?'

We had left *Mischief* safely anchored in a small harbour in Mallorca. On our way across from Sardinia the old mainsail, which I had been hoping would see us through another year, had finally blown out. It was repairable, but not sound enough for the voyage that we had planned, home through the Bay of Biscay in early winter.

Ted had returned to the Navy, confessing with a chuckle that he had not spent so long at sea since the war ended. So *Mischief* sat tranquilly to three anchors in Andraitx Harbour, secure behind the small breakwater. She was looked after by a local fisherman who had promised to pump her out once a week and open her hatches every fine day.

There is always a certain excitement about a city, even if you dislike it, but for the first few weeks we felt like visitors from another planet. The ugliness of most of the architecture, the steady undercurrent of noise, the increasing vulgarity of the newspapers, the eternal preoccupation with money in order to buy more things that were unimportant, the staccato beat of the advertising posters urging one to buy so as to work harder, so as to be able yet again to buy—these things were difficult to accept. If the world lasts, men of the future will probably look back on our civilization with the same distaste which we reserve for the sanitation of the Middle Ages and the intolerance of the Inquisition.

One curious thing was that, despite my dislike for the life to which I had come back, I had an enthusiasm for work and a vitality which old friends and acquaintances seemed to lack. I still had the sun in my bones and a health of body which they, who had been tied over the intervening years to a city routine, had lost. It is not just the Northern climate that kills the life in man, but the climate allied to an industrial civilization. Better fed, better clothed, better shod, and better educated, they all of them lacked the simple spring of life which many an illiterate peasant retained.

I adapted more quickly than Janet to our change of circumstances and environment. It was easier for me. I had an interest in my work and was busy on articles, broadcasts and a book, so that I had no time to savour the sadness and frustration that rises like steam off the great bowl of London. Besides, we had come back for only a limited number of months; long enough to earn a new mainsail, to put a few pounds in the bank, and to secure a lifeline of work that would keep us another year while we sailed

Mischief back to England. As long as one has an objective life is never entirely meaningless.

Meeting old friends was often a disturbing experience: disheartening, perhaps, for both of us. We had drifted so far apart that we were no longer in contact. We were working on different wavelengths, for our conceptions of what constituted success or failure had radically altered. One would need great arrogance to be sure that one's own wavelength was the right one.

I was sitting one day with Jack, after a mellow lunch, in his club. We had known each other for many years and could talk without restraint, even on those subjects which the Englishman is trained to avoid.

'All that stuff we used to dream about when we were young,' he said. 'Do you ever think about it now?'

'Sometimes. Yes, I do when I'm at sea. And when life is quiet.'

'But where does it get you? Honestly? I'm not trying to point any moral. But where does it get you? All those adolescent queries about life and death and the purpose of man on this planet? I never bother with them now. I don't allow myself time to think about them. I work damn hard, as you know, and when I enjoy myself—well, I enjoy myself too. But if ever I feel the blue mood of useless thinking coming over me I just get straight to my desk—wherever I am—and get on with some more work.'

'You've made a success, Jack.'

It was a true statement, without irony. He had a handsome wife, two good-looking children, a pleasant house, a car, and an income of three thousand a year net. There was a newspaper lying next to us on the club table. He looked at it.

'These bloody Russians! To tell you the truth, I don't trust the Americans a great deal more. They've certainly sold us down the river in the Middle East. And income tax is going up again, you can take that as gospel.' He looked at his watch, a slim gold Swiss one, fine as a sovereign. 'I must get along! Our South American traveller's coming in after lunch. Things are in a mess out in the Argentine. Give me a ring, though, and come round any evening—well, almost any evening. Talk to Brenda, she keeps my home diary.'

'I'll do that, old boy. God bless.'

The porter called him a cab as we stood outside on the steps watching the traffic rumble up and down St. James's Street. It was one of those December afternoons when the air is crisp and sharp as a razor, and the mouldings on old buildings seem to jump down into the street.

'Can I drop you?'

No. We were going in different directions.

Janet and I were sitting in the basement drawing-room of the small flat we had taken for the winter. It was dark outside although it was only four-thirty. The spring was still a month or two away, just discernible sometimes in the mornings by a new lift in the tired air and by the faintest featherings of green, an almost indetectable shadow, round the bare branches outside our bedroom window.

I pulled the last sheet of paper out of my typewriter and clipped it to the others that lay on the desk.

'How's it going?' she asked.

'I've just had to rewrite it all. I saw them this morning. They like it, but it wasn't exciting enough.'

'How not? I'd like to see old man Travers in a gale of wind!'

'Well, there it is. What I wrote was true; it was exactly what happened. But he thought it wasn't exciting enough. Perhaps he's right.'

'You know damn well he isn't right. You've just had to falsify in order to sting their jaded palates.'

'That's exactly what you have to do all the time these days. Unless you scream nobody hears you.'

'Nobody in a place like London.'

'London isn't so bad.'

'That's nonsense, and you know it. London is a cess-pit.'

'Some of the people are all right.'

'Oh yes—you have to falsify, cheapen, and scream in their ears so that they believe you.'

There was a deep rumble under our feet and the flat shook a little as another train went through.

'We're nearly home, anyway,' I said. 'There's a lot more work on the horizon. The mainsail's ordered—and paid for. Things aren't so bad.'

'I believe you wouldn't mind staying here.'

'Where? In this flat?'

164

'No. In London.'

'I don't hate it as much as I used to. Besides, I've got my work to keep me interested. It's different for you—your job only interests you for the money it brings in. I quite see that. So long as I've still got a typewriter or a pen, and someone who likes what I do for them—and pays for it—then I can get on nearly anywhere.'

'How about Greece? And Sicily?'

'No work. Not enough even for the locals.'

'If you've once lived the kind of life that makes sense it's impossible to come back to a second or third best.'

'Not impossible at all. People are doing it every day of the week.'

'Only because they're not single-minded enough. They haven't got the real guts to strike out for what they want, no matter what the cost.'

'You're probably right.' I looked at the clock. 'Coming out for a drink?'

'No, I won't bother, thanks. Every shilling saved here can be better spent somewhere else.'

'It's not good for you to come back every day and never give yourself a break. And at week-ends too.'

'Anything's good for you that gets you where you want to go.'

It was quite cold outside and I was glad I had put on my heavy coat. The sky was clear; there was a slight frost, and the pavement under the street-lamps glittered with a thousand miniature stars. It was difficult to see the real ones because of the orange glow of London. I remembered coming on leave early in the war, just a weekend's leave from Portsmouth, and seeing from the halted train the glow of London burning. That was the night when most of the city went up. A long time ago now.

I had been to the passport office and the Spanish Consulate during the morning, and renewed our passports and collected our visas. Janet was leaving in a month to crew for some friends on a voyage to Greece. I was going out the month after to start work on *Mischief*; to get her ready for the late summer when we would sail back to England. Those were our plans.

15

Cada vez que considero
Que me tengo que mori
Tiendo la capa en el suelo
Y me jarto de dormi.

OF COURSE the sun has a lot to do with it. After a fortnight of being back there I felt like another person. Something dropped away from me and fell, like an unregretted cloak, somewhere in the sea between Barcelona and Andraitx.

It was late spring when I got to the island. The almond blossom was fading, although the long valley that swings back from the port of Andraitx to the blue mountains inland was a moving sea of foam; when the wind blew over it the undersides of the waves were green and brown as the tree-trunks and the earth showed through. *Mischief* lay secure in her anchorage; she had not shifted through the squalls of winter. Dry below, and aired out, she was ready to be sailed to Palma for the slip. Janet had been busy scouring and scrubbing; the ship's sides gleamed; the decks were fresh and white; the stove was going in the saloon.

Just before she left on her cruise to Greece we took *Mischief* to Palma. Guy, an old friend who had come out from England to help us, sailed round with us. The day after that I waved Janet good-bye as her boat drew away into the blue rim of sea and sky. It was the first time that we had not sailed together.

Mischief lay at anchor, stern to the wall, by the Palma Yacht Club. With her heavy, old-fashioned gear and her working-boat appearance she had the look of a bulldog among whippets. Seen next to the sleek hulls of the yachts and racing-boats that lined the end of the quay, she had a plebeian look. For the first time in some years I was anchored in the same waters as the international yachtsmen. Here idled, sailed, drank and gossiped the expatriate British, American and French who preferred to live afloat in

Spain rather than ashore, and taxed, in their own countries. Some of them I liked, but even in England I had never been greatly drawn to the yacht-club bar, to the whole social pattern that comes under the heading of 'Yachting'. I preferred to call any vessel I owned a 'boat' rather than a 'yacht'. In Customs' documents and harbour master's forms I was pedantic enough to list myself as 'sailor' rather than 'yachtsman'; the latter suggested a wealth which I did not possess and an outlook towards sailing which was very different from mine. I lived on a boat in preference to a house, and used it as my place of work; to the yachtsman on the other hand a boat was a form of sport or social relaxation not so far removed from a bag of golf clubs or a pair of skis.

Guy and I soon had a name for the serried line of craft that graced the yacht club wall—'Yachtin' Row'. There was a book to be written about it one day; about their owners and their way of life. They ranged from retired English businessmen and their wives, who had found that the restrictions governing foreign currency could be more easily circumvented by living in a boat, to the fantastic and the plain crooked. Some of the crooks and smugglers were entertaining enough. Others were no more than sad figures who had slipped right through the *dolce far niente* into so deep a dream that the only way they could keep living it was by a little trafficking in those goods which are dutiable in Spain but not in Tangier. These were not the real crooks. The latter were usually high-level confidence tricksters, some of them men without countries, and some men with many countries. They shared one secret in common: that a large, well-kept yacht in the Mediterranean provided a background and an aroma of wealth as attractive to the rich and guileless as a jar of beer to summer flies.

It was midsummer two months later, midsummer and the alleyways of Palma were still hot at nights as if the sun had never set. During the day it was scorching. A sultry sea breeze drew on to the land lazily at noon, and at night the faint damp rustle of the land breeze went out to sea again.

Mischief was up on the slip. She cried with heat at midday and relaxed to the level of a warm fire at night. All of her iron ballast was out in the yard, being chipped and painted. Her mast, stripped of its rigging, shrouds and blocks, lay newly scraped in one shed; her boom in another; her rudder on the ground under the stern; most of her interior fittings were ashore, locked in a shed. Living aboard her was like living in the simplest of huts. The galley still worked; there was fresh water laid on to flow through the upper deck tanks; and there was cover when it rained. It was poor cover though, for the overheated decks were opening under the sun.

Guy, with his red beard and sunburnt nose, had stayed on to help me with the work. We were stripping the old boat and going over every inch of her so that, at the finish, she should last another thirty years. By day we sweated over scraping, and varnishing, and supervised the Spanish workmen who were stripping her paint and cleaning the ballast. By night we went ashore and ate in small cafés or bodegas that were off the tourist beat.

We went to 'Fat Jack's' most of all. The Bodega San Pedro, to give it its full name, was a small workman's bar off the Plaza Ataranzanas in the dockyard quarter of the town. It was run by Fat Jack and Fat Jill, an eternally smiling couple who must have weighed thirty-six stone between them. Guy and I were the first English people who had ever come to their bar and, when they found that we liked our vino and our anis as much as the locals, they adopted us. Soon we were eating with the family, paying about one-and-sixpence for a three-course meal, and introduced as 'amigo' to their other friends. When Fat Jack called you 'amigo' he really meant it. If you had gone to jail the next day he would have been round to visit you and would have had a meal ready when you came out. If you were 'friend', short of something as unlikely as an attack on his wife, you would remain 'friend' as long as you lived. Sometimes, if Guy or I were short of money, he would haul out a thick wad of much-thumbed pesetas and say, 'How much do you want, friends?' One day he loaned us more than four pounds' worth, no small sum in a working-class district.

'But, Señor San Pedro,' I said—he was no churchman and rather enjoyed the nickname—'supposing we don't come back again? Or supposing we're run over and killed?'

'You'll come back. Red beard here,' and he gave Guy a wink, 'would never run away from that pretty little dancer in the cabaret down the road!'

One evening we had been working late and had gone ashore for a drink without bothering to change. We were both grimy, covered with paintflecks, and had thirsts that would need a litre of wine to quench.

'Fat Jack's?' said Guy.

'Where else? I could do with a bowl of soup, some bread, and a drink. Let's go back and change afterwards. I feel like a night on the town tonight. After all, it's Saturday—the workmen won't be along tomorrow.'

'Thank God for that, I could do with a lie-in.'

On weekdays the workmen started at seven in the morning. There was no chance of sleep once the shrill scream of their scrapers had started on the ship's side, and Guigliemo, the foreman, had a habit of popping his head down the hatch, wishing us 'Good day' and sharing a breakfast cup of coffee.

Fat Jack's bar was crowded; fishermen, dockyard workmen, sail-makers, ropemakers, and all the local characters having a sundown drink, *pour chasser la honte du jour*: a good habit.

Jill gave us a huge smile that lingered like the Cheshire cat's and seemed to hang in the air long after she had turned away to draw us off a bottle of wine from the cask. Jack came down the stairs from the small room that served as their bedroom, drawing-room and parlour, and held out a huge hand across the bar. He was still pasty and sleepy-eyed from his siesta.

'How does it go, friends?'

'Well. And you?'

'A little tired. But I'll soon fix it.'

He got a small glass down from the shelf behind him and gave himself a large shot of Spanish gin. As he began to come to, muttering to himself and shifting his giant belly slowly along the edge of the bar in front of him, he noticed that we were still in our working clothes.

'Eh! Been working late tonight on the little boat? You oughtn't to let him work so hard, Captain.' This to me, and laying a finger against his nose as he winked. 'Red Beard will have no strength left for his little dancer if you keep him too long on the boat.'

Jill came back and pushed a plate of olives in front of us. 'There will be some soup, if you like it, in a few minutes?' Behind us a group of workmen were playing a coin-tossing game on the square flags of the floor. Jack leant across and pointed to the sheath-knife at my side.

'That looks good. May I see?'

I drew it out and flipped it on to the marble counter. Jack held it up to the light, tried the edge on his finger, and smiled.

'Beautiful English steel. Stainless, too. We don't get steel like that in Spain.'

I was just handing it to one of the workmen who had asked to have a look when I saw Jack gazing intently over my shoulder towards the door behind me.

'Put it away, Captain!' he said in a low voice. I slid the knife back into my sheath and picked up my drink. The bar had fallen silent. Jack was talking over my shoulder in his formal 'on duty' voice.

'No. No one has come in here in the last few minutes. Quite sure, señor. No. No, all these gentlemen have been here for twenty minutes, more or less. They are all known to me. Certainly, señor. Yes, if I see anyone like that I will report it. Good night, señor.'

A babble of talk arose. Fat Jack hitched himself round the bar and gave us a wink. He went over to the group of workmen and they started talking. A man in a shabby white mackintosh came in from the street, recognized Guy and myself and waved. He was a sergeant in the 'Armed Guard', a lean Madrileño come to Mallorca to visit his parents.

'What's up?' Guy asked.

'A man's been stabbed down in the Plaza. Didn't the lieutenant of the Guardia Civil just come in here?'

'That's what it was!'

Jack came over and took his arm. He was shaking with laughter and the tears were running down his cheeks among the day-old stubble.

'Just as the lieutenant comes in and asks "Have you seen a stranger round here with a knife?" the captain here—who is, after all, a stranger—is standing in front of me with a knife in his hand! Ah, amigo, I nearly turned you in then! You know you're not allowed to carry a knife in Spain?'

'Yes,' I said. 'But——'

'Of course, everybody does—but it isn't legal.'

There was a laugh and one of the workmen tossed a knife on to the bar. A few seconds later the marble top was tinkling and rattling as every man in the room produced a knife of one description or another. Fat Jack unhitched from the back of his pants a thing that looked like a butcher's cleaver. Even the little cobbler, who normally sat silent in the corner, saw the joke and released a spring-loaded blade that hummed and quivered between his lean brown fingers.

'And you, señor?' said Jack to our friend in the mackintosh.

He slipped his hand under his armpit and laid a small blue Biretta on the bar. There was a shout of laughter.

'We are a law-abiding people, we Spanish!' Jack sat down shaking with laughter on a chair in the corner. 'No one is allowed to carry any offensive weapon—that is the law. Even fishermen must leave their knives behind on their boats when they go ashore for a drink!'

'Have another gin,' I said. 'Just for not turning me in!'

The knives disappeared from the counter. Our friend from Madrid slipped his revolver back into its holster, and there was nothing left to show that every man in the room carried his defence in his pocket.

'What happened down in the Plaza?' Guy asked.

'Trouble over a woman. The husband returned to his home, met the lover, picked up a kitchen knife, and stabbed him.'

'Badly?'

'In the belly. He'll live. He's in the hospital now.'

'They know who did it then?'

'Oh yes. That's why the lieutenant from the Guardia Civil was going round the bars—looking for the husband.'

'They'll arrest him?'

'Probably not. You see, our Spanish law is different from yours. Especially over a matter of honour. What will happen is that, if the man who's injured leaves hospital within fifteen days, there will be no charge made. If he's still there after fifteen days they will charge the husband with causing him grave damage. What often occurs in a case like this is that the relatives of the wounded man try to see that the doctors keep him in hospital for *more* than fifteen days. The relatives of the attacker, for their part, try and get the doctors to have him out within the time-limit.' He winked. 'It is possible that money changes hands.'

Guy and I laughed. 'What a system! Better than the National Health Service! Either way the doctors are in clover.'

'It seems strange to you? It works though. And usually, if

the wounded man is not too gravely hurt, the doctors will have him outside in time so that no charge is made. After all, it is a question of honour. A woman is concerned.'

We had our soup, some bread, a plate of beans, and polished off a bottle of red wine.

'We're going back to the boat to wash and change. We may go to the cabaret later.' We shook hands formally with Fat Jack and Jill and our friend from Madrid. Jack slapped his wife's huge backside with a friendly hand.

'Perhaps I shall see you in the cabaret. They tell me there are two new gipsies come over from the mainland.'

Jill knocked away his hand with a contemptuous gesture as if she were brushing away a fly.

'Don't think that they would look at you. You are too old and heavy. When they have these young English to dance with why should they care for a man who cannot even dance?'

Jack, who was on his fifth glass of gin, snapped his fingers in the air and did a small twirl, for all the world like an elephant in a circus.

'I can outdance Red Beard and the Blonde One any time. Besides, gipsies are not only interested in a man's dancing.'

Back on board the boat we heated up two large saucepans of water and had a wash. I shaved, Guy combed out his beard, and we put on clean shirts, socks, canvas trousers, and polished our shoes. It was no white-collar cabaret that we were going to, just a small place frequented by sailors from the Spanish merchant ships, commercial travellers on the spree, and the occasional fisherman or local businessman whose wives were either visiting relatives or engaged in child-bearing. There was a four-piece band—pianist, drummer, guitar and mandolin. The mandolin-player was an Italian from Naples who loved to cry over his remembered home when drunk, and who would gesture round the smoky room with a white shaking hand, saying: 'Spaniards are savages! Why did I marry one?'

Guy and I were well received by the manager, a portly Barcelonian with a plump 'fairy' behind which he waggled round the room like a dowager at a deb party.

'Señores! Señores! But it is a week, more or less, since last you were here! Come to the bar with me and take a little Fundador before I find you a table.'

We had a glass of Fundador with him and listened to the band starting up in the next room. We were the first arrivals and he had sent out word to start the music and bring on the dancing girls. Two of them came in and joined us, the little dark one 'Chicita' and Lola, the big swarthy girl I called 'Mia Mexicana'.

'*Alma de mi corazon!*'

'She loves you!' said the manager. 'Ah, you are lucky, señor—love is so difficult a thing!' He gazed at Guy's beard. Mia Mexicana had settled herself on my lap, all twelve stone of her. Chicita hovered round Guy like a humming-bird.

'Buy me a drink!'

'Buy me a drink!'

'No, kids, wait till we've got our own bottle on the table.'

They both pouted. Their drink at the bar was called champagne and cost twenty-five pesetas—out of which the girls got ten each.

'We'd better buy them one,' I said to Guy. 'Otherwise old Fatso here will be a bit sick. Besides, the girls have got to eat.'

'*Si. Si. Debemos comer!*' They had picked up a little English, a good deal more than they pretended to in fact. Little escaped them.

Round about two in the morning the room was blue with smoke, all the tables were occupied, and the band was doing its heavy Flamenco routine while the consumptive girl they called Dolores held the floor. More than any other regional music, the Spanish puts a light inside you, especially when you have drunk a lot of brandy and your skin still feels warm from the day's sunshine. The clacking of the castanets was a kind of madness in the ears, and the heavy stomp! stomp! of Dolores' feet as she bounced and postured on her steel-tipped shoes was like a quick heart-beating.

It was Lola's turn to dance next: she left our table to go and put on her costume. Chicita was only a hostess, not one of the artists; she was taking dancing lessons so that by the winter she too could qualify for the higher grade and make a few more pesetas. She had a small oval face, black eyelashes like fans, and the real blue-black hair of Andalusia. Her eyes were a deep nigger-brown and her skin, of which she was very proud, was as white as an English girl's. She was twenty-two, and had an illegitimate child by a picador who had left her in Barcelona. He

173

was not much good as a picador and had recently been badly *cogida* in Madrid.

'Bastard he was!' She was telling Guy all about it. 'Spanish men are selfish and cruel. Pigs! How I would like to come to England where all the men are kind and have red beards like you.'

I gave Guy a wink and filled their glasses. We had a bottle of Fundador on the table for ourselves, and a bottle of medium Jerez for the girls. They preferred 'champagne' because they made more money on it, but we were regulars by now and they no longer treated us as if we were casual tourists who had drifted in out of the dark Plaza. The brandy and the sherry together only cost fourteen shillings. Even if we stayed until dawn we would have change left out of two pounds. Pepe, the guitarist, came over.

'Get yourself a glass, Pepe, and have a drink.'

'Many thanks, señores. Good to see you again. How goes the work on the little boat?'

'Well enough. We shall have completed it in another month.'

The lights dimmed and Lola came on in a poster version of the Spanish dress; red and white balloons on black. She had the usual strident voice of all Spanish women and her dancing was poor, but she conveyed a wonderful animal vitality. When her big body moved and her round brown arms lifted above her head there was a kind of sigh from the men in the audience. Chicita nudged me.

'She is beautiful, my friend Lola, isn't she?'

'Yes. Very attractive.'

'You are wrong—I am attractive. Lola is *beautiful*.'

They shared a flat together and were truly fond of each other. Chicita's old mother looked after the baby while the two girls went out at night to their work. They had great honesty and lived their lives with that passionate intensity of which only the Southerner is capable. Neither of them ever read a book or a newspaper, and they never indulged in the melancholy of thought. They were brilliant, admirable animals, with all the flashing grace of that surface life and vitality which brings a lump to the throat because it will so soon die. Before they were forty they would be shapeless old women.

Watching Lola dance, watching the lift and ripple of her big

174

cat-like body, I felt all the sadness that lies at the heart of the old pagan world. The brandy, the night and the music suddenly seemed to sweep over me like a great wave and for a brief second —as on that night years ago in Alexandria—I seemed to grasp the whole meaning. But even if you have solved the riddle you can never formulate it or put it into words.

We came out into the dawn where the air smelled damply of earth and flowers. The girls lived a few streets back from the Plaza and we walked them home through the alleyways that were cool with the new day coming and with the land breeze drawing off the open countryside behind the city.

'It's Sunday today. Shall we meet for a bathe in the afternoon?' I asked. 'We'll hire a taxi and go out to Cala Azul.'

'Yes. Yes. We can leave the little one with the old mother. It would be good to swim and lie in the sun.'

'*Mia Mexicana!* Always the sun for you! I'll lie in the shade.'

She leaned softly against my arm—a musky, cat-like scent of sweat, tobacco smoke, sherry and warm brown flesh. I had drunk enough so that the walk down the streets seemed like floating in a slow balloon, my feet lifted a little above the pavement.

We stopped and said good-bye to them a few yards from the old house where they shared the top flat. The neighbours were not very happy about having two gipsy girls there anyway, and it was tactful not to give them any cause for complaint. I had given Lola a gardenia. It hung heavy and luminous against the darkness of her hair, its scent like a drop of oil on the clean morning.

Although in my heart I was disturbed and unhappy, there were moments that summer when the brief brilliance of life seemed more lovely than ever before. What were the words of that song she was so fond of? 'Every time that I remember I am destined to die, I spread my cloak in the shade and lie down and have a sleep.'

> *Cada vez que considero*
> *Que me tengo que mori*
> *Tiendo la capa en el suelo*
> *Y me jarto de dormi.*

175

16

IN THE late autumn of that year six of us and a dog set off from
Gibraltar in the yacht *Electra*, bound for the West Indies.
There was a Levanter blowing and the Rock had drawn its
familiar grey cowl over its head. On either side Spain was tawny
in the sun.

Electra was one of the loveliest boats I have ever sailed in,
forty-five foot on the water-line, teak, and ketch-rigged. She had
been built by Camper and Nicholson in 1936 as an ocean racer,
but she was as comfortable to cruise in as she was fast, and her
fittings and accommodation were of a pre-war standard. Bob
Crytser, an American friend of mine, had bought her the year
before and was now taking her over to her new home on the
other side of the Atlantic.

In midsummer, just after the work on *Mischief* was finished
I had sold her to H. W. Tilman, the explorer and Everest
climber, who wanted her for an expedition to the Patagonian
ice-cap. I was sorry to see her go but she was too big a boat for
my pocket; another drawback was that for comfortable cruising
one always needed four people on board. Finding crew when you
want them is not always easy, and finding congenial companions
is even more difficult. She had proved herself a good boat in the
year and a half that I had sailed her about the Mediterranean; she
had taken us from Malta to Sicily and across to the Balearics; and
then, during that summer, we had sailed her to Corsica and back,
round Menorca, Mallorca, Ibiza and, finally, down the Spanish
coast to Gibraltar.

On the eve of our return to England Bob had suddenly
dropped in down the sun's track: Bob and his wife Glenda, their
friend Don, and their Spanish pointer, Duque.

'Where you going, kids?' he shouted. 'I hear you sold *Mischief*.

Want to come for a sail in a real boat? No topsails here! No lousy great gaffs shifting around over your head, no dead-eyes and lanyards—all as sweet and simple as the American genius can make it.'

'The boat was built in England,' I pointed out, 'and the rig was invented in Bermuda!'

Bob laughed. 'You'll be telling me next the Limeys built the *Queen Mary*. And invented radar!'

Perhaps it was Bob's special Martinis that did it (Take one bottle of gin, remove two small tots, top up with French and place in the ice-box for an hour) or perhaps it was the sudden challenge of the opportunity, just at the moment when I was on the point of buying our tickets home. Within an hour Janet and I had moved our gear on board and joined the *Electra*.

'How about old Guy here?' asked Bob as we were sitting around on the upper deck. Guy shook his head.

'No, Bob, I've got to get home and do some work.'

'Come on! You can't go back to England when I'm offering you the opportunity to see the New World. Where's this Elizabethan spirit of adventure we hear so much about? Glenda, give Guy another drink.'

Don came over rubbing his hand over his crew-cut head.

'Yeah. Come on, Guy. They haven't seen a beard like that on the other side since the seventeenth century. Gee, I just want to take you back to L.A. and show the folks what they've been missing since razors came in!'

Half an hour later Bob had his crew. With six of us it meant easy watch-keeping on the long run down through the Trades from the Canaries across to Barbados. Guy cabled home and acquainted some astonished employer with the news that he would not be back, but was sailing to the West Indies for Christmas. Janet and I got in some fast letters and telegrams.

'You'll be able to write about this,' said Bob.

'It's been overdone, Bob. Out in the far spaces of the Atlantic you can hear the rattle of typewriters for miles off.'

'I know. But we're going to do it different. No hazards, no perils, comfort afloat, take it easy. No one's in any hurry. We'll drop off from here tomorrow. Gibraltar gives me a pain in the neck. No offence, but what do you Limeys do when you find yourself a piece of Mediterranean?'

'It's just like Malta,' I said. 'We turn it into a kind of Wimbledon.'

'Well, I don't know what Wimbledon is, but there's a kind of stuffiness about this Rock I don't care for. Even the climate's English. Yes, we'll drop off down the coast and take a look at Casablanca and a bit of Morocco, cross over to the Canaries and then, maybe, run down to the Cape Verdes on the way over. I've got a feeling that the Trades will be better the further south we go. Most of these guys nowadays have found it pretty airless up on the old Trade Wind route. We might drop down to about thirteen degrees, take a look at the Verdes and then—over to Barbados for Christmas!'

Bob had been in the salvage business in the Far East and he and Glenda had lived most of their lives in the Pacific. They had just spent a year's holiday in Europe, in the course of which Bob had bought the *Electra*. He was a fine seaman, had owned boats all his life, and had raced his own boat in the longest race of them all, from Los Angeles to Honolulu. He had an easy, relaxed outlook on the subject of sailing, one which I found preferable to the eager-beaver style of so many racing yachtsmen.

'Let's reef, what do you think?' he would say.

'No need to yet, Bob. We could hold on for another hour.'

'Yeah, I know. And then we all come up at the rush, get soaked through, strain our guts out, and end up by congratulating ourselves for having hair on the chest. Hell, no! We're doing this for fun. Besides, if we leave it an hour it will be time for chow and if there's one thing I hate it's having cold chow. And Glenda's making a special *suki-yaki* tonight. Let's reef.'

Sailing with other people in their boat is always a test, especially if you are used to sailing your own. But of all the people I have ever sailed with Bob was the easiest to get on with. We were a happy team and, if you visualize six people all of different temperaments in a small boat for weeks on end, that means a great deal. *Electra* was a comfortable boat for six. Bob and Glenda had their own cabin aft; Guy and Don slept in passageway berths just abaft the saloon; Janet and I had the fo'c'sle to ourselves. Duque, the liver-and-white Spanish pointer whom Bob had collected in Majorca, slept in a basket under the saloon table, or curled up on a rug in the cockpit. He was an amazing dog, with a liking for raw fish—no doubt acquired in the fishing village where

Bob had found him. We none of us had realized how deeply ingrained was this taste of his until the first night out of Gibraltar when a flying fish leapt on board. Duque was after it like a flash, eyes gleaming, lips bared in a snarl and hackles up. He soon found that flying-fish were not unlike his old Mediterranean favourites, and would despatch them in two neat bites and a swallow, like a gourmet eating an oyster.

One of the things I will always remember about the voyage was Duque's morning round. He would come up on deck at about six o'clock, tentatively clamber over the cockpit rail and wander forward. When we were in the Trades the boat would be rolling heavily and he would scrape, slither and slide as he tried to keep his balance. An inspection of the mainmast, which he used as a lamp-post, was followed by his morning prowl for flying fish. There were always a few that had come on board overnight, and one's tender morning stomach would often be affronted by the sight of Duque slithering back towards the cockpit with the tail of a fish sticking out of his mouth.

Crossing the Atlantic in a modern yacht today does not present half such a problem as people are often led to believe. A dozen or more yachts cross every year going both ways, either by the Trade-wind route for America or coming over to Europe in the Westerlies of the North Atlantic. The sensational stories of hazardous crossings which reach the daily papers are usually engineered by yachtsmen in need of hard cash and publicity. They are the product, only too often, of inattention to essentials such as seaworthy gear and adequate supplies.

Like mountaineering, or any modern hazardous sport, ocean sailing calls for organization, team-work and a knowledge of the craft. The successful voyages are not the ones which meet the public eye over the breakfast table. Only the year before we ourselves sailed the Atlantic, Rear-Admiral Goldsmith, who was then over seventy, had crossed with a crew of one. There was never a mention of this almost unique achievement either in the daily Press of America or England. In the same year, however, an expedition that set out from England to sail round the world ended in disaster before leaving the Channel. It was hailed by the popular Press as an epic of seamanship and endurance: it was an epic of inefficiency and muddle.

Keeping watches was little problem, as six hands were more

than enough to handle *Electra* under cruising conditions. We came to a good arrangement which was to move the watches round and stand down one member of the crew every day to do cook's duties. An unenviable chore was thus equally shared, and it also meant that every day one had a different watchkeeping partner. The change of cook also led to a friendly rivalry which varied and bettered the menu. Bob and Glenda, coming from the Far East, gave us Chinese or Japanese meals; Don, from California, introduced American salad such as pineapple and carrots. These shocked the Europeans, while Janet and I rattled the others by a heavy hand with the garlic. Guy plumped for solid English fare, insisting on meat, two veg., and a pudding. Fortunately *Electra* had a large ice-box so we were well placed for fresh food throughout the voyage.

On the second night out we were running down to Casablanca with the wind just abaft the beam, and the yacht travelling at an effortless seven knots. The sky was a deep plum colour and the stars seemed to pulse, twice as large as usual. The wind was off the land, warm from Africa, and we were rolling slightly in the beam sea. Don sat on the foredeck, strumming his guitar; Bob and I had the deck; the others had gone to sleep.

'Look at that wake!' said Bob. 'You don't get it that bright in the Med. We'll see more of it as we get down into the Trades.'

Phosphorescence is something which I never tire of watching. That night it was rolling astern of us in a broad swath of fire; sometimes eddies of it would surge up and burst in sudden flashes like fireworks. Occasionally a fish would questioningly sally up to have a look at us. You could see the shine of his body and then the bright explosion as he flicked his tail and made off. The waves themselves were lipped with phosphorescence, and the sliding lines that moved up out of the night and lifted us in their swell broke, as they felt the touch of the boat, into flowers of foam. There was no sound but the plangent guitar, faint on the wind like a memory of Spain, and the chuckle of water against the hull. Just occasionally the mainsail would rustle as we lifted over the crest of a big roller. Bob had the wheel, and I sprawled out on the cockpit cushions.

'This is the life,' he said. 'Cigarette?'

'Thanks. I'll make some coffee in a minute.'

'Good idea. Well—you've seen the last of Europe for a bit. Maybe you won't ever go back.'

'*Quien sabe?*'

I watched the smoke of my cigarette against the night. It would be cold in England by now and the queues would be forming at bus stops and Undergrounds as people went home after an evening out. Yes, this was the life all right, but I would add a rider to Bob's words, 'Provided it did not unfit you for any other.' It would be too easy—and I knew people who had done it—to become a yachting 'bum', permanently sailing the world, professionally or as an amateur. There was no difficulty in that, provided you were a good hand and that people liked you. There was the North American circuit you could cover for part of the year; then the Bermudas; the Bahamas; the West Indies; the Mediterranean; and the Pacific even. You could keep sailing twelve months of the year. 'And getting nowhere fast,' added my northern conscience. 'Where does anything get you?' murmured another voice, and there was the sound of a guitar and the memory of a song—'*Cada vez* . . .'

Next morning Casablanca rose up before us out of the sandy coast, white, glistening, modern—the most American of all the North African cities. Her towers and shining buildings were sharp against a sunrise of saffron and rose. We hardened in the sheets and set ourselves to beat to windward as the breeze began to draw ahead.

After a quick visit to Marrakesh we sailed down the coast to Safi, stayed there a night and then took our departure for Teneriffe in the Canaries, some four hundred miles away. There was a fine off-shore wind for our crossing and I think we were all glad to see the low coastline of Africa slide away astern of us. It was a bad time to see that part of the world. The bitterness spilled over the edges of life and, being uncommitted, I could only see the virtues and the vices of both sides.

I was glad, though, I had had the chance to see Marrakesh; to swing down into it from the desert and see the eternal green and the liquid splash of water against the far blue of the Atlas mountains. Wandering through the market Janet and I had the strange experience of meeting a friend whom we had known six years before in London. Literary and epicene, he had swum towards us in a haze of Arabic accompanied by his faithful companion.

181

'You two?' he said. 'And still together after all these years!'

I could have said the same. It was curious to think that I had met him in Alexandria during the war and that once, in the lulls of a wardroom party, we had dreamed of the London life we were going to make for ourselves when it was all over. He had been living in Marrakesh for two years, having drifted down there from Tunis. We drank a lot that afternoon and grew mildly nostalgic.

'We'll never meet again, my darlings,' he said as he waved us good-bye. 'I feel it in my bones. Everything changes, as your friend Heraclitus said.' I shook his soft boneless hand and was a little ashamed of feeling moved. The brandy must have sparkled in my eye, for he noticed it and smiled. 'You too! Ah, you're not such a hardened old warrior as you pretend to be.' He winked at Janet, all his old charm falling again over features that were tired beneath their suntan. 'I knew the Ancient Mariner during the war.' The last traveller boarded the bus. The driver started the engine and the door was shut. We leaned out of the window to hear him.

'Youth!' he said. 'Remember? "It eluded us then, but that's no matter—tomorrow we will run faster, stretch out our arms further.... And one fine morning——" Ah! You never were good at quotations!'

The wind that lofted *Electra* so easily from Africa to the Canaries had other travellers on its wings. On the first morning Glenda, who was at the wheel, suddenly called out: 'Look! Bob, that's a funny cloud!'

It moved up astern of us, wispy and straggling, yet having a life of its own so that it bent and twisted without the wind. Here and there a dark fold sagged into the water. A few minutes later our rigging and sails were thick with locusts. They crunched underfoot, crawled through our hair, and sent Duque crazy. We beat them down, shovelled them up, and hosed them off the decks. For more than two days and nights these insect clouds passed over us. Luckily it was only the first one that a freak of air current drew down onto the boat, but every now and then we would come upon great clusters of locusts struggling in the sea. Strange, sprawling insect-land! They clambered on each other's backs until the weak point of the mass would tilt and break and then, individually, they would bob away into the blue that drowned them.

The strong off-shore winds of that year carried them as far as the Canaries. When we reached Teneriffe, we had some difficulty explaining to the local fishermen that the insects really flew all the way from Africa. One old man whom I spoke to was contemplating a great pile of locusts washed up on the beach and exclaiming: 'They know how to make rafts, señor, and then they drift over! These are some that fell off and were drowned!'

The port of Santa Cruz in Teneriffe was backed by a wall of smoke when we arrived; the farmers had lit smudge pots to try and stop the insects landing. Even so, the banana trees sagged beneath their pink bodies and much of the crop was ruined. Up on the mountain of Teide the trees, the scrub, and even the road were black with them. Our taxi driver smiled sourly as his wheels crunkled over their bodies.

'As if the Canaries weren't poor enough!'

We stayed in Santa Cruz for over a week, attending to the final details of storing and fitting out. During the day we sat in the sunny plaza and passed slow dreamy hours over olives and sherry. At night we dined off prawns and lobsters fresh from the ocean that surged and sounded just beyond the breakwater.

All the same, I think none of us were sad to leave and to feel again the motion of the boat as she lifted to the slow Atlantic swell. The land is good for a while but, as Fat Jack used to say, 'The sailor has an itch under the skin.' After which he would draw himself off another glass of gin, rub his giant belly and smile. 'How happy I am to stay ashore and never wander the waters!'

That first evening as we breasted out into the dark slow movement of the ocean we had a shared peace and companionship that is rare among human beings. How good the night air was after the dust and the smoke of streets and cafés! How sparkling fresh and clean it was, rinsed through and through by the miles of water that surrounded us.

Don sniffed the air. 'Gee, that's better!'

Bob felt the deck with his hand. 'Dew. Do you know I never felt a dewfall in Santa Cruz.'

Glenda brought up the martinis. 'All right, kids? Better at sea, isn't it?'

A whir of flying fish went over the bows.

'Did you hear them?' Janet asked.

'There's a porpoise close behind us,' said Guy.

'There really is!' I said.

'Three!' said Don, who was accurate. Their indrawn sigh of breath reminded me.

'Do you remember them on the way back from Greece?' I asked.

Bob laughed. 'Poor old Ernle has Greece on the brain. Did he ever tell you, Guy, how he sent us there? Told me it was the best place . . .'

Janet left us. She was cook for the day and it was nearly time for supper.

'Listen, Guy. I went there on his recommendation. Fine sailing, agreed. Fine islands, agreed. But—Hell!—never a civilized hotel or bar anywhere! And let's face it, kids, once you've seen one beat-up old statue you've seen the lot. One headless marble body's the same as another to me!'

'You barbarian bum!' I said. We were all laughing as he gave his impressions of scrabbling over the ruins of Delos.

'. . . Everything broken! Not a drink on the island except some lukewarm wine that tasted like disinfectant!'

Our days now fell into a regular routine. We rose for our watches, ate our meals, did our share of navigation, sail-tending, or clearing up the ship—and slept. Out there you have a deep simple sleep like that of childhood, and you wake in the morning with the same eagerness for the new day. Sometimes, coming off watch at night, I would lie with a farewell cigarette between my lips and listen. Like everyone I had my worries, but I could forget them as I lay there, listening to that sigh of water, hour after hour, night and day, an inch or so from my ear—like the rhythm of the world breathing.

After seven days we saw the gaunt cheeks of the Cape Verde Islands rising up ahead of us. Sunbaked, almost barren, the Verdes are the last islands where one can stop for fuel or water. Beyond them lies the Atlantic and the Americas.

We spent a brief day there, topped up our tanks, took on some fresh vegetables and bread, and were off again. As we left, the Danish training ship *Danmark* was coming in under full sail, cadets manning the yards, ready to brail up at the order. She stood in out of the open sea, a fully-rigged ship under her breasts of canvas, with the white chuckle at her bows that showed she was moving fast although she seemed to be frozen in time. She was a ghost ship, a memory only, and no more, of the days when these islands regularly welcome out of the ocean the most beautiful vessels ever made by man.

From the Cape Verdes to Barbados, a distance of some two thousand miles, we were thirteen days and ten hours at sea. It was an average speed of just under seven knots: good going, for we never pressed the boat and we sailed under no more than two working staysails boomed out on either side. If we had tacked downwind under plain sail, or carried a spinnaker, or set large twin staysails, we could have cut our time down by days as well as hours. But, as Bob rightly said: 'What the hell! If I was trying to get there fast I'd have had her shipped over from Europe and taken a plane. We're doing it because we enjoy it—I hope!—and so long as it doesn't take a month that's okay with me.'

In the long following seas of the Trades (and we had really found them in the latitude of the Cape Verdes), the motion of a small boat takes some getting used to. The rolling was continuous —in our case something like fifteen degrees each way, three times a minute. Like all high-masted Bermudan boats *Electra* was not so comfortable as an old-fashioned hull and rig like *Mischief's* would have been. But, once one had grown to accept the roll as part of the rhythm of living, it was no longer a worry. It was tiring, though, for every muscle in one's body, silent and unnoticed, was being brought into play every waking minute. Even when you slept, your body was swaying and shifting endlessly with the motion. To be comfortable in a bunk it was essential to wedge yourself in with cushions and pillows.

But all this was made up for by the ever-changing face of the sea, by the phosporescent wake at night, by the fluffy Trade Wind clouds, and by the great clean bowl of sea and sky in which we lived. I came to know the dawn and sunrise over a great ocean as I had never known it before. The sky at night, altering its face gently as we ran down our latitude, became part of my world and remembered for ever.

One morning of bright sunshine and clear horizon, the green back of Barbados stood up out of the sea.

'Dead on the nose!' said Bob chuckling and patting his chest.

We rounded the southernmost point of the island and dropped anchor in Carlisle Bay. Officials, Customs officers and friends

185

came out. The surf was breaking on a strip of coral sand, so white that it hurt the eyes.

'It must be good to be ashore again!' said a welcoming voice in the Aquatic Club.

'Yes. Yes, it is.' Our response was a little slow, as if we were not quite sure. The land, however lovely it may be, is always something of an anti-climax.

17

THE beautiful indolence of the islands digs under the skin and infects one with a happy *je m'en ficheism*. The rhythms of blood and breathing change, and with them the patterns of behaviour. The eternal afternoon of cloudless skies, broken only by the violent downpour of a passing cloud belt (after which the bright tropical green steams and you hear the plants growing), the brilliance of the sea and the white monotony of the coral beaches have a disruptive effect on the European. Those twin pillars upon which our society is based—that work is important, and that the individual is important, too—begin to crumble. Something that sighs in the Trade Wind and that sounds in the collapse and sizzle of every breaking roller speaks of the futility of effort. Life is here and now, in this bright moment, to be enjoyed while we are still capable of enjoyment.

My typewriter was rattling away. It was mid-afternoon in Barbados and I had to mail my clean typed copy by the evening to catch the next day's flight. Janet had gone ashore to swim. Bob and Glenda and Don had left for Christmas in Los Angeles. Guy was on his way home by steamer. I heard the plash of oars nearing the boat.

'Anyone aboard?'

I could lie low and say nothing. It was unlikely to be anything important. Then I heard the rattle of someone making a dinghy-painter fast to one of the stanchions.

I went up on deck and saw Bill's brown face peering over the rail capping. He had a girl with him and they were both full of rum.

'Hi! Thought we'd just come over and say Hi! This is Jacky.' He pointed to the girl who waved in a regal way as if to say: 'I'm not tight. Not at this hour in the afternoon.'

'Jacky's from England.'

'Come aboard,' I said. 'Don't sit there too long or you'll get cramp.'

He scrambled awkwardly over the gunwale and Jacky screamed as the dinghy lurched and shipped a little water. She was an attractive girl, dark-haired, with a tanned skin, somewhere in the late twenties. I got them both safely landed and sat them in the cockpit.

'Brought a bottle with us,' said Bill. 'You got any ice?'

'Surely. I'll bring some up.'

I got some glasses out and a tray of ice and a can of beer for myself. When I got back to the cockpit they were in a deep swooning clinch. I coughed gently and put down the things.

'Excuse us, kid.' Bill sat up. 'Here have some rum—the very best!'

'No thanks. I've got a beer here. I've some work to do, and if I start on rum at this time of day I'm finished.'

They both began to laugh.

'Did we see you last night? Jacky and I were on the town. She's just arrived. Well—just arrived here, haven't you, honey?'

'Twenty-four hours ago,' the girl said slowly in a Kensington voice, and then: 'I wonder how Richard's getting on?'

They both laughed again.

'That's her husband,' said Bill. 'They sailed over about the same time you all did. Just she and her husband. They went to Antigua.'

'We went to Antigua.' She began to cry. Bill put his arm round her shoulders. She stopped after a few seconds and said fiercely, 'I'm never going back to that bastard as long as I live!'

'That's the girl. You're better off in Barbados, honey. Antigua's a lousy hole.' He topped up their glasses again and I finished my beer. I could see that I was not really essential to the conversation.

'I must get on with this work, Bill. I'll be up again as soon as I've finished. If you want to swim off the ship you know where the rope ladder is. You know where the heads are if either of you want them. There's more ice in the box when that lot's melted.'

I went down to the saloon and started off again on my cleantyping. Bill was a nice enough character; an American ex-naval officer living on a small pension. He owned a beaten-up old cutter and, whenever funds were low, did an occasional tourist trip round the islands. When he was on one of his jags he started on rum for breakfast. I had never seen the girl before, but there were quite a lot like her round and about in the islands. The sun and the indolent heat got at them; they hardly needed the extra boost of rum. If the moral standards of Kensington were right they ought to be victims of acute despair: the curious thing was that, except for the odd fit of tears, they usually seemed happier than they would have done at home.

They were still up there, groggy and half-asleep, when I came out to go ashore.

'Got to go to the post,' I said, 'and collect Janet at the Aquatic Club.'

'Okay, thanks for the ice. We'll be seeing you. Must get ashore ourselves.' He looked at my clean shirt and shore-going trousers. 'Jeez! What's up? A dance on?'

'Good-bye,' said the girl. We'll be seeing you. Didn't you live in Chelsea? We must have some mutual friends.'

Barbados still had a colour bar. It was the most conservative of the British islands and was run on Victorian lines. The Yacht Club was strictly for Europeans and the best sailor on the island (he always carried off the club dinghy-racing trophies) was not eligible because of his ancestry. Most of the yacht club members were not interested in sailing at all. They either sat in deck chairs in the shade or sprawled out sunbathing on the strip of restricted beach which belonged to the club.

Sometimes, looking across from *Electra* at the nearby shore, I would be struck by the strangest of contrasts. There on the yacht-club beach lay the master-race, hairy and brown, or smooth and somewhat blotched, and there—a few yards to the left—were the beautiful bodies of the dispossessed. The young coloured men and women were like dark bronzes and their wide-eyed, curly haired children were plump with life and laughter.

The beauty of the visual world in the islands helps to justify the absence of thought. One evening, leaving Bridgetown, I was crossing the bridge by the Careenage where the island schooners were mirrored on the water. Music was coming out of a shanty bar and the glow of a paraffin lamp lit up the faces of four card players. Standing just outside, leaning against a rickety wooden pillar stood a young girl in a bright green dress. One arm was folded back behind her neck and she was scratching her back with the ease and indolence of a sleek black cat.

'You got the time on you, suh?'

I looked at my watch. 'Eight,' I said.

'Thank you. My fella's late.' She disengaged her arm and stretched lazily, her whole body from her lean ankles to her oiled hair shifting in a slow ripple. Two sailors from one of the schooners passed me as I wandered on. They walked with the same relaxed flow of life that had shone in the girl against the doorway.

'You sailing soon, Captain?'

'Next week, I think. My friends will be back by then.'

'We're off in the mornin' for Port of Spain.'

Their voices had the same soft buzz as hers, a little like the West Country accent, but with the sun in it.

Often, if there was no rain in the Trade Wind clouds (and there was little now, for we were in the dry season) we slept out on the upper deck. The island had a sweet smell and the sound of the tree frogs was clear over the water, a persistent throbbing like a tooth-ache. Sometimes it would touch an angry nerve and I could not sleep for it, while at others it was no more than the background to silence. In the morning I would wake to the sound of the flying-fish boats going out for the day.

Clunk! Clŭnk! I would hear them and roll over sleepily, then clunk! clunk! clunka! Propping myself up on an elbow I would see one of the boats tacking past under our stern, making a long board out to clear the reef.

' 'Mornin', Captain! Sleepin' well?'

Several others would pass, and soon the blue horizon would be spotted with the gulls' wings of their sails.

They were open boats, cutter-rigged, with perilously long bowsprits on which they set great ballooning jibs. They were over-canvassed and had no keels. All their ballast was internal in the shape of scraps of old iron, bits of motor cars, bricks, and anything heavy and portable. The way the ballast was stowed, a good half of it had to be manhandled before a boat could be put on to another tack. This was the noise that woke me in the mornings. I would watch the helmsman putting down the helm and, as he did so and the boat hovered up into the wind, his mate would be hurling old iron across the boat—clunk! clunk!

offers from agents, but found it impossible to leave the island: his love life was very complicated. His versions of the calypsos were not the ones recorded for popular consumption overseas; they were coarse, witty, and very much to the point. One night an imposing American matron from a cruise ship asked him for the old favourite 'Mary Ann'—and left before he had finished. 'Cakes' looked surprised and went on with a ballad about a German watchmaker; an old music-hall song which had suffered a surprising sea-change. He would play my own favourite:

> Brown-skin girl stay home and mind babee
> Brown-skin girl stay home and mind babee
> Ah'm gwine away in a fishin' boat
> And if ah don' come back—
> Just mind de damn babee!

In the small hours of the morning we would walk down to the Careenage, get the dinghy from the steps, and row back to the anchored yacht. The schooners were silent, sidling gently against their mooring ropes, and the sky was rich and clear. It was a long pull back to the yacht, nearly a mile; it was good exercise that cleared one's head and lungs of rum and tobacco fumes.

In the spring of that year we sailed to many of the islands. Bob was prospecting the West Indies with a view to settling down and putting capital into some business there. It was fine sailing, with the Trades blowing steadily day and night, easy sailing with nearly always a soldier's wind on the beam as we cruised between one island and another. After island-hopping in the Mediterranean the distances seemed vast, but the steadiness of the winds meant that we could calculate our departures and arrivals with something like the precision of a power vessel.

'You ought to stay out here, kid. Wadd'you want to go back to England for?' Bob leaned back in the cockpit. We had just set the big fair-weather jib and the boat was pulling hard, northward towards St. Lucia. The night was fine and there was half a waxing moon. Water burbled, sails slopped in the troughs of the swell, and the log clicked busily behind us.

'Work,' I said. 'I have to earn a living like everyone else.'

'You could do that out here.'

'I know, but I've got lots of ends to tie up in England.

Besides, I've seen very little of books and plays and so on since I've been away sailing.'

'Go back and have a look then. But I'd advise you to come right back out here. This side of the world is on the up. Europe's a fine place all right, but it's had its time. Look at it on the map.'

I had. It is curious thing when you get on the western side of the Atlantic and look at the map. How small Europe seems, an unhealthy appendix to Asia, and how vast and potentially grand seems the New World. A few hundred miles away from us was Venezuela, spouting with oil, and rich the way England was in the nineteenth century. And Venezuela was only a flea-bite on the continent.

'You're not too old to make the break,' said Bob. 'Why go back to write articles or edit a paper for peanuts in a place where it always rains?'

'Wind's heading a bit,' I said, and we busied ourselves over the sheets, winching in the jib and staysail, and hardening in the main. A fast-flying group of Trade Wind clouds crossed the moon and a little rain fell. The mountains of St. Lucia were in sight before the end of our watch.

One week I flew down to Trinidad for Bob, to take a look at the dry docks with a view to slipping and hauling deep-keel yachts. The plane flew over the Grenadines, then Grenada, and then there was Tobago sprawled out shining on our port hand. The islands looked very beautiful and peaceful in the sun. You could see the water shoal in towards them, the dark blue changing into pale cream with only a trace of colour where the sea made up against the coral reefs. They were fine islands, but they did not stir me like the islands of the Aegean or the Mediterranean. They had too few associations and what history they had was short and brutish—or was that my mistake in thinking of history solely in terms of what got into books?

The light of Port of Spain was like an explosion. It was hot, too, for the Trades did not blow all the way home as far as this island. It was not an oppressive heat in the same way as it often was in Martinique or Guadeloupe, for the brilliance of the scene somehow relieved the feeling of ennui which built up in the French islands. Music was spun on the air and the crowds were confetti-patches of colour. There was no darkness anywhere except the asphalt, and even the shadowed recesses of doorways or courtyards were plum or purple. The jazzing and the drumming and the plangent tremor of the steel bands beat against the nerves. Snakelike I shed a skin in Port of Spain and have ever since moved differently, felt differently, and even thought differently.

In the evenings, after a hot day among the docks and the harbour offices, I went out with some American friends. We started in the cool smart bars where the waiters wear white jackets and the air purrs in fresh and damp, and we ended in the riot of the cheaper night-clubs among the squirming dancers and the smell of sweat and cheap scent.

'D'you enjoy yourself, kid?' asked Bob as he met me at Barbados airport. 'Quite a place, isn't it? Still thinking of going back to England?'

It was January and the road that drifted through the cane fields was dusty under the sun. A plane was coming in from the north, silver, high up in the clear sky. Beyond the pier of the Aquatic Club a schooner was just hoisting her sails and the waves were lipped with foam. It was bursting white on the outer reef where the heavy surf of the noon-day Trades fetched up.

'Who's that with Bill?' I asked pointing.

'Another rummy.'

The two figures wavered towards us.

'Hi, kids!'

Bill's friend was thick-set and fortyish. He was laughing and his eyes had the transparent look of the drinker who is living in a private dream. I knew that to him he seemed to be dancing, although his feet dawdled a long way behind the dance.

'That's the trouble with these islands,' said Bob as we got into the dinghy. 'You've got to have a job of work or you go to pieces.'

18

I HAD wanted to visit Martinique ever since I first came across a description of the island in the works of Lafcadio Hearn. That strange wanderer and inquiring traveller had drawn an exciting picture of Martinique's brilliant hibiscus flowers, of its giant tree-ferns, inaccessible forests, and sultry Creole beauties—whose skin he described as 'a rich brownish yellow'. The island has the beauty of a painting by Gauguin: steep mountains, short swift rivers and dense, dark-green jungle where the deadly *fer-de-lance* moves like a whip.

I first saw the mountains of Martinique from the deck of *Electra* at dawn. We had sailed up from St. Lucia, some twenty miles to the south, overnight. It was a swift sail under the press of the Trade Winds which funnel between the two islands, and the night air was cat-tongued on the skin, and heavy with the salt smell of the Atlantic.

We arrived at Carnival time, two days before the beginning of Lent. Even at five in the morning, as we dropped anchor off the island's capital, Fort-de-France, we could hear the sound of the beguine drifting across the water. Like all West Indians the natives of Martinique are born dancers, and the beguine is their national dance rhythm, just as the calypso is that of Trinidad.

Later that morning, standing in the Savane which is the park of Fort-de-France, I got talking with a French bank official. He had seen me looking at the statue of the Empress Josephine.

'She was born here, you know. Yes, in Trois Islets, just across the water. But we have something else that you should see in Martinique before you leave.' We made our way to the nearest café and ordered two coffees. 'Tonight, of course'—he offered me a Gaulloise—'you will see the dancing and the gaiety of Carnival—but you should visit St. Pierre.'

St. Pierre, the name which he let fall into the bright impartial sunlight, had a sullen ring about it. For the moment I could not recall what echo it stirred in my memory. But, the other face of the island—I knew what he meant by that. For Martinique is not all sunlight and tropical flowers and green mountains wreathed in Trade Wind clouds. It is a place of harsh contrasts, and the tranquillity of its cloudless days, the languor of the sun and sea, is only on the surface. In the last three hundred years Martinique has suffered thirty-three hurricanes, seven earthquakes, three volcanic eruptions and eleven tropical storms with tidal waves. Life here is either lethargic—or violent. It is an island of extremes.

Later that afternoon, leaving the others who were going on a bathing-party, I set out for St. Pierre. The car was one of those pre-war open American tourers whose speed, shape, and power seem to mark them as having been designed for characters like Al Capone or 'Pretty Boy' Floyd. As we drove, I tried to piece together from memory, and from my driver, the story of St. Pierre.

At the turn of the century Martinique was very prosperous. Its sugar and fruit fetched high prices in France, prices which were reflected in the comfort and luxury of the plantation owners and shippers of Martinique. (I remembered, too, that about a hundred and fifty years ago, at a time when sugar was at a premium in Europe, there was serious discussion in England as to whether it might not be a good idea to exchange Canada for Martinique. After all, people argued, who wanted a barren and semi-frozen country like Canada when they could have rich, fertile, and luxuriant Martinique instead?)

When I told this story to the cab driver I said in conclusion, 'Lucky for us that we thought better of it.'

'No,' he replied. 'You would have kept Martinique and some-how or other have regained control of Canada!' The legend of Perfide Albion dies hard.

In 1900 the island's capital was not Fort-de-France, but the busy, booming town of St. Pierre on the north-west coast. With a population of forty thousand and a fine anchorage sheltered from the prevailing Trade Winds, St. Pierre was one of the most thriving cities in the Caribbean. It had the reputation also of being the wickedest. It was a reputation that took some earning, for Port Royal, Jamaica and Port of Spain, Trinidad—rip-roaring towns and homes of the latter-day buccaneers—were no mean competitors.

St. Pierre was a colourful place fifty years ago. Rich Creoles swaggered through the streets; the sailors of a dozen nations diced and drank in the waterfront bars; and at night the music of the dance drifted out from the open windows of the merchant's houses, mingling with the frou-frou of silk skirts and the tinkle of crushed ice in tall glasses.

But the town was overshadowed by a genie; a genie long bottled up, yet still prone to acts of fury. This was the sombre mountain, Mont Pelée, a volcano four and a half thousand feet high. On April the 25th, 1902, the giant began to stir uneasily, and a heavy fall of ashes disturbed the planters' dreams. On the 2nd and 3rd of May there was an eruption that destroyed a number of plantations north of St. Pierre, killing about a hundred and fifty people.

It was at this point that both the lotus-eaters and the hard-working residents began to worry. Some of the more fearful left the city, moving either to Fort-de-France or to their summer villas in the mountains. In the main, though, people remained where they were. Lulled by pleasure, indifference, or that feeling of '*mañana señor, mañana*,' they continued to disregard the warning. Their feeling that all would be well was strengthened by the news that the volcano of Souffrière on the neighbouring British island of St. Vincent had begun to erupt. The pundits interpreted this as an indication that Mont Pelée would be relieved of most of its subterranean pressure. They were unaware that the main escape vent of Mont Pelée was blocked by old solidified lava, and that it was acting like a plug in a safety valve. On the 8th of May, 1908, the pent-up pressure inside the volcano blew the plug sky-high and lifted the top off the mountain.

I had been piecing together this history of St. Pierre, and of its sudden death, while the taxi scorched along the road towards the old city. At times we would dive through an area of steaming green forest—the jungle there comes up at you like a hot hand in the face. It is a tangible presence, powerful and dark. (There is something strange and frightening about the smell of century upon century of vegetation.)

Sometimes, though, while the driver gesticulated and talked away in the soft island patois, the road would skim out onto a cliff edge, and there below us would shine the Caribbean Sea, the tops of the waves turning under the Trade Wind.

We dropped down into St. Pierre and the ruined city advanced to meet us, grey and preserved for ever—a modern Pompeii. In the morning of May the 8th, when the volcano exploded, a rain of ashes, fire, molten lava and dense gas swept down over the city of St. Pierre. It was Sodom and Gomorrah all over again. The merchants who, the night before, had been toasting the eruption of Souffrière, their ladies who had danced and gossiped by open window, the consular officials of many nations, the Creoles, the 'poor' whites and the 'poor' blacks—all were dead. Within a few hours forty thousand people, the entire population of St. Pierre, were wiped out.

The blue bay over which I gazed was turned into an inferno of blazing ships. Out of the dozens at anchor, only one escaped. There were many ships at anchor then, graceful ships, for those were still the days of sail. I have an old photograph which shows the harbour as it was, and one can easily pick out the different types—tall clippers, square-rigged on all masts; barques and barquentines; island schooners; men-of-war; and scruffy trading vessels with sails of patched sacking.

Now, as I looked over the bay, I saw only one small island schooner coming in to anchor, her single-cylinder diesel engine blowing smoke-rings through a rusty exhaust. The quiet of St. Pierre which is like the quiet of Pompeii and of all destroyed cities (as if the sudden cessation of activity had left an indelible trace on the air) was all around us.

It is true that some attempt has been made to rebuild; but the small shanty town, which sprawls along one edge of what was once the island's capital, seems only to intensify the loneliness of this place of sudden death.

The driver got out and walked beside me. Together we traced the old streets, elevated several feet by the ashes so that we walked on a level with buried window sills. It is the small things which move one most among the relics of old disasters. A child's doll at Pompeii speaks more eloquently than a mummified body, and at St. Pierre, in the museum which commemorates the disaster, it was an electric light bulb which gave a twist to my nerves. It was one of those old light bulbs with a spike at the top, and filaments so thick that you can see each one even when the bulb is alight. It had been trapped and preserved unbroken in the lava. The museum's curator pointed it out to me and then, taking a wandering lead, touched it to the base of the bulb. Immediately the filaments warmed up, the bulb glowed, and I was looking on the light that had shone, over some drawing-room perhaps on the evening of May the First, fifty-three years ago. It had lit the white throats of planters' wives, or run like gold along the amber arms of Creole beauties.

'Dear, dead ladies with such hair too!'

Outside, the sunlight was like the glare from a furnace door. A small coloured boy played in the dust. It was the sight of him which reminded me of the one survivor, for there *was* a survivor from the city of St. Pierre—just one. He was a middle-aged coloured convict, and he was serving his sentence in a small cell almost underground, a cell dark and damp. If he had been in a modern well-lighted cell above ground, he would undoubtedly have died with the others. As it was, the search teams and rescuers of many nations who flocked to St. Pierre found him still alive though badly burnt.

The coloured convict of St. Pierre lived a further fifteen years, a member of Barnum's circus. He had little to do—merely show his scars and be gazed at respectfully by fascinated millions—the sole survivor out of forty thousand people.

That night, back in the brightly lit streets of Fort-de-France, with the sidewalks gay with brilliant dresses, I saw the other face of Martinique. Guitars and drums spun Caribbean rhythms out of the bars and dance halls. The air was spicy with flowers and fruit and rum; a rich scent made piquant by French tobacco and the astringency of freshly sliced limes.

The beauty of the island women, many of whom combine Gallic features with Caribbean grace—they move like panthers—the vitality of the scene, and the dark-velvet voices singing across the bay were a long way removed from the dead city of St. Pierre.

My acquaintance from the Bank sauntered past. He spotted me among the crowd and came over.

'You went there?' I nodded, and he began to talk about the island's history since the tragedy, and about the decline of Martinique. But I was no longer listening. I was thinking how sinister the streets of St. Pierre must look under this tropic moon. I was remembering the electric light bulb and the small boy playing alone in the lava dust.

Then, suddenly, all around us was the sound of the movement of the beguine—the grace of the dark dancers.

19

THE feeling of being back in the nursery was even more
accentuated this time. After the youth and vitality of the far
side of the Western Ocean, after the innocent American belief
that life was really worth living, England seemed more than ever
like an old man denying that spring would come again. Even the
kindness of old friends, even the peace of country villages, bore
a worn and faded air—like the sepia faces which emerge to mock
us from old family albums.

I had been back in London four months, and already the long
Atlantic creased by the Trade Winds and the islands leaning before
them under the sun were no more than a memory. Janet had gone
to Greece and was not returning. When someone has discovered
the way of life that makes sense to them then, if they have any
strength of character, they must follow it at all costs. The self-
sacrifices of which most people boast are only the concessions of
weakness.

I lived alone, and worked hard—I had been commissioned to
write a film—and learned for myself the strange lonely world of
bed-sitter London. Behind all the closed doors of those decaying
Victorian houses in South Kensington I could hear the rumour of
a thousand-thousand lonely lives. Unlike the poor of Italy and
Spain they had no Church to comfort them. Unlike the scare-
crows of Martinique or Guadeloupe they had no sun. Unlike the
derelicts along the harbour walls of Peiraeus they had no violet
mountain over their shoulder.

I had been back four months and the film, except for final
details that could not be arranged until next year, was complete.
It was autumn and the swallows were gathering along the tele-
graph poles. On the umber Thames the tugs at twilight had the
same husky voices that had moved me years before.

I had made my arrangements to leave and the lean colonel's widow who ran the vast echoing house in which I lived gave me my bill.

'You're off again?'

'Only for a few weeks,' I said.

I intended to make it months, but I did not want to hurt her by arousing envy in her heart. She, too, often longed for the sun; and her crowded drawing-room was full of pictures of Kashmir, and of lean, dead faces under solar topees.

'What's the gimmick?' she said.

The word was incongruous coming from those precise lips and that long-nosed face framed in its oval of grey hair. 'Gimmick', however, had moved out of Wardour Street, into the popular Press, and had been taken up. 'Angry Young Men' had recently been discovered and the normal healthy criticism of youth was being headlined as if it had never happened before.

'None,' I said. 'It's just that I've finished this film, and a magazine has asked me to write them a few articles about little-known places in the Mediterranean. I thought I'd go down to Spain and live there cheaply while I did the job.'

I went third, overland to Seville. France was paralysed by strikes and I was held up in Paris for three days; an embittered Paris that lacked its old *joie de vivre*. Prices were high and I made do with one meal a day in a workman's café behind the Eiffel Tower. It rained crossing the Pyrenees and it was raining in Madrid. It was not until we were fifty miles from Seville that the grey overcast folded back and the blue came through; a pale, rainwashed sky opening softly southward all the way to Africa.

I found a small *pensione* used by Spanish commercial travellers in the old Santa Cruz quarter and moved myself in for a month. It was cheap living: 11s. 6d. a day, including wine, and the house was spotlessly clean. I would hear the old maid-of-all-work start her scrubbing at six in the morning, and when I came out for my coffee at eight, the whole house and the tiled courtyard of the patio were gleaming and smelled of coarse soap and fresh water. Even the leaves of the plants and the winter-roses round the courtyard had been sprayed bright so that they shone in the pale pale autumn sunlight. Most days the sky was cloudless, a simple childlike blue with none of the heaviness of summer.

In the morning I took my notebooks and paper and pen into

the gardens of the Alcazar. I had found a quiet summer house, once the haunt of the kings of Spain, and now given over to silence, a black cat and myself. Just outside the summer house a fountain trickled leisurely into a basin, and through the cobwebbed windows the golden globes of oranges and tangerines gleamed among the rich leaves. It reminded me a little of the garden in Quinto's house at Palermo. I thought often of that Sicilian winter in those days.

The gardeners soon got used to the sight of the lone 'turista' sitting in the old house scratching away with a pen, and would come in and chat. They seemed happy men and, though their pay was poor and their conditions of living primitive, they possessed a tranquillity which I had not seen in my London friends.

One day an old Englishwoman came up and asked me the time.

'The gardeners told me to come to you. My Spanish is very poor. It's a funny thing, because I've been coming here every winter for twenty years. With the exception of the war, of course.'

'It's a wonderful city. Very peaceful.'

'Not in the spring,' she said. 'You've never been here for the Feria? No? Oh, we used to stay here for the Feria—my husband and I. Ever since he died I've always left Seville before it started. He used to enjoy it so much. We both did. But somehow I can't enjoy all that noise and gaiety again. I like it in the winter, though. My husband was very fond of this garden. We came here on our honeymoon.'

The cat stretched lazily and jumped from my lap to the ground.

'What a nice cat! Do you speak Spanish to him?'

'A little,' I said. 'But I don't think he understands my accent. I learnt my Spanish in the Balearics and Barcelona. It sounds a bit odd here.'

She gave me her name and address—staying in the big hotel.

'I go up sometimes in the evenings,' I said.

What I did not say was that I went up and gave one of the waiters ten pesetas and took a bath—unknown to the management—in one of the lavish marble-and-chromium bathrooms kept for the visiting rich of Feria week. She was the only English person I spoke to in over a month in Seville. With the background pattern of a foreign language constantly with me I had time to think quietly and alone in my own tongue. That is something one never has a chance to do at home; always bombarded by the common coin of one's language one loses touch with careful definition, and before long one finds the clichés of journalism and catchphrases of advertising forming part of one's mental pattern. With Spanish as my workaday language, and with the patter of the Sevillian accent in my ears, I had English to myself.

It was curious how at home I felt in Spain—in Spain, or in Italy or Greece, for that matter. It seemed as if I understood the conventions of those countries better than those of my own. Was it that a classical education had impressed me so deeply in youth that I could only feel at ease among the cicada-haunted walls of the old classical world? Or was it some strain in the blood inherited from an Irish grandfather? The indolence, the charm, and the quick anger of the Irish have much in common with the Mediterranean temperament.

From Seville, my work finished, I made my way up to Barcelona. On the way I stopped twenty-four hours in Madrid, finding myself a room above a small bar just off the Puerta del Sol. The bar was noisy and cheerful, frequented by soldiers and working men. The local whores slopped in and out, for a glass of wine, or a plate of tunny and onions in between clients.

'English?' asked the barkeeper. 'I thought you weren't American. You have the look of a European.'

I knew what he meant; I had not got that look of almost surgical cleanliness which distinguishes the American from the European. My trousers were cavalry twill and in need of a press; my jacket a friendly but shabby old Harris tweed; my hair was too long; and my eyes belonged to a citizen of a tired and wary world.

'There are many of them here.' He made a gesture of distaste. 'Too much money and no code of behaviour.' He took a peseta from his pocket and pointed to Franco's head. 'They are helping *him*. Without them he would be gone by now.'

I had seen the long lines of guns, weapon-carriers, jeeps and military cars stacked along the sidings as I came into the station that morning.

'They give much work, though?'

'Ah, yes. But the prices rise and the people are no better off.

The rich grow fatter, that's all. Eh.' He shrugged his shoulders in the eternal gesture of resignation, the almost Arabic fatalism of Spain. 'Eh—*Come triste la vida!*'

The rain came down in small quick bursts like machine-gun fire and it was cold in the streets that night. I was glad to leave for Barcelona in the morning.

It was nearly a year and a half since I had last seen the Mediterranean. The first glimpse of its humanized waters—it is the only sea where man seems to have left an imprint—stirred up many memories. I spent nearly seven years of my life, both in war and peace, under sail or in the lean steel hull of a destroyer, active upon its changeable surface. As the train neared the city the sea invaded the view more and more. It was a day of shifting cloud from the north, and the sea's face was alternately blue and bright or grey and sullen. A steamer was coming into harbour from the East, her funnel smoke trailing over the water and hanging in greasy patches in the troughs of the waves.

I got a taxi at the station and told him to drop me off at the bottom of the Ramblas. I could get a coffee and an *ensaimada* there, and then make my way to Mario's bar and find out about a room. I was travelling light, with only a small kitbag and a portable typewriter.

After the sleepiness of Seville the salty vitality of the Ramblas was as stimulating as a large brandy or a glance from a pretty girl. The lottery ticket sellers were prowling about with their boards of potential happiness fluttering in the wind: the flowers on the stalls were a bright challenge to winter; the smells of roasting coffee, of meat turning on spits, and of wine and garlic were all blended in the crisp air—the air that was cold enough to rouse an appetite, yet not so cold as to kill one's zest for the simple visual world.

After breakfast I humped my things across the road and turned down one of the narrow alleys into the 'Chinese quarter'. I never know why they call it that; I never yet saw a Chinaman there although there were members of almost every other race, from drunken Nordic sailors to cat-graceful Africans, and blanket-swathed Moors threading their way through the narrow streets. They jostled each other at the bars or moved with sliding or with stumbling steps out of the way of the Guardia Civil. The Guardia always went in pairs in that quarter.

Mario was out, but his old father greeted me as if it was only the day before that I had dropped in there, thirsty from the sea.

'Hey, Captain! How goes it? You sold the little boat?'

'More than a year ago,' I said.

'So long? Wait a minute, I'll get some prawns. They're good—just come in today. I know you like prawns.' He shouted for his old wife to go and get us a plateful, then brought the bottle of Fundador over to the table. I was looking through the bullfight magazines. Mario's was the 'fight' bar in that part of the world and there was nearly always a lean old veteran drinking in one corner and a group of youths listening to him. The journalists came there, too, although it was far from being a 'Press' bar, just a sawdust-on-the-floor working-man's pub, with nothing but the bullfight posters and the magazines to show that it was any way different from the other bars in the street.

'Hold it!' I said. The old man was always lavish-handed with the bottle. 'It's too early in the day.' He looked over my shoulder at the magazine, at the serial of the life of Belmonte.

'Always they are writing up that broken-winded trickster!' he said. 'He was never any good. Manolete was something different! Well'—raising his glass—'health and money and love!'

'Health and money and love!'

Mario came in shortly afterwards; he was amusing, smooth, good-looking, and in his late twenties. I never liked him as much as the old man; in acquiring his charm and his gaiety, the son had somehow lost the true values of the mother and father. Mario was on the way up. He had an interest in a garage, a share in a schooner, and was thinking of adding a proper restaurant to the old bar. He spoke American as well as Spanish, and had worked as an interpreter for the U.S. Forces.

'Hi!' He put his arm over my shoulder. 'Where you been, pal?'

His father shifted a little uneasily in his chair.

'Now you speak English,' he said, 'and I don't understand. I'm too old to learn it.'

'I speak English,' I corrected. 'This one speaks the dialect of colonials.'

The old man laughed. 'Like the Mexicans!'

Mario laughed, too, but he was not entirely with us. 'American's more use than English these days,' he said. 'The Yanquis have the money.'

He sat down while his father went to get another glass, and began to tell me about his latest love affair. It was a German girl this time. Two years ago it had been a French widow. Mario's taste was catholic and his proud boast was that he had made love with every race in Europe. I thought it quite likely; he was attractive enough, and Barcelona during the summer was thick with tourists. Mario's speciality was playing the dashing young Latin for the benefit of matrons or virgins from Northern Europe.

'The ugliest woman I ever had,' he said thoughtfully, 'was a Milanese of forty. But—she was the best. The most beautiful was that little English from the ballet company. She was no good, though. Englishwomen are ashamed of themselves. The Italian was never ashamed!'

I had another drink with them and Mario gave me a card to the owner of a small hotel round the corner—'He won't charge you tourist rates'—and I went off and signed myself in. It was a dark, scruffy-looking place but the floors were clean, the bedroom had a polished air, and the sheets were fresh and well-ironed. I went back to Mario's for lunch and had a bowl of soup, some spiced sausage and a salad. There were a lot of people in the bar and I read quietly while I ate my meal. Just as I was getting up to order myself a coffee from the shop across the road Mario came over.

'I've got an old friend of yours here. The captain from one of the Palma schooners. Says he remembers you from the Bodega San Pedro. He's just come in from Mallorca.'

I recognized Pablo mooning across the room. He was one of Fat Jack's regulars, and no lean one himself, either. He had the stub of a black cigar between his teeth, a basque beret on the back of his head, and his eyes were a little bloodshot. His hand had the rough feel that one gets from a lot of salt water and cordage.

'How was it coming over?' I asked.

'Pretty good. Seven knots with the engine, and another two with the sails up. Wind from the north. We unload today and load again tomorrow. Then we sail for Ibiza.'

'You're busy?' I said.

'Busy all right. But it comes and goes. Running a schooner isn't what it used to be. And now that much-loved son-of-a-bitch, the General, has made a law that no new schooners are to be built.'

'I read it. The only new construction is to be of iron or steel.'

'You know why? It's because Franco and his friends have all their money in the big steel yards. Where is a man like myself ever to get the pesetas for new construction in steel!'

I remembered his schooner, a good one, of about a hundred and fifty tons; some fifteen years old, and called *The Most Holy Conception No. 3*. The name had always amused me. Pablo's grandfather had built the 'No. 1' at the turn of the century.

'What are you doing down here?' he asked. 'I hear you sold your little boat. Bought another?'

'Not yet. I can't afford it. I've been in Seville.'

He made a wry face. 'All among the Holy ones. Peasants and priests! There are no free-thinkers like you and I in Seville. Would it interest you to come to Ibiza?'

I thought it over for a moment; weighed it against the return to London that I had planned—and decided in favour of going to sea again.

Next day I shifted my gear into the schooner, gave the Customs officer a handshake containing a hundred-peseta note, and joined Pablo in his cabin on the poop.

'Everything all right?' he asked. 'Good. He's a nice fellow that Customs man. You see—I'm not allowed to carry passengers and I couldn't sign you on as crew because you're a foreigner. I explained you were a friend of mine and Mario's, and that you were a sailor and not just a tourist. You gave him the hundred? That's enough. There'll be no trouble at Ibiza. You know how it is there—just a small island. Anyway, the sergeant of the Guardia is my brother-in-law.'

There was a cold grey sky on the day we left. The wind was in the north and there was quite a swell running outside the breakwater. We were loaded with a general cargo for Ibiza: manufactured goods, some grain, part of a winch, drums of oil, and a motor-bicycle. Pablo and the crew had been up since dawn, completing the stowage and getting ready for sea. It was pleasant to lie in my bunk and feel that it had nothing to do with me, and that I need not get up until we were out at sea. I heard the hiss and thud as the diesel started, and came on deck as the long quay walls of Barcelona fell away from us.

'Going to be rough,' said the old man hitching a battered

oilskin over his shoulders. You could see by the way the torn clouds came down that it was blowing hard to the north—probably a full Mistral up in the Gulf of Lyons. Still, on the course we had to take for Ibiza, it meant that the wind and weather would be astern of us. We might wallow a bit but we should not roll, and it would all be helping us along the way we wanted to go. I noticed that they only set the foresail, leaving the main where it was, bundled up along the top of the coachroof. Pablo saw me looking at it and shook his head.

'Bad old canvas. We shan't need it with this wind that's coming. You see—we shall make our ten knots on passage. The main would be too much for her. Even if the canvas held.'

There was sun along the tawny coastline as we eased away onto our course, and the smoke from the factories was blowing fast to the south. The hills behind Barcelona were very sharp and clear. The mate who was another regular at Fat Jack's bar came up and gave me a nudge.

'You like to be out again? I saw your gipsy a few weeks ago—the dark one, you remember?' He held his hands out in front of his stomach as if supporting a great weight. 'She's very fat! Not married, either.'

There was a big enamelled jug of coffee in the wheelhouse and the mate was pouring me a cup when Pablo came in.

'For the señor,' Pablo said and added a tot of brandy. 'I remember you at Ballester's yard when you used to take your breakfast in the canteen. I remembered that if it was cold you liked something in your coffee.'

We had settled down on course now, and the old boat was going well. The foresail was bent out full and hard, and the steady thump of the slow-revving diesel gave one a warm, secure feeling. The following sea had got the schooner by the tail and it lifted her up, gave her a push and then corkscrewed gently. She had quite a high freeboard, but even so there was water sloshing across the well-deck forward of the wheelhouse.

'We'll be in harbour tomorrow morning if this keeps up.' Pablo was laying off the course on a fly-marked old chart. The compass bowl had a big bubble in it: I don't suppose it had been corrected since the boat was built.

'We'll have to get the sail off her later on,' Pablo said, 'or we'll be fetching the island during the dark.'

Like most schooner skippers he hated to make a landfall at night. He never quite trusted the Spanish lighthouses and, having found out myself how unreliable many of them were, I could not really blame him.

At midday the cook came out of his small galley with a huge iron pot full of stew. It was heavy with olive oil, rice, garlic, and odd bits of fish. There was a demijohn of rough red wine beside the table and Pablo kept filling our glasses with the remark, 'Against the cold!'

I slept through the afternoon, and when I woke up the dusk was coming down over the sea. It looked bleak and cheerless, and even the fat helmsman whom they called 'Franco' had lost his happy look. The foresail was swaggering in the wind and I wondered whether the foremast would stay with us.

'We're going to get it down,' Pablo was standing beside me. 'Will you take the wheel while I send them all forward?'

I nodded and relieved the helmsman while he cut down the engine so that its sound died and became only a whisper under our feet. The four hands and the mate went slithering forward along the wet deck, with the wind plucking at their loose clothing.

It had really blown up during the hours that I had been asleep. Even inside the wheelhouse I could hear the cry of the wind in the mainmast shrouds and the seas were running big and long. They had the full sweep all the way down from the mouth of the Rhône. I could imagine how the Mistral must be booming through those valleys and flattening the smoke from the kitchen chimneys of Arles.

'Right!' said Pablo.

I put the helm down and we began to come up into the wind. When we got the sea full on the beam the schooner laid herself down as if she would keep on going, right over. I hoped to God they had stowed the cargo well; if it shifted now we might look rather dead. No, we were lifting and coming to the vertical again, and the wind was drawing ahead. The big heavy gaff of the foresail was swaying and stooping over the heads of the working men. I could see that one of the vangs had broken, and the loose end was flailing across the deck making them all duck. Pablo went outside and shouted something. The sail came down with a run and the gaff plunged with it, just missing fat 'Franco'.

Pablo put his head in through the door and nodded. I spun

the wheel and headed her off again downwind. A few seconds later he joined me and stepped up the engine revolutions.

'You saw what happened? Not only the vang—the peak halyard broke just as they were starting to lower away. I renewed all that rope in Palma last summer.'

When the men came back he sent the cook to make coffee and spiked all their mugs with a liberal tot of brandy.

'You were lucky, Franco!'

The fat man felt the top of his head apprehensively. 'Just missed me!'

'A pity it wasn't the General himself underneath,' said the mate. 'Then we might have arranged things better!'

The wind came up harder as the day died and by nine o'clock it was blowing half a gale. I gave Pablo and the mate a hand to lash down the cranky old dinghy on the poop; it was our one and only lifeboat, and a boat that I would have mistrusted even if it were only carrying me across the calm waters of Andraitx Harbour. Out on deck the wind had the feel of ice in it, and you had to hold on for fear that the lift of your coat or oilskin would spin you away like an autumn leaf. The sea rolled up and sat right under our stern, then fell away again with a long-drawn sigh, leaving a gulf like the opening to an unlighted cellar. We had eased the engine, but the log showed that we were still making over eight knots.

We were cold and wet when we got back inside but Pablo, who was full of wine, was still cheerful. He nudged the mate.

'You see, the señor here? This is what he calls a holiday. I tell him, why doesn't he come to Spain like all the tourists do—just for a fortnight in the summer and lie on a beach and make love?'

'Too much sand,' I said. 'I'd rather be in a bed.'

'You used to go out to Cala Azul in Mallorca,' said the mate. 'Remember? Plenty of sand there.'

The cook was taking a spell on the wheel. He turned and gave me a wink. 'You should marry a Spanish girl, Captain. Cook well, make good babies, keep the house clean.'

'The cook has four sisters,' said the mate. 'All beautiful.' A little rain came up with the wind and lashed around the wheel-house.

'Think!' said the cook. 'On a night like this you could be in your house with your woman, after a good meal, with a bottle of wine, and with sons to look after you when you are old. The trade of a seaman is the trade of a dog.'

'Never say it!' I lit him a cigarette and put it between his lips. 'It might be that the woman had an evil tongue and that the sons were not yours, and that the wine was sour.'

'He is crazy like all the English,' said Pablo.

'The English and the Spaniards are all right,' said the mate. 'It is the others who are no good.'

The old boat was heavy to steer and the iron cable that ran through primitive blocks to the heavy rudder was difficult to shift. Compared to a yacht or a battleship, you really had to work to keep her on course. The bubble in the compass irritated me and I told Pablo that I would top it up with gin when we got to harbour.

'When we get to Ibiza,' he said, 'you will meet my brother-in-law, the sergeant of the Guardia, and my sister and my uncle. We'll *drink* the gin, not put it in the compass!'

There was a rice dish for supper and afterwards I smoked one of Pablo's small black Cuban cigars. I took the helm for three hours and then, before turning in, went out on the upper deck. The noise of the wind was high in the rigging; and the seas, lit every now and then by patches of moonlight, were heavy and pewter-coloured. The foam from their crests was lifting a little. Before long the air would be clouded with the blown spume.

Down in the cabin the air was hot and humid, yet friendly with its smell of human life. Pablo rolled over in his bunk when I came in and switched on the light.

'How goes it?'

'All right. It's a big sea, but she's moving easily.'

He was wearing long grey woollen underpants, over which he began to pull his canvas trousers.

'I must go and look how things are. I think we might ease down a bit more. I don't want to run up on Ibiza before the sun comes.'

The cabin swayed and creaked, but it was dry enough. The exhaust went out under the cabin-sole and chuntered away some few feet from my ear. Pablo lit a cigarette and ran his huge hands over his eyes to massage away the sleep.

'Three or four days in Ibiza,' he muttered, 'then down to

Alicante. Then back to Barcelona. We'll be about a fortnight. Will you stay with us?'

'Is it possible? If not I'll get the steamer to Mallorca.'

'Surely, it's possible. You might write something about us for your English paper. I would like to read about myself in a journal.'

In the morning the sea was still high, but the clouds had lifted and the air, though cold, was lit by a feeling of expectancy. The sun ran along the tops of the foaming crests and the decks were drying white with the salt on them. The wheelhouse windows were pasted with salt and 'Franco' was just starting to get around them with a rag and bucket of fresh water. Pablo was on the wheel and the mate had just come back from the galley with a pitcher of hot coffee.

'Look!' said Pablo.

There was the island ahead of us, with the sun full on it and the hills looking curiously green after the burnt-out winter of the mainland. I could see the shine of the white houses where they climbed the hill into the old town, and the mountain behind was feathered with happy clouds.

20

L YING in my bunk aboard *Kay* while we ran back under bare poles before that Atlantic gale, I had time to remember my other days at sea. The criss-cross pattern of many ships and boats, of many landfalls and many lands laid their coloured threads against the dark night of my eyes. I lay with a cushion at my back to hold me secure against the boat's motion, and my face deep in a pillow. I could hear the tap of a jib sheet block above my head, and the sigh and creak as it lifted under pressure from the sail.

What, I wondered, had my sailing years taught me? It was over fifteen years now since I had first gone to sea, an eighteen-year-old ordinary seaman, just after the withdrawal from Dunkirk. One thing I had learned was that wisdom did not reside among the publicized philosophers and the men of many books. I had found it in other places. The less you earned and owned, the freer you were—that was true, at any rate. It was only if you were trying to safeguard a position in life, and maintain what was called 'a good standard of living' that you put fetters on yourself. If all your worldly possessions would go in a kitbag you were free; if not, not—and no apologist had ever yet been able to explain away that hard saying about the rich man and the eye of a needle.

There were certain basic truths about life and living and when you met men who knew them, then you recognized them. They were not confined to any particular country, and certainly not to any class. It was just a fact that there were some men—and women—who knew how life must be met. They were neither sentimental nor cynical; neither squeamish, nor hard. They accepted the things that had to be accepted; and fought hard against the things that were wrong, and that could be changed. Most of them had never heard of Seneca, but they would have recognized him if they had met him. Fat Jack was one of them. It was a curious thing. It was like belonging to a club, but a club where there were no candy-striped ties, no distinctions of class, race, or income, and no club premises with deferential waiters. Mario's father had been a waiter once—and he was a member all right.

'Are you asleep?'

Arne's voice. It was two days after the big gale and we were headed back west again, making good the hundred miles and more which we had been forced to throw away.

'Just dozing. How is it up top?'

'Not so hot. The glass has begun to fall and the damn wind's going back into the west. I don't like the look of it. Seems as if we're just standing into a series of depressions.'

I sat up and lit a cigarette.

'I'm afraid that's just what it does look like. Still, we knew we had to run that chance at this time of the year. The whole question is whether we're ever going to get a lucky break and really scud for little old New York—or whether we may not spend another ten days battering back and forth over the same stretch of ocean.'

'Come and have a look at the chart,' he said. 'I've left Ronnie on the wheel. The others have all got their heads down.'

It was half past three in the afternoon. Frank and Bob lay in their bunks in the saloon; Bob with his huge feet jammed against the end of his bunk; Frank with a grin on his face as if his dreams were full of laughter. Arne spread the chart out on the table, while I fetched down the U.S. weather maps and the Admiralty Pilot for the North Atlantic.

'It's six days since we had a sight, as you know. Nothing but this overcast all the time. I've figured out our position as near as I can make it—puts us about here'—he pointed to a small cross on the chart, some 400 miles north of the Azores and a little to the east of them. 'I'd like you to check it.'

'I'll get a plotting sheet,' I said, 'and work out as accurate a position as I can from our last fix.'

The hatch behind us opened and a cold splatter of rain blew in. Ronnie's bearded face, dripping with water, appeared.

'Steamer, Arne. Coming up from ahead.'

We rushed up on deck. Arne took the wheel, while Ronnie and I went forward to bend on the signal hoist that gave our name and asked them to report us to Lloyd's. She was only a quarter of a mile away from us—an old wartime Liberty boat, lifting and plunging heavily in the swell, and showing the red of her anti-fouling paint as her bows chopped up and down. She had already seen us, and was altering course in our direction as we gave the watch below a shout. She was the first ship we had spoken in over a fortnight, since leaving the Channel in fact.

'Greek,' said Bob. He had caught a sight of the lettering on her bow. She was only a few hundred yards off now, a tired old boat, her plates streaming with rust, but she looked very big and comfortable to us. There was a crackle from her bridge and a second later a Greek-American voice boomed above the wind and the noises of the sea.

'Are you okay?'

We waved.

'Is there anything you want?'

Frank told him, and it was just as well that his words were whipped downwind. We were still laughing when the Greek came back again.

'Okay. Got your name. Will report you to Lloyd's. Good voyage.'

Her crew were lining the decks looking down at us. I wondered whether by any chance my old acquaintance from Levkas was aboard her, or whether there were any men from Hydra or Missolonghi in the crew. We must have looked very small to them and I could imagine their practical comments. 'They do that for fun?' and 'Her masts are too tall. I never saw a caique with masts as tall as that, and a caique is bad enough in rough weather.'

'God, I'd like to go aboard and have a hot bath,' said Bob.

Stig muttered something in Swedish to Arne who translated:

'Stig wonders whether they'd take him back to Marstrand. He doesn't think New York can be worth all this trouble.'

The Greek circled us in farewell, the crew and the officers on the bridge giving us a wave, then she squared away on her course and wallowed off towards Europe.

The wind was still freshening from the west and it was growing colder as the sun went down. We were under all plain sail, but it looked as if we would be reefing again before night-fall. The kettle was steaming when we got below and Frank was clattering about making tea. Arne and I took a cup and went back to the chart table. The glass was going back steadily, the wind was rising, and it looked as if we were in for another dirty night.

'Suppose we ran off to the Azores,' he said. 'We could be down there in less than three days. I've a feeling that only by going a bit further south are we likely to get out of these Westerlies.'

'There's less chance of them three or four hundred miles south. The percentage is much less. Here—you can see on the wind chart.'

Kay bounced into a big one and a wave broke over her bows and slapped along the deck, its greenish-white back undulating past the charthouse window. Night was coming on, and suddenly it seemed as if we could all do with a little sun and a bit more comfort. It was over a week now since we had been in the bad weather area, over a week since the boat had been really dry or anyone on board fully rested and free from cold and wet.

'Okay. Let's do it. You tell the boys what the plan is, Arne, and I'll work out a course.'

Half an hour later we freed the sheets and turned to the south. It was still cold and wet as ever, but the fact that the ship's head was pointed towards the sun seemed to send a flicker of warmth through the boat.

'Better,' said Stig.

With the wind and the sea on the beam we were tramping along at a happy seven to eight knots. The motion of the boat was easier and Ronnie, who was cook for the day, excelled himself by producing an almost professional steak and kidney pie. Afterwards Arne opened our last tinned cake, mixed it thoroughly with half a bottle of sherry and several tots of rum, and called the mixture 'trifle'. It was so rich, so fruity, and so heavy with alcohol that two or three spoonfuls made one crawl somnolently towards the bunk and lie there faintly groaning.

'Wind aloft, wind alow,' Frank remarked. 'And any more wind down here and we'll have to take a reef in the deckhead.'

I was glad that we had finally come to the decision to run south. In those eight days of steady bad weather we had been lucky in having no damage to sails or gear, and no one hurt. But every time work had to be done on the foredeck, or even routine jobs like setting the trysail or reefing the main, we had moments of anxiety. It was not always possible for people to work wearing safety-belts, and there were times when a small slip or a piece of ill-luck on the bouncing foredeck might have meant a man overboard. In the seas that were running most of the time it would have been impossible to save a man in the water. In any case, the weight of his clothing would have taken him down like a stone.

The North Atlantic is often cold, but that spring the wind seemed to have ice in its teeth and the spray on our chapped faces felt like a handful of finely ground flints. Bob was singing when I came on watch, his feet wedged comfortably either side of the compass. The boat was going well, with a long sighing hush of water, and the round, full feeling of her eased sails.

'I'll give you a spell, Bob.'

'With pleasure, my lord. Course, south.'

> 'He asked for a candle
> To light his way to bed,
> He asked for a pillow
> To rest his weary head. . . .'

'Cigarette? I'll make a cuppa in a minute.'

He sprawled out along the seat as I moved over behind the compass and took the wheel. She was steering very easily and it was pleasant to take her and to know that we were headed for the Azores, some warmth and a brief rest. The prevailing Westerlies had beaten us, but we could feel that we had put up a good fight and not run at the first sign of trouble. Perhaps it was the large meal that gave us such warmth and confidence, but even the occasional shot of spray could not douse our spirits.

We were singing when the next watch came up to relieve us:

> 'She's a big fat girl
> Twice the size of me—'

'You two feeling all right?' asked Frank. 'Or have you been at the spirit locker? Midnight, wet, cold, and you're sitting there making a noise like a bunch of drunks at closing-time.'

'Due south,' I said. 'And keep her rolling.'

Twenty-four hours later we got our first sight for nine days; a little to the east of our estimated position. It was odd to think that, when we had taken the last sight, we had been west of the Azores, and now we were east of them. We had certainly learnt that bucking the spring westerlies in a small boat was doing things the hard way. Pehaps we had been unlucky, but at any rate the attempt had been worth it. Now we should run to Fayal in the Azores, stretch our legs, top up the water-tanks, and get in some fresh bread and vegetables. From there on, if fate was kind, we might expect better weather. Every day now the spring was truly coming over the cold sea, and the sun at noon would stand higher over our yard every mile further south we went.

The morning that we sighted the Azores was soft and clear, and you could feel the sun on your skin like the touch of a fire-warmed glove. The upper deck was littered with sails, clothes, bedding, ropes, blankets, and most of the interior fittings of the boat. We were washing everything down with fresh water—we could spare it now—and shining the metalwork and polishing the varnished wood. The whole boat steamed happily and it was warm enough to get buckets over the side, strip off and have an all-over wash. Porpoises were playing round us in the gently lifting swell and there were many land birds. Mother Carey's chickens had deserted us shortly after we turned towards the happier southern zone. The sea was full of the beautiful, but sinister, violet sails of Portuguese men-of-war. Looking down into the water one could see the long drifting lines of their stinging tentacles.

Arne and I stood watching them for some time and then we both remarked on the same thing.

'Do you see? They really can beat to windward!'

I had always thought that the inflated bladder which serves the Portuguese man-of-war as a sail could only be used like a square-sail—that the jellyfish could only go downwind, in fact. But now we could both see that many of them were truly going to windward, not pointing very close to the wind's eye, perhaps, but certainly doing better than a square-rigged ship would have done.

'Turtle soup!' shouted Frank. He was standing in the bows waving and pointing ahead of us.

'By God, so it is!'

Two large turtles cruised slowly down the ship's side while we fell over each other trying to get hold of nets and gaffs.

'Missed them!'

'More coming up!' he shouted again. 'I'm going to have a crack at one of these.'

Frank had been taking a bath, and was stark naked except for the belt and sheath-knife which he now buckled round himself.

'Where's the camera?' said Bob. 'This is something which should be on permanent record. *Health and Efficiency* would buy it!'

But Frank had already dived over the side and was swimming towards a turtle. A few seconds later we heard his shout:

'Got him!'

He drifted alongside the yacht, which was only idling through the water, and then we saw that he had both his large hands firmly latched on to the back of a three-foot turtle. With some difficulty we got Frank and his catch safely on board, and captor and captive confronted each other panting in the cockpit. The turtle moved its flippers uneasily and stretched out its leathery old man's neck and looked at us. Stig was sharpening a huge kitchen knife.

'How do you make turtle soup?' asked Bob.

'I'm not quite sure,' I said uneasily. 'Do you know, Frank?'

'Haven't an idea.'

Stig said something to Arne, who made a grimace.

'Stig says to cut off its head and scrape it out of the shell.'

'It'll make a hell of a mess. Besides, it wouldn't be easy to get it out of the shell.'

Frank gazed thoughtfully at the turtle which looked more than ever like an old member of the Athenaeum fallen into the hands of bloodthirsty revolutionaries.

'Perhaps we ought to put the damn thing back,' he said.

'It's your turtle,' said Arne.

Stig saw what was in the wind and began to scowl. He finished sharpening the knife and came forward and got hold of the turtle's shell. Frank took one look at him and with a swift movement picked up the beast and threw it back into the sea. We were all relieved—all except Stig, who burst into a torrent of Swedish and refused to speak to anyone for the rest of the day.

Late that afternoon we dropped anchor in the small port of Horta in Faial. The land looked wonderfully green, the small houses were whitewashed and shining, and the brown leathery faces that beamed down on us from the jetty were the faces of friends. The men of the Azores are seamen with a tradition of centuries behind them, and they gave us all the help and the welcome that one brother could extend to another. They showed us where to buy food and wine, where to get the best milk and bread, and the cleanest ice—and then they sat down and introduced us to the local wine. By nightfall it seemed as if we all had known each other for years. They had shown us their boats: the long open ones in which they still go after whale in the fashion of Captain Ahab. I had been shown one by the local shipwright which had the whole bows stove in from the stroke of a whale's tail. The boat's coxwain grinned.

'You should come back next year and we will take you out.'

I remembered the flying-fish boats of Barbados, and reckoned that if I had been frightened then it was nothing to what a day's whaling would do to me.

'Don't worry,' he said. 'We hardly ever lose a boat!'

We left the island a day later. The weather was fair and we could not afford to waste time for we needed two weeks in New York to bring *Kay* up to scratch for the Bermuda race.

'Set all fair weather sails!' was the cry as we stood out westerly for America. The wind was a little abaft the beam, drawing softly over the deck as we ran up the spinnaker, the spinnaker staysail, and the ghost-like nylon bubble of the mizzen staysail. *Kay* felt the easy power of her new wings and began to surge ahead. It was, indeed, like sailing through silk. For day after day we ran off the miles under every stitch of canvas that she could carry. In seven days we logged 1,354.5 miles, with one noon-sight to noon-sight run of 202 miles—an average of a little over eight knots. I remember a day when a tramp steamer that we sighted on the eastern horizon at dawn was still no more than abeam of us at sunset. Driving hard, although not as hard as if one was racing, in a boat of *Kay*'s quality was as fine a sensation as I have found in life.

Only the dedicated artist or scientist can know the satisfaction that comes from an achievement that is abstract. But even the artist and the scientist are nearly always concerned with the potential bread-and-butter that their work will earn them. In sailing—which nowadays has no commercial attachments to it—

a man's dedication and devotion to his boat are as pure as anything in human life can be. There are no creditors at the door to spur him on, and no money being made out of the achievement. It is something done for love alone. Along with a few sports like mountaineering, deep-sea sailing is the only thing in the modern world which can give a man that sense of selfless and abstract dedication which was once to be found in monasteries. But it does not matter how you get to the still centre; once you have discovered it, it is always with you. Once you have well and truly found it you can even go back into the corruption of the great cities and still retain what Seneca called 'the diamond-hard axis round which revolve the petty happenings that make up our daily existence'.

The nights were as fine as the days, and soon we drew into the southern edge of the Gulf Stream, or Western Current. The temperature rose, and the water was swaying with the yellow bundles of gulf weed. Sometimes looking down at the weed we could see small crabs and shrimp-like creatures crawling in and out of the strands. Bo'sun birds with their long, feathered tails were often about the boat and we passed whales lolling and spouting in the easy swell.

'Flying fish. Hundreds of them!' said Arne one night as I was taking over the watch from him. Every now and then as a shoal of them rose in front of the boat you could hear, so silent was our motion, the swift wild buzz of their gossamer-fine wings. The scuppers were full of them and Stig, with memories of the turtle, was busily popping them into a saucepan.

'We'll have a good fish fry for breakfast. Pity we've got no fresh limes.'

The log entry for that midnight holds something of the freshness of the world in which we were living. 'Brilliant fine night and a few scattered cumulus clouds moving over. The boat is going easily and well. Today has been perfect. Very warm, deep blue sea, pleasant breeze over the quarter and tonight the phosphorescence of the wake and the movement of countless porpoises and flying fish make the sea shine so that it vies with the stars. This is how the sea settles its score. After a day like this even the most crotchety of sailors must admit that he has been "Paid in Full".' Yes, in hours like those one comes as close to the perfection of life as man can ever get.

Bob's cigarette-butt glowed in the dark. Just to the right of him I could see the pale shine of the Kenyon speedometer, with its needle wavering between seven and eight knots. The sighing, silken hush of our passage was in our ears and the rising grunts of the porpoises had the friendliness of a shared life.

'We'll find New York a bit different after this,' he said.

'You're going to stay there, aren't you, Bob?'

'I think so. I have a job fixed for me. You going back to England?'

'I'm not sure. I've no ties. I'm going to Bermuda anyway. The race should be fun.'

He relieved me at the wheel and I went forward to check over the sails, and see how they were drawing, and that there was no chafe at the lead points or in the blocks. The mizzen staysail brushed softly against my face as I worked my way towards the mainmast. The moon was behind the sail and, as it lifted in the wind, it shone like a clay-pipe bubble of childhood. The mainsail, too, was drawing well, with just a slight shift and crackle as the yacht bowed to the waves.

Up in the bows I had the lift and swagger of the green spinnaker above my head. I could see that it would draw better if we eased off the sheet a little. Right up in the bows there was no sound except the slight crunch under her forefoot as she shouldered her way over the swell. The sea seemed to shine from within, and sometimes the phosphorescence trailing away in our wake would shudder up and form itself into round soft bubbles like balloons. They swirled and burst like flowery bombs in the velvet water.

'Are you okay?' Bob's voice.

'Just coming back.' I must have been lounging there idly some five minutes or more. The decks were slightly damp and the air was soft and humid. On the white teak the drops of salt spray stood out a darker and different colour from the overall dampness of the rest. If you bent your head and looked through the thin rain of spray on the weather bow you could see, flickering and shining, an opalescent moon-bow.

'What a night!' said Bob. 'I wish life was always like this.'

Five days later we eased our way through a white Cape Hatteras fog over the last fifty miles towards New York. The drumming boom of steamers' sirens was in our ears for a night and a day, and once a Norwegian tanker sliced through the thick air only a few hundred yards ahead of us.

'Oh, for a warm bar!' said Bob. 'Slick chicks with Martini eyes. This last lap has me nervous.'

We were under power and plain sail, with an errant light air shifting around on the port beam, but not strongly enough to keep us going under sail alone. We had hoisted the radar reflector to the main yard, but the Norwegian rather shattered our faith in it.

'Those things are all right,' said Ronnie, jerking his thumb towards the yard, 'if you could only be sure that the merchant ships were using their sets. Or if you could be sure that the third officer or whoever's supposed to be keeping an eye on the radar screen knows what he's looking for.'

I was asleep next morning when the fog began to peel away. Then Frank's shout 'There she blows!' and the general scramble on deck brought me out of my bunk. The white, low-lying clouds were peeling off the face of the sea and the towers of Manhattan stood up shining a few miles ahead of us.

'There she blows!'

We were thirty-seven days out from Falmouth, with no damage to crew or gear, and the boat looking as if she had only just left Long Island Sound. Arne was opening a bottle of champagne.

'A fine dry Louis Roederer!'

'After you, André Simon!'

'A firm little Circassian of a wine!'

So we stood on deck and toasted the rising skyline, while the giant hull of the *Queen Mary* slid slowly out from New York as if she had come to meet us.

Yes, there are many roads and many keys. For me at any rate the sound of the pleasant place is in the waves of the sea. And the smell of it is damp cordage and wood, on a fair morning when the off-shore breeze just carries the scent of the land. And the sight of it is a dolphin breaking clean and shining out of a foam crest—or the curve of a wind-washed sail, at evening, when the sea's line shines.